The Most Beautiful Girl in the World

Jenny Ellis

Copyright © 2014 Jenny Ellis
Head Editors: Katie Beam and Maya St. Clair
Assistant Editors: Nancy Ellis, Audrey Hessler, and Lindsay Janik
All rights reserved.
ISBN-13: 978-1499765595
ISBN-10: 1499765592

For my dear friend, Elena,
who is a joyful inspiration.

For my sister, Katie,
who is a conqueror because of Christ.

For my girls, Elsie, Hannah, Lindsay, Rachel, Sarah,
and Sydney, who are beautiful inside and out.

For my biggest fan, Alexandra,
who will always make me smile.

And for my blue-eyed encourager, Corey,
who helped me remember that Jesus is
and will always be the one true Lover.

In the eyes of the Creator,
you are each a MOST BEAUTIFUL creation!

"**He has made everything beautiful in its time.**"

Ecclesiastes 3:11a

Table of Contents

Introduction 9

Prelude 11

Grade School
Welcome to Reality 13
Chunky 14
Follow the Leader 15
Picking Teams 16

Middle School
Hair Scare 18
School Ridicule 20
The Running Game 22
Be Afraid . . . of Me 25
Enter Riley 27
P.E. Should Be Called Pee-Yew! 31
Janey Loves Riley 36
Running Buddies 39
Into the Darkness 45
Running is Pain 50

High School
First Dance 56
The Stocky One 61
Basketball Blues 64
Record-Breaking Heartache 68
Pudding in Time 72
Running Low 75
Second-Chance Dance 78
Good-Bye Normal 88

College
Exit Riley 89
Running on Empty 92
Running is Bliss 98
The Donut Queen 102
Bangs 'n Fangs 104
Dessert Desertion 105

I am NOT a Pig 107
Dropping Seconds by the Pound 109
Hide 'n Seek 110
Sub 100 112
Word Wake-up 113
The Hot List 114
Milkshakes, Anyone? 115
Game Changer 117
Build Up 124
Running Victorious 130
Christmas Crush 137
Christmas Crushed 143
Running on a Prayer 147
Just Dance 150
Enough is Enough 151
Listening to the Wrong Voice 153
Bring on the Marathon 158
Suddenly I See 160

Post-College
Kayley is Beautiful 166
PAJET 168
Enter Ryan Darling 172
The Moment of Truth 179
Just Friends? Really? 191
Best Day Ever 194
Spreading the Good News 197
I Could See Myself Marrying You 199
Sub-Three Isn't What It's Cracked up to Be 203
They Say I'm a WHAT? 211
Raging Sea 214
Like a Sister 215
Writing Away the Sorrows 222
Still Writing 223
You're Beautiful, Baby! 224
Hope Destroyed 226
Fresh Start 229
Healing Rain 231

Postlude 234

Introduction

The idea for this book came to me over a year ago when a girl I was close to started struggling with an eating disorder. Having been there myself in college, I wrote out my story for her to read, and it impacted her in a big way. Following that, I gave my story to various other girls, and they too were affected for the good. Because of this, I decided it was time to write out my ENTIRE story from when I was a young girl up until several years ago. I wanted the hurts of my life to be able to reach those who have struggled similarly because I knew God did not bring me through the heartaches for naught.

Throughout the course of this book, you will see how the mind and heart of a growing girl—from the age of three to twenty-five—is impacted by the world around her. You will see how the successes and failures of life have influenced her, as well as the words and actions of others.

Because this book is autobiographical in nature, each story is based on events that actually happened. All of the interactions between the characters are written how I, the author, remember them occurring. Everything is meant to be as accurate as possible. However, in order to protect those I have written about, names of characters and other finer details have been changed. My intent is not to vilify anyone but to show how both negative and positive exchanges have left an impact.

The purpose of this book is to explore how a person's perception of beauty is formed throughout his or her life. My hope is that the reader will come to see that what is truly beautiful can only be connected to the One who has made everything beautiful. As it is stated in the lyrics of the song "The Shadows," from Tenth Avenue North's album *The Struggle*, "Beauty never intended to be more than a reflection." The purpose, therefore, of this book is not to point the reader towards the beauty of creation but towards the Creator—towards the One from whom all beauty flows.

Prelude

Giggles erupt through the vibrant spring sunshine. They are quickly followed by high-pitched shouts of joy.

"Ginger! Ginger! Come here, Ginger! Giiiiiiiiinger!" A curly-locked little girl races through the lush, green grass, feet flying to and fro.

"Ginger! Stop that! Ginger! Ginger!" Clad in a crocheted jumper as blue as the sky overhead, she is tearing after her best dog friend in the world, her beloved Ginger. Her long brown waves fly in the wind as she chatters and chuckles. She is a beautiful little girl. Pattering through the grass, she is all smiles, without a care in the world.

"Ginger!" Finally she grasps the velvety-brown scruff of her furry pal. Clutching on for dear life, she is practically at eye level with the dog. She warmly embraces her patient companion and giggles some more.

"Oh, Ginger!" There is a light in her eyes that seems to dance. It is a joyous, unquenchable fire of bliss. She leans once more into the soft, milk-chocolate coat of fuzz as the screen fades to black.

*****

When the color returns, a quaint living room comes into view. Warm sunshine spreads throughout the house as a mother sits in her rocking chair with her half-asleep daughter on her lap. We deduce that this is the same little girl from the first scene. We also discover her name.

"Janey Lynn. Janey Lynn. Janey Lynn's my little girl. Janey Lynn. Janey Lynn. Janey Lynn's my little girl." The melody is soft and cheerful.

Leaning back contentedly in the arms of her glowing mother, Janey is familiar with this simple serenade. She quietly enjoys its comfort as her newborn sister, Kayley, also quite content, lies asleep in the cradle.

"She's the best, beats the rest. No one else could ever do. Janey Lynn. Janey Lynn. Janey Lynn's my little girl." Janey's mom holds her close, reminding her that she is loved, as the screen once more fades to black.

*****

When the color returns, we find Janey has aged a full five years. She is now joined by not just one little sister but two. We find them in the same quaint living room we last saw them in, but, this time, things are a little more upbeat.

"Pretty woman, walking down the street. Pretty woman, the kind I'd

like to meet. Pretty woman." Dressed in the most ridiculous of outfits, the Eller family frolics around the house as the oldies music blares.

Tasha bobs up and down to the music, with the spastic sort of flailing only a one-year-old can tolerate, while Janey and Kayley stomp and twirl around the house, winter scarves flailing. Sporting a Beauty and the Beast tank top and shorts set, a tiny skirt she once wore in first grade, pink-rimmed sunglasses, a floppy hat, and, of course, the scarf, Janey could pass for the most stylish, prettiest little girl in the third grade. Mrs. Eller, her mom, dons a black leotard, the kind she wears when she does her aerobics.

"I don't believe you, you're not the truth; no one could look as good as you . . . . . Mercy." Janey taps her foot back and forth as rhythmically as an uncoordinated eight-year-old can, and Kayley punches an invisible person with an air of toughness.

"Kayley has some moves!" Mr. Eller calls out from behind the video camera.

Every Friday night, this is their routine. Mr. Eller turns on the oldies station, and the girls dance as he catches as much of it on film as he can. They aren't dancers in public, but they love to bust a move under the cover of their own roof. To the outsider, they may look like a freak show, but they could care less.

We focus one last time on Janey as she spins around, brown waves whipping in a fantastic circle.

Then, the colorful world dissipates one last time into darkness.

Welcome to Reality

When you are a little girl, there isn't a whole lot that can faze you. Yes, you sometimes don't get what you want when you want it. And yes, you may throw a tantrum every now and then. But you never seem to question your worth as an individual. It is only as you age that the critique and ridicule of others makes you start to question why you were ever truly able to frolic through the world footloose and fancy-free. It is as you age that you wonder how you ever pranced around in a short skirt and a winter scarf without anyone noticing.

And it is at this stage, this stage of aging, that I, Janey Lynn Eller, the little girl in the previous scenes, start finding myself. I still am very much free to be me, but those around me seem to only have one goal—to rip that magic carpet of freedom right out from underneath me.

Chunky

"You should really get her into swimming or something," I overhear the doctor tell my mom, as she gazes with some concern in my direction.

Ooh, swimming. I just learned how to do that this summer. I can glide beneath the surface like a dolphin.

"Take a look at her charts." The doctor hands my mom a graph of some sort. "As you can see, Janey is in the 50th percentile for her height but in the 80th percentile for her weight."

I swing my feet back and forth and listen to the statistics. If weight were a grade, I would be sitting at a B minus.

"Is that bad?" My mom inquires.

Of course it is bad, Mom. B stands for BAD. Remember that B + on my report card last year in the third quarter of third grade? That was BAD. And it was in MATH, my best subject!

"It isn't bad, but she could stand to lose a few pounds. It isn't the best when weight percentage exceeds height percentage."

What is this lady trying to say about me? I'm not fat, am I? I mean, I was the fastest girl in my class at the 100 meter dash in second grade. How can a fat girl be fast?

"She is just a tad on the chunky side, and we want to combat that issue as soon as we can."

Chunky? So she IS calling me fat. I search for my reflection in a nearby mirror. The girl in the pink sweat suit smiling back at me looks perfectly happy and healthy. This lady must be crazy.

"Well, we are a pretty active family," Mom pauses, "and Janey even joined a soccer team in the spring."

Yeah, BAM! I play soccer, Dr. Know-It-All. What now?

"Hmmm. Well, that might not be enough."

It might not be enough? What does this lady want from me? Okay, so maybe she could say it wasn't enough when I was a four-year-old and picked dandelions in the middle of a soccer game, but not now. Now, when I play soccer, I give 100 percent. I am feisty and aggressive and may even have the chance to play forward next season.

"Well, it is the summer, and our family does a lot of biking and hiking on our camping trips. I'm sure she'll be fine." Mom sounds a little defensive.

"That sounds good to me. Whatever you can do to get her active would be great." The doctor grins my way, as if she has been ever so complimentary.

I give her a half-hearted smile in return.

I am not sure I really like this doctor anymore.

Follow the Leader

"Janey Eller! Follow me! We are going to play horses."

I step out onto the playground for another day of torture. Jillian Mills, the queen of the horse stable, is ready to boss us around for yet another forty minutes of recess.

"Now, horses, I am the main horse. You all have to follow me." Jillian crouches down and begins to prance across the pavement.

I want to say something but hold my tongue.

The other girls pretend to gallop after Jillian.

Even Clara Whitaker, my sweetest friend, pretends. Like me, she doesn't really have anyone else to play with at recess.

I just walk, still following but not having the heart to be a horse. It is rather silly if you ask me.

To the left of me, I watch as Erica Grein happily swings from one monkey bar to the next. She looks like she is having fun. If she wasn't the only girl in the fourth grade who people tease more than me, I would gladly join her.

"Janey Eller! Why aren't you galloping?" Jillian is aggravated.

"Why do I have to?"

"BECAUSE. I am in charge, and you have to do as I say."

"I don't really like playing horses though," I mutter, no longer able to hold it inside.

Jillian looks like she might explode. "Then DON'T play." She quickly glances at the other girls. "Come on, horsies. Janey isn't playing with us anymore."

Clara looks over at Jillian and looks back at me. She is torn. If she comes with me, she will officially become an outsider. If she stays with Jillian, she may still have hope.

"It's okay if you play with them," I mouth to her.

She smiles and gallops away.

I stand completely still on the pavement, unsure of what to do next. I can be brave and ask to join the boys playing soccer. Or I can be courageous in a different sort of way and join Erica on the monkey bars.

I choose to join Erica. She may be different, but she always enjoys my company.

I run over to the monkey bars and don't look back.

Picking Teams

Fifth grade comes, and recess is just as frustrating. I choose to play soccer, which is better than horses, but it is still no stress reliever.

"I pick Trisha."

"I pick Amie."

When picking teams is involved, life is never fun.

I stand on the pavement with Jillian Mills (yes, we are actually friends now) and Keeley Hanes, waiting for our names to be called. We all play on the same soccer team, the Purple People Eaters, so we have no reason to fear being picked last. Do we? Keeley and I are the leading scorers, and Jillian is a stud on defense.

Name after name is called until I finally hear my two friends being chosen.

"I pick Keeley."

"I pick Jillian."

My two best friends jog to their teams, leaving me all alone on the sidelines.

"Okay, let's play!" Trisha Rink dribbles the ball to the middle of the field.

"Um, whose team am I on?" I am completely taken aback. No one will even CHOOSE ME?? That is much worse than being picked last.

Trisha looks at me and scowls. "Not mine."

"She's not on mine either," Tamara Atkins adds in a mean tone.

I can tell that Keeley and Jillian are nearly as furious as I am.

"Can't I be on SOMEONE'S team?" I never thought I would be asking this question.

"No. You play like a freak." Showing off her moves with a smug laugh, Trisha takes the ball to the goal.

I am frozen.

"I'm not playing unless Janey can play," Keeley states firmly.

"I'm not either." Jillian puts her hands on her hips.

"Come on, Janey." Keeley grabs my arm. "Let's go talk to Mrs. Jensen."

"You mean 'The Cow Lady?'" Mrs. Jensen is this lunch lady that is obsessed with cows. She wears cow-patterned clothing and probably collects cow figurines.

"Yeah, that one."

"Moo!" Jillian adds just to lighten my mood.

We march as one to Mrs. Jensen.

"Excuse me. Mrs. Jensen?" Jillian seems to be the most confident of the three of us when talking to adults. "The girls will not let Janey play soccer. This is RECESS. Everyone should have the chance to play."

"And Janey is GOOD at soccer." Keeley is adamant.

Mrs. Jensen jiggles her glasses and stares down my two small friends.

"They are being complete jerks," Jillian adds.

Mrs. Jensen studies us some more through her crooked spectacles. And then, she marches straight over to the soccer game. She is the ultimate authority on the playground.

"Girls! Everyone that wants to play soccer gets to play."

I can see that some of the girls are scared. I mean, Mrs. Jensen is a legend. Trisha, however, still looks rather defiant.

"I don't want her on MY team."

Maybe I shouldn't have even tried to play. Maybe I should see if Erica Grein stills spends her recesses on the monkey bars.

"Well, someone needs to pick her."

Most of the girls look down at their feet.

And that is when I make a decision.

"Mrs. Jensen, I think I will just join the boys."

"Are you sure?" She raises her eyebrows.

"Yep. The boys are actually NICE, and THEY don't care how aggressive you play." I look straight at Trisha.

"Well, then we are playing with the boys too," Jillian says.

"Yep!" Keeley adds.

"Okay then." Mrs. Jensen looks back at the paused soccer game. "You can continue playing, girls!"

Together, Jillian, Keeley, and I head over to where the boys are playing soccer, on the opposite side of the paved playing field.

Once we arrive, we join their game without a hiccup. They are welcoming and even a little bit excited.

"I want Janey on my team!" Bryan Kaiser yells. He sits next to me in class, and we are pretty good friends. I might even say I have somewhat of a crush on him.

"We'll take Keeley and Jillian!" Eric Nielson calls.

And just like that, we are playing soccer with the boys—running around, laughing, and having a great time.

That is the last time I ever ask to play with the girls.

"Mom, can you cut my hair?" I elephant stomp from Gramma's room into the living room holding a shiny silver pair of scissors, my weapon of choice. My hair is long, frizzy, and uncontrollable, like a wild mane on a mustang. (And you know how I feel about looking like a horse.) It needs to be tamed BEFORE I go back to school.

"Okay, just let me finish taking these cookies out of the oven."

I hurriedly sit cross-legged on the carpeting and run a brush through my hair as my mom finishes up in the kitchen. She is always cooking something delightfully delicious. I glance up at the many Wal-Mart portraits of my sisters and I on the wall. My hair looks so lovely in every picture, up until the one from this summer that is. Yuck. My bangs are nearly freakish. Something needs to change.

"Okay, now you need to tell me how much you want me to cut off." Mom plops down behind me, whisking up the gleaming scissors from the floor.

"Um," I pull at my hair and inspect, "how about right here." I point to somewhere near my shoulder.

"Okay!"

I hold my head as steady as possible, and my mom goes in for the snip.

"Uh . . . oh."

That is never good to hear when your locks, no matter how crazy, are being chopped from your head.

"What's wrong?" My voice is only slightly anxious.

"The scissors bounced."

"The scissors WHAT??" Okay, now I am a little more anxious.

"They bounced. I went to cut where you pointed, and the scissors bounced off your shoulder to nearly your ear. And . . . that is where I cut."

How do scissors bounce? They are made of metal, not rubber.

"Well, I already started cutting, so I had better finish," Mom continues.

"Well, be careful. Don't cut any higher than you just did." My apprehension is only increasing. Who knows what Mom will do next?

When the deed is done, I jump to my feet and run into the bathroom. I gaze into the mirror and yell out, horrified, "MOM!!!! HOW COULD YOU??!!"

"You ASKED me to cut your hair, Janey. I did my best."

"MOM!!! I look like a freak!" Peering even deeper into the mirror, I stare into the triangular formation that has become my hair. If I thought it looked bad before, it looks a hundred times worse now. Why did I ever ask her to cut my hair?

I am fuming as I gallop from the bathroom to my parents' room. I grab the first ponytail holder I can find and try pulling what is left of my hair back with it. Only about one third of the brown frizz holds within the clutches of the hair tie.

"MOM!!! My hair doesn't even fit into a ponytail! How am I going to go to school??"

"You will just have to wear your hair down, I guess."

"WHAT??!!" I nearly explode. "I HAVE to wear my hair in a ponytail!!"

"I'm sorry, Janey. I know you don't like it, but I can't just glue your hair back on. What's done is done."

Gawking back at my reflection, I silently mourn the loss of my hair.

It is doubtful this school year will have a fairy-tale ending.

All I can do is groan.

"She has a fro, and she looks like a crow . . ." Serena Langley's words sound like nails on a chalkboard.

I choose to tune out the rest of the little ditty as I blaze through the crowded hallway of the grade school. It is only September, and, already, half the sixth grade has latched onto the fact that I don't exactly have the most attractive head of hair.

Mom and her scissors have ruined my life.

But it isn't just my triangular fuzz that is causing a buzz.

"Why do you smile so much?" Now, Jessica Donner is in my path, about to ridicule me for something even more moronic. The hair I somewhat understand, but not THIS.

"Excuse me?" I am taken aback by the apparent accusation.

"You are always smiling. And you never talk. It's just weird." She rolls her eyes and flips her glossy brunette hair over her shoulder.

"I talk . . . I talk a lot. Just ask my friends. And I smile because I'm happy." I know I am slightly defensive, but I have the right to be in this situation.

"Okay . . . whatever you say." She sends me a fake grin and turns into the nearest classroom.

I send a steely glare into her spine.

I don't always smile.

When I find Jillian and Keeley, a weight is lifted. These are the girls that are always in my corner. We refer to ourselves as "The Three Musketeers."

"Are you ready for our skit?" Keeley, who is nearly a foot shorter than me, is enthusiastic.

"I sure am! I can't wait until everyone sees me in my grandma costume."

We all giggle as we head out of the doors of the grade school, carrying numerous props in our arms. We are the lucky few that have the chance to walk to the middle school each day for the accelerated reading class.

"Jessica Donner told me I smile too much." I spill what is on my mind as we enjoy the warm fall breeze. "And Serena keeps singing her dumb afro song every time she sees me."

"Well, they are just stupid, Janey. Don't listen to them. You are faster and smarter and sweeter than all of them, and they are just jealous. Do you think any of them could run a seven-minute mile?" Keeley is firm in her encouragement, and she gives me a quick side-hug. She is one of the only people I know that always knows what to say.

"So, Janey," Jillian lowers her voice, "I hear you have a crush on Aren Jannis."

"I DO NOT!!" My face explodes into purple as I shove her playfully.

"I see how you look at him in band," Keeley nudges me.

All I can do is blush.

"I am not looking at anybody in band." I deny what she has said but am smiling.

"Maybe he will be in the indoor soccer league with us this year," Keeley adds spiritedly.

"Maybe." I try to whisper because he could be right behind us. He is in the accelerated class too.

Soon, we are climbing the stairs of the junior high and are entering Mrs. Prattle's room.

"Hello, girls!" She smiles our way.

"Hi, Mrs. Prattle!"

We find our seats and eagerly await the presentation of our skit.

Aren walks in shortly and looks my way. Giving me a small smirk, he sits in the block of seats on the other side of the room.

This day started off pretty cruddy, but now I can only smile.

The Running Game

My stomach flutters as I try and sit through my Algebra 1 class.

Today is the conference cross country meet, our last meet of my first season of running. Mr. Barney's words, "She's a star!" have finally driven me to try my new favorite sport.

I look back at the clock and notice Melanie Wales, one of my favorite eighth-grade running friends, staring at it too. She looks my way and makes a goofy face. I know she is worried about the big race as well.

In one minute, the bell will sound, and the time of reckoning will come.

"Riiiiiiiing!"

I spring from my seat and dash out the door.

"Slow down, Janey Eller!" Mrs. Gelanis, my teacher, calls out in vain.

I fling open my locker, and all of its contents fall to the ground. I madly scramble to recover each notebook, folder, and textbook before they are kicked down the hallway. Sometimes I move too fast for my own good.

"And there's Janey, lying all over the floor again," screeches the annoying Reese Hunker. He can really get on my nerves, especially when I am already in a frantic frenzy.

When I finally make it to the bus, I find a seat by the window and sit in scared silence. I can't talk when a major race is approaching.

"Hey, it's the hairy ape!" Lupe Gomez exclaims, as he passes my seat. I continue to stare out the window, trying to ignore him. I am sick and tired of people calling me names just because I don't shave my legs. I am twelve for goodness' sake!

Once we reach Cherry Lake Forest Preserve, it takes everything within me not to vomit right there on the bus. I can see the white starting line stretched out across the field like a foreboding monster. There are ten boxes for the ten conference teams: Berkley, Crawley, Johnston, Lees, Morrison, Northwest, Norwich, Parkville, Waveland (our school), and Whitson.

We file out of the bus and, once we place all our backpacks under a tree near the finish, start our course walk. We have practiced here earlier in the week, but nearly everyone went the wrong way. My race, the sixth- and seventh-grade girls' race, is first, and I, for one, want to make sure I know where to go.

"Did you hear the Parkville girl is running eighth grade today?" Melanie catches up with me and tells me the good news. "And a couple other girls might be running up as well."

"Really?"

"Yep! You could win this!"

I gulp. I took first place in two other races this season, but to win the conference meet would be an even greater victory.

"That would be awesome!"

"Janey!" I turn around and see Keeley sprinting after me. She has come just to watch me run. "I heard a bunch of girls moved up to eighth grade for the race today! You could win!"

"That is what Melanie told me." Now everyone knows I am supposed to win! I don't think I can take all of this pressure.

When we arrive back at our pile of bags, I sit in the grass and stretch. Melanie, Nicolette McFadden, Lynnea Rend, and some of the other girls are spraying silver paint in their hair. I lay back and do the quad stretch as I stare up at the puffy, white clouds.

"Janey, do you even have a stomach?" Above me, I see Lisa Bucks eyeing my waist. She lightly presses down on my abdomen with her shoe. "You are lucky to be so thin."

Ha, if only my know-it-all doctor from fourth grade could hear what people were saying about me now!

I jump up and pace a little by the starting line. I appreciate the compliment, but I need to focus. There are only a few minutes before the gun sounds.

When we are all lined up to go, like a long rainbow of runners, I finally feel ready. This is my race.

After a few anxious moments, the gun sounds its thundering cry, and I shoot out, like a cannonball headed for enemy territory. My chicken legs fly in front of me, and I can feel the breath of an angry mob on my back. They are close behind, but not for long. As I round the first bend, I keep my quick pace. The woods are like a big shadow covering me, hiding me from my pursuers.

Passing by a glittering lake, a song enters my head. It is "The Bunny Song." Well, actually, it is "The NEW and IMPROVED Bunny Song," which is the kinder version of the original.

"The bunny, the bunny, whoa, I ate the bunny. I didn't eat my soup or my bread, just the bunny. The bunny, the bunny, oh, I love the bunny. But now I feel sick in the head from the bunny."

Why on earth is THAT song in my head? It is not only a ridiculously silly Veggie Tales song but has a very slow beat.

I try as hard as I can to think of another song, but it is useless. I guess this is my anthem that will carry me through this race.

As I charge up a hill and approach the crowd once more, I hear a familiar voice. "GO, JANEY, GO!!!!" Keeley is cheering her heart out for me. She is sprinting as she cheers and crosses right in front of me. I almost run her over.

"WAVELAND, GET OUT OF THE WAY!!!" Mr. Faraway's voice booms over the crowd. By Waveland, he means Keeley.

I tear off towards the bird house and feel my legs starting to tire. My mouth is as dry as a desert, and I am definitely slowing down.

Dig deep, Janey.

I hear the crowd cheering for someone behind me.

The angry mob is gaining ground!

I press on, reeling in the last tree, and hang on for dear life as I approach the finish. I know my form is quickly falling apart.

"Run, Janey, run!" My teammates chant. "Run, Janey, run!"

As I cross the finish line, the clock reads *"5:55."*

My heart soars.

I not only took first in the conference but broke six minutes on the mile for the first time in my life.

I am handed a green ribbon with the word *"finisher"* in gold lettering. It may not say "first place," but it is like an emerald to me.

That is when my jello-legs give out, and I collapse to the ground.

I am finished.

Be Afraid . . . of Me

"Janey! I'm going to beat you to Mrs. O'Connor's room!" Micah Hadley jogs past me, giving me a small smirk, as we both head to our Language Arts class.

"Hey, you can't run!" I lengthen my walking stride until I am speeding as fast as I can without actually jogging or running. I find myself smiling as I race after my newest crush. Micah may only stand at four and a half feet tall, but he is hilariously awesome.

I make a quick right turn at the stairs and rush down two at a time.

I am halfway down the second flight when I am suddenly airborne. I am flying, flying, flying through the air, superman style. When I finally make contact with the earth, I land in a belly flop at the bottom of the stairs. I just lie there stunned for a couple seconds.

"JANEY!!! Oh my goodness!!! Are you alright??!!" Micah has turned around and is just staring at me, the corner of his lip quivering. He is trying so hard not to laugh.

I don't say anything at first because the floor has knocked the wind out of me.

"Uhhhhh, yeah. I'm good." My face is raspberry red as I jump to my feet and catch up to my friend. "I just fell down half the flight of stairs." I still can't even believe that just happened.

We both burst into giggles as we walk side by side the rest of the way to Language Arts.

As we enter my favorite class, I glance up at the board.

"What scares you?"

That is our journal topic of the day.

It is Halloween, so the question is understandable.

I head straight to my seat, still chuckling from my epic fall while simultaneously listing all my fears in my mind.

Once I pull my notebook from my enormous, blue binder, I start to write. I already know my list will be quite long.

"What scares me? Well, I am afraid of many things. My fears include tornadoes, lightning, black widow spiders, snakes, the dark, my closet, bridges, crossing train tracks, heights, being alone, my house burning down, sharks, flying in an airplane . . ."

After about five minutes, Mrs. O'Connor wakes me from my thoughts.

"Does anyone want to share his or her journal entry with the class?"

I immediately raise my hand. I love to participate.

"Janey?"

I stand to my feet and read what I have written.

Micah chuckles in response to my list.

After I share, Chrissy Girdling slowly raises her hand.

"Chrissy?"

Chrissy pushes her nearly jet-black hair over her shoulder and rises to her feet.

"So, Chrissy, what scares you?" Mrs. O'Connor asks.

"Janey Eller."

That is all she says. And then, she sits back down in her seat.

My mouth drops open. I am more stunned by her words than by wiping out on the stairs.

I swing my head over to look at Keeley. She is staring at me, just as stunned.

Mrs. O'Connor looks confused as to why Chrissy said what she said but just moves on to the next raised hand.

"Yes, April, what scares you?"

April Reiser jumps to her feet and spits out the words before anyone can stop her.

"Keeley Hanes because she is friends with Janey Eller!"

Did I just hallucinate, or did she just include me AND my best friend in her list of fears?

All Keeley and I can do is stare at each other, mortified.

This is worse than people saying I look like a crow.

This is worse than the eighth-grade boys calling me "Hairy Ape."

This is even worse than not being chosen to play soccer at recess.

I now SCARE people.

And Keeley scares people because she is my friend.

I am not sure if it is my hair, my clothes, or my personality, but I now know there is something about me that frightens others. And that knowledge gives me a sinking feeling in the pit of my stomach.

"Okay, that is enough sharing for today." Mrs. O'Connor looks a little shaken, but she doesn't admonish the girls for what they have said.

Earlier this month, I was on the top of the world, taking first place at the cross country conference meet. Now, after this Halloween journal entry, I feel lower than a measly worm.

Enter Riley

"Come on, Janey. Please? Pleeeeeease sing 'I Love My Lips' for us!" Mark Rogers' wavy blond hair bounces up and down in the sunlight. He knows I have memorized every Veggie Tales song and is adamant I sing it for him. We have just finished our track workout, and now we need to fill our time with something. Apparently, Mark thinks I should fill it with singing.

I start to open my mouth but stop myself. Mark and, more importantly, Riley Gray are both watching me.

I am not sure I can resist those sparkly green eyes.

"Oh, okay. Well, if you really want me to sing." I pause and then break out into my favorite Veggie Tales song. *"If my lips ever left my mouth, packed a bag and headed south . . ."*

Riley is looking right into my eyes.

I pause and then start walking towards the school.

Riley and Mark follow me.

"Come on, Janey!! PLEASE sing it for us!" Mark whines.

I blush. "No." I can't sing in front of these boys, even if it is only a silly song.

Riley continues to walk alongside me, but Mark runs off to goof around with Joshua Maloney. He is tired of waiting.

I glance down at my little follower as we walk into the dimly-lit multipurpose room. He is small for a sixth grader, with short chestnut hair, freckles, and emerald eyes. He is one of our fastest boys on the team, and I am the fastest girl. Maybe this is why we are starting to become fast friends.

We both see the drinking fountain in the distance and take off sprinting.

We giggle as I start to take a drink, the victor in the miniature race.

"You ran so well today, Riley," I smile, looking up at my running buddy, who is waiting to properly hydrate himself.

"So did you, Janey."

I wait for him to drink his fill of water, and, together, we walk back across the multipurpose room.

"Would you two stop flirting?" Robin East laughs melodically as she walks past us.

I stop dead in my tracks and give Riley a quick look. His face, like mine, flashes a hot red. Within milliseconds, he is a runaway train, racing out into the sunshine.

I cannot believe Robin would say such a thing.

I was NOT flirting.

I was just talking to a friend . . . a friend that I might actually have an itty-bitty crush on.

I walk slowly out of the gym, contemplating what just occurred, and watch as Riley tears around the school. He must be running laps.

In less than two minutes, he passes me again.

We give each other a quick smile. Robin and her comments are forgiven.

This routine continues for quite some time until he is on lap seven, then eight, then nine. Is he ever going to stop?

I step back into the gym for a bit, as to not appear like I am obsessed with Riley, and watch as Maggie Williams begins an attempt at the high jump. Her feet soar from the ground, and all seems well until her head collides with one of the metal poles. My mouth drops open as Mrs. Murky races to her side. Her poor head is dripping with blood. Poor Maggie!

I step back outside, just in time to see Riley round the school once more.

"I'm on my thirteenth lap!" he proudly tells me.

"Good job, Riley!" I cheer. I am the only person watching.

I yell this out each and every time he comes around the corner.

Soon, Keeley Hanes is at my side. "How is my skinny, little wimp doing?" she asks, wrapping her fingers around my bicep. She is always teasing me about my stick-like arms. I can't believe I ever had a doctor that thought I was chunky.

"I'm good."

She nudges me with a giddy smirk when Riley completes his seventeenth lap. I know exactly what she is thinking.

When it comes time for everyone to start heading inside, Riley rounds the school for the twentieth time. He comes to a halt, putting his hands on his hips, and I run over to his side.

"That was awesome, Riley! You ran at least five miles!"

He is beaming.

"And that is on top of the block workout we did earlier."

I am proud of my little friend.

We both head inside and make our way to the locker rooms.

Another day of track practice has come and gone.

As I leave the school, I hear some track athletes talking and laughing.

"This one little sixth grader ran around the school like twenty times."

"He must be crazy or something."

"What's his name?"

"Riley Gray," I slowly answer, feeling the need to interrupt their conversation.

"Oh, well, why did he do it?"

"He probably just wants to get faster," I remark, sticking up for him.

"Are you talking about Riley?" Keeley sneaks up behind me and pokes me.

I don't even answer her. Instead, I start walking towards my dad's white twelve-passenger van. She jogs to catch up with me. I am her ride to soccer practice.

As we walk, I catch a glimpse of Riley hopping into an aquamarine minivan. I smile to myself.

We start the drive to practice, and I notice that the same van is following us.

"Hey, Janey," Keeley nudges me. "Isn't that Riley behind us?"

"I don't know," I reply in a grumbly voice, even though I clearly know it is him.

"Ooh, Janey. Like five people have told me he likes you, including Johnny Rend." Johnny is a close friend of hers.

I slump down in my seat and attempt to wrestle her mouth shut.

"Some people even say he ran around the school to impress you," she says, when her mouth is set free.

Dad just laughs from the driver's seat.

When we reach the soccer field at Crocker Park, I take off out of the van with water bottle in hand. Keeley takes off after me, her long blondish-brown ponytail swinging in the spring air. I set my water bottle down and begin to hop up and down the small set of bleachers. Keeley starts to hop up and down with me, and we begin to beat out the song of "Mary Had a Little Lamb."

"You do like Riley, Janey."

"No, no, no, no!" I sing back at her.

"Yes, yes, yes you do!"

"MARY HAD A LITTLE LAMB!!" I sing out even louder.

"BANG! BANG! BANG! BANG! BANG! BANG! BANG!" call out the bleachers under our feet.

"What are you guys doing?" Tammy Spader laughs, clad in her grey track sweats. She is a fellow runner.

"Oh, nothing," Keeley giggles, as I give her a playful glare.

Pretty soon, Coach Freeman and the others arrive, so practice can begin.

"I heard you are doing a pretty good job in track," Coach says.

"I guess," I shyly say back to her.

Mr. Gibbous joins our conversation. "Didn't you run a 6:13 the other day?"

"Yep! It was our second track meet of the season!" I smirk and skip onto the field.

It is sort of fun being slightly famous—slightly famous AND slightly in love.

P.E. Should Be Called Pee-Yew!

The bus comes to a halt, and I am ready. Hopping to my feet, I scurry out of the parked vehicle. Keeley and Mason tear after me down the steps and towards the heavy, blue middle-school doors. Keeley giggles and yells at Mason to grab onto my backpack.

I am too fast for their efforts.

My frizzy, brown braid bounces against my purple backpack as I come to a crawl outside the office doors. I quickly scribble my name onto the sign-in sheet and grab the latest packet of announcements.

Let's just say this is an everyday routine for me and my Algebra 2 pals. Every day, we are dropped at the high school for an hour of smarty-pants math and then take a short bus to our actual school. Every day, they all race to beat me to that sign-in sheet, but they rarely ever do.

I lightly skip up the stairs, flipping through the announcements. On the last page, I find a brief summary of the previous day's cross country meet versus Crawley, Northwest, and Lees. *"The eighth grade girls won . . . Janey 'Pace Master' Eller came in first."*

I smile as I turn the corner and walk to my locker. Once I fling my jacket and backpack inside and pull out my enormous binder, I tear over to Keeley.

I spin like a ballerina beside her. "Look at me twirl," I sing out, just as Micah Hadley turns the corner.

I come to a blushing halt as Keeley and I burst out laughing.

Micah shakes his head with a smile.

"Riiiiiiiing!" sings the bell. It is time for second hour.

Speeding down the stairs, I make my way to the girls' locker room. I careen through the open door, which greets me like the mouth of a tomb, and hurry to change into my gym suit before anyone else arrives. I like to turn everything into a race.

I guess I didn't walk fast enough today though because Tanya Spires is already there, waiting for me.

Dang it.

Before I can even pass her, she quickly lifts up her shirt and bra and bares her chest to me.

"Hi, Janey," she whispers darkly, her long auburn hair cascading around her devilish eyes.

I gasp, turn the color of a watermelon, and sprint the rest of the way to safety.

I reach for my lock and spin it three times to the left, two times to the right, and once to the left. I jostle it open and . . . all of the contents are gone.

What the heck?

I already had my school lock stolen from me three times in the past two weeks, along with several of my notebooks. The rebellious Max Rivers, my one time rival in all things running-related, had found a way to tear into my secret cove, making my life one annoying series of disappearances.

Now, a girl in my gym class has done the same.

I want to cry. My day started off so well, and, now, it is quickly headed towards a dark abyss.

I look at the number on my locker to make sure it is actually mine.

It is.

My gym suit is gone.

I rifle through the lost and found.

"Jessie Currillo."

"Katie McCoy."

"Abby Yates."

No "Janey Eller."

I circle the locker room, scanning the floor and any possible hiding place.

That is when I see the garbage can nestled in the corner by the emergency door.

They wouldn't go that far, would they?

I dare to look in the least expected location, and, right there, on the top of the trash heap, is my gym suit.

I stare at it for a couple seconds, wrestling in my mind as to how it ended up there.

Was it Tanya's doing? Or was it Gabby Rader's? (Gabby is this rather heavyset girl that likes to randomly ram me into the wall whenever she sees me.)

After a few seconds of thought, I rip it from its hiding place and march over to Mrs. Pfeiffer, my P.E. teacher.

"Mrs. Pfeiffer! My gym suit was in the garbage!"

"How did it get there?"

"I don't know." I really want to cry now.

"Did you lock your locker?"

"Yes. I always lock my locker. I don't understand how people keep opening it!"

Mrs. Pfeiffer looks a bit flustered by the situation but gives me a reassuring smile.

"They probably just wish they were as athletic as you. My daughter, Maddie, has to try so hard to run, but you do it almost effortlessly."

I grin at the compliment.

"Well, thanks! Kids used to say I ran like a chicken with its head cut off."

"You don't! You are a natural."

So, once Mrs. Pfeiffer has given me a little more motivation to continue attending this awful class, I quickly head to my corner to change in the fastest time possible. I have already lost crucial seconds in my race to be the first person dressed.

When I finish, I speed walk to the end of the hallway where we wait for our teacher to dismiss us to the gym.

I am still the first person there.

Score.

I sit down and rest my head against the wall. This is going to be a long day.

The girls, one by one, line up behind and across from me.

Susy Latham, one of my so-called friends, eyes my legs curiously.

"Why don't you shave your legs?"

"Um, what?"

"Why don't you shave your legs? They look kind of hairy."

"I DO shave my legs, just not above the knee." My mom forced me into it the day before the first day of school. I wanted to remain a kid forever, but she wanted to put a stop to the needless teasing.

I guess her efforts were in vain.

"Well, you should definitely shave your WHOLE leg. Do you really want all the boys to keep calling you 'Hairy Ape' behind your back?"

Is Susy just trying to make me feel even worse? I KNOW what they call me. I don't want to be reminded of it.

"Yeah, don't you want to impress Riley Gray?" Keeley nudges me as she sits down beside me.

"What are you talking about?"

"I see you flirting with him at the cross country meets, Janey."

Can somebody pull the fire alarm or something? Or pinch me and wake me up from this horribly nightmarish dream?

"I don't really care what you or any guy thinks. They are my legs. And I DO shave them!"

"Yeah, but you could do a better job," Susy scoffs.

"Well, at least I don't look like a cucumber riding a skateboard."

There, maybe that will shut her up. People don't seem to know how to respond to a Janey Eller original comeback.

"What does that even mean?" Susy rolls her eyes, but Keeley just laughs.

Soon, Mrs. Pfeiffer blows her whistle, and we file out of the crowded hallway and into the gym.

Finally.

Being in an all-girl gym class may not be the best, but it is better than being in a crowded hallway surrounded by an entire flock.

Who on earth ever decided to segregate classes in middle school?

They should be sentenced to life in jail.

"So, today, we are going to play flag football," Mrs. Pfeiffer announces. "But first, we are going to do some sit-ups and push-ups."

All of the girls, except me and Keeley, groan.

"Fifteen push-ups. Ready, go."

I am nearly done with the fifteen counts when Mrs. Pfeiffer blows her whistle.

"Girls! I need to see you all trying a little harder."

My heart sinks a little. I WAS trying.

"Janey, can you come up to the front?"

"Sure." I am unsure of where this is headed.

"Now, most of you girls are just bobbing your heads or dipping your bodies a couple centimeters on these push-ups. That isn't going to get you anywhere. Janey is going to demonstrate the CORRECT way to do a push-up."

I don't know if I should be happy to be picked out of the crowd or slightly embarrassed.

Some of the girls give me a disdainful look.

Keeley gives me a thumbs-up sign.

I demonstrate three of my best push-ups for the class.

"See how she keeps her back straight? That is how ALL of you should be doing them."

Someone in the back of the gym snickers.

Great, now I'm going to be teased even more for being the teacher's pet.

When we are done with stretching and various abdominal exercises, we head outside to the field.

"One lap!" Mrs. Pfeiffer shouts.

I sprint out the black double doors and take off around the perimeter of the field. My one arm flails crazily, and I lean a little too far forward, but my legs are flying regardless. I love to run. It is like pure freedom.

After our lap around the field, in which most of the girls walk or jog at a pathetically slow pace, it is time to pick teams.

Whoever thought this was a good way to divide up a group of girls should also be sentenced to life behind bars.

Tanya Spires and Jessica Donner are chosen as captains.

"I pick Gabby."

Gabby Rader trudges over to Tanya's side.

"I pick Josie."

Josie Jamison swaggers over to Jessica's side.

"I pick Reina."

And so the picking continues.

And it continues until Keeley and I are the last two remaining.

Jessica squints, scrunches her nose, and sighs.

"I guess I choose Keeley." Keeley smiles just a bit, happy to not be picked last. She gives me a reassuring glance as if to encourage me in my predicament.

I feel as if I have been sucker-punched in the gut.

Last again.

And the stupid thing is that Keeley and I are probably the only two girls who care about sports or will even try in a game of flag football.

I attempt to not look too disappointed as I jog on over to Tanya's team.

How fair is it that I have to be with the girl that flashes me every day of my eighth-grade life?

I will show those girls how dumb they were to pick Janey Eller last.

Three minutes into the game, I have already scored two touchdowns. My chicken legs are flying, my braid is bouncing, and my energy is high. The only person that comes close to pulling my flag is Keeley.

"Ouch!" Josie lets out a whiny yelp as I plow past her.

"Calm down," Jessica grumbles, as I make a dive for the waving flag on her hip.

"Geeze, it is just gym class," Gabby growls.

"You guys should at least try," I whisper to myself.

I brush off their comments and continue giving 100 percent.

I don't really care if they like me anyways.

And besides, I know that Keeley is my only true friend in this gym class.

"Hey, Janey," Keeley whispers, as she, Johnny, and I walk down the hallway together. "Look!"

I gaze in the direction she is pointing and nearly stop in my tracks.

It is Mrs. Gray.

She must have dropped something off for Riley.

I look down at my feet and blush.

"There is your future mother-in-law," Keeley giggles, as she pokes me.

"Shhhhh!" I shove Keeley softly, trying to keep her from spreading my secret any farther.

I look over at Johnny, and he can't help but smile. He knew about my love for Riley long before Keeley made this declaration.

The three of us, along with the rest of the band, are headed towards the bus that will take us to Contest, the one competition we partake in each year. I know that Riley will be somewhere on that bus, and I also know that sometime, in the midst of the music and the fun, Keeley will ask him how he truly feels about me.

Once we reach the bus, we run up the stairs, and I sit near the front of the bus. Keeley sits beside me.

"Have you seen Riley yet?" she softly asks.

"No, not yet." I have thoroughly scoped out the bus in the couple of seconds it took us to find a seat, and I know Riley has not yet boarded.

"So, you really want me to ask him if he likes you?" she asks, grinning back over at me.

"Yeah," I whisper. "I'm sure."

Keeley has done my dirty work on numerous occasions throughout our middle-school years—with Bryan, with Aren, and with Micah—but in all of the previous times, the guys gave her an unfavorable answer of "no." Now, I am truly hoping the answer is "yes." Of all the other boys I have liked, I have never felt as sure of my feelings as I have now, with Riley. He is what makes me look forward to going to school when I have no other reason to go. Amidst the ridicule, rejection, and constant bullying, I always know I will see my sweet, green-eyed buddy.

Once Riley, who smirks shyly over at me as he boards the bus, and the rest of the band are seated, we begin our short journey to Weeks High School.

We have only been traveling for a few minutes when Susy Latham leans towards our seat and asks, "So, Janey. Is it true that you like Riley?"

"Shhhhhh," is all I can say. This is not the time or place to talk about Riley. He is only a couple rows behind us.

"Ooooooh, Janey! You like Riley?" Maggie Williams, who is sharing a seat with Susy, leans in, eager to find out all the little details.

"No, I don't!" I deny it and turn to face the window. I am pretty sure the red glow on my cheeks is a dead giveaway to the fact that I am lying.

"Oooooh! Janey loves Riley!"

I lunge across Keeley, trying to stop Maggie before she repeats herself.

"Maggie, DO NOT say that!!"

"JANEY LOVES RILEY!!!!" Susy exclaims, while my focus is on Maggie.

"STOP!!!!" I yell over at the both of them.

Out of the corner of my eye, I glance back to where I know Riley and Johnny are sharing a seat. Riley, like me, is blushing . . . but he is also smiling. He doesn't seem at all disgusted by the announcement. He actually looks kind of proud.

"JANEY LOVES RILEY!!!" Keeley feels the need to repeat the statement once more.

"Keeley, STOP!!" Since she is right beside me, I wrestle her into the seat.

Luckily, after this, the declarations cease.

But the damage is already done.

Now, the entire band knows of my secret.

Once we arrive at Weeks, we head to a practice room. This is where we will stay before we perform.

As we are heading to our seats, Julia Blue's little sister, Kerry, taps me on the shoulder.

"Are you the girl that likes Riley?"

Oh my word. I barely even know this girl.

"I was just kidding," Keeley answers for me.

"Yeah, they were all just joking," I add.

"NO THEY WEREN'T!!" Julia proclaims. She is a trombone player who sits by Keeley and Riley in band each day.

Once we are seated according to instrument, the talk of crushes ceases, and we all focus on the music. Finally, I can sit in peace.

For the rest of our time at Weeks High School, there is little disturbance. We practice and perform our songs quite well, and I am able to play my clarinet solo without squeaking. I am fairly certain that all minds are taken off me and Riley. Or so I think.

Once we pile back into the bus, Keeley makes a beeline to sit beside me.

"Janey, I did it! I asked him. And, this time, he gave me an actual answer!" She is about to burst from the seams with the information she now possesses.

"What did he say?" I try not to act too intrigued, but I am desperate to know.

I give her my full attention.

Keeley is practically dripping with excitement as she begins her story.

"Well, we had a few minutes before we were going to perform, so I asked him, 'Riley, did you hear what those girls were saying on the bus?' He glanced sideways at me, smiled, and said, 'yes.' I told him, 'Janey wasn't the one saying it. It was Maggie and Susy.'"

"It was you too, Keeley!" I interrupt, giving her a small nudge. She is not getting off the hook that easily.

Keeley continues once I have said my peace.

"So, Riley gave me this really weird look, and I told him, 'Janey was pretty embarrassed.' And then, I asked the question, 'Riley, do you like her?' He again looked sideways at me and said, 'Let me think about it.' I said, 'Tell me yes or no. Do you like Janey?' This time, he replied with, 'Fine, I do.' But, since he still didn't answer my question, I said, 'Do you not understand? It's a yes or no question. DO YOU LIKE HER??'"

I am holding on to her every word.

"This time, he softly answered, 'yes.'"

"Reallllly????"

"Yes, really. Riley likes you." Keeley is radiating with happiness. It must be a reflection of the glow on my own face. "Isn't that so exciting?"

"Yeah," I whisper.

For the rest of the ride home, I am sailing down a river of bliss.

All Keeley, Johnny, Veda Redding, and Robin East can talk about is the possible future Riley and I have together.

"At least he finally admitted the truth," I can hear Johnny say, as they chit chat about the situation. "I asked him that same question so many times, and every time he just looked away."

"I have asked him before too," Keeley chimes in. "Each time he would either say 'no' or 'maybe' or just look all around and avoid answering me."

"I knew he liked her," Robin sighs. "He LOVED the valentine she gave him, AND he is always flirting with her."

"We should set 'em up!" Veda happily adds.

Although I am not exactly in the conversation, I thoroughly enjoy all that they are saying.

I smile contentedly, excited for what the upcoming track season may have in store for us.

If only I was eighteen so that we could actually date each other.

"Okay, guys. It's already four o'clock. If we are going to go for a walk, we need to go NOW." Mom jumps up from the couch as Tasha makes a face.

"Why do we always have to go for a walk?"

"Hang on, the Cubs game is almost over," Dad responds, mid-snore.

"You know they are just going to lose. And, besides, you weren't even watching the game. You were asleep."

"No, I wasn't."

"Let's go." Mom turns off the television as several family members groan.

I, however, am not a part of the groaners.

"Are we going to Mavis Woods?" I ask excitedly. I just love our Sunday walks, especially at the state park.

"Yeah, I think so," Mom answers.

"Good! Maybe I will run part of it."

Mom gives me a smirk and then says, "You should call up Riley and see if he wants to come with us."

I scrunch up my face as if that is the dumbest idea ever. Inwardly, however, I am rejoicing at the notion.

"Really?"

"Yeah, it would be safer than if you ran all alone."

"Ooh, Riley," Tasha giggles.

I give her a glare, mid-blush.

"Are you sure?"

"Yeah. We could pick him up on the way over."

I just stand there, weighing the options. I would love to run with Riley, especially since I now know he likes me too. But I am afraid of the teasing that might ensue if we do pick him up and bring him with us.

I take a deep breath and ponder for a few more seconds.

"Should I give him a call?"

"Sure," Mom replies.

I slowly walk into Gramma's room and close the door.

Seven months back, before I was certain of Riley's love for me, he called me to join him and the guys for a run at Cherry Lake Forest Preserve. It was the only other time we talked on the phone to each other. That time, when I asked who was calling, he responded by saying, "It's me." (Like I should automatically know who "me" is.) It was the most adorable thing ever.

I count to five several times, trying to work up the courage to pick up the phone.

And then, I do it.

I dial the number that I know by heart and wait, heart pounding.

"Hello?"

It's him.

"Hey, Riley. It's Janey."

"Hey! What's up?"

"I was wondering if you were going running today."

"Yeah. I am actually about to go over to the track." He pauses. "Do you want to meet me there?"

"Well, my family is actually going to Mavis Woods."

Silence.

We appear to be at an impasse.

"Well, not much to talk about," Riley quietly states.

He mumbles something else unintelligible, and that is when I decide to hand off to my back-up.

"Do you want to talk to my mom?"

"Sure."

After giving her the phone, I listen attentively.

I have fled the awkwardness for at least a few moments.

"Do you want to go to Mavis Woods with us?" she asks.

Silence.

"Oh, don't worry. We can pick you up."

Silence.

"Yeah."

Silence.

"Okay, see you soon."

I am not sure why I couldn't have had the exact same conversation with Riley, but, for some reason, I couldn't even formulate a cohesive thought with him on the other end.

Soon, my family and our doggies, Shiloh and Stormy, are all packed into the van, ready to go.

"I hope our dogs are nice to Riley," I mutter with a laugh. Shiloh and Stormy are nut cases, and they aren't really all that great around people.

"Ooh, Janey. You are going to run with Riley." Tasha can't contain herself.

I turn around and pummel her with my eyes.

When we roll down Riley's street, I feel my pulse quickening. We are almost there.

When I finally see him standing there, waiting in the driveway with his parents, I feel like I might actually vomit.

"There he is," Tasha chuckles.

Oh, PLEASE just be quiet.

"Hi, Eller family!" Mrs. Gray calls as we pull to a stop.

"Hello!" Dad responds in a friendly manner.

"Thanks for picking up Riley to run."

"Oh, no problem."

Riley sheepishly makes his way to the door and climbs in. He is wearing a white tee-shirt tucked into a black pair of soccer shorts.

"Hey," he whispers, with a shy smile.

"Hey."

I can practically feel Tasha's grinning face burning into my back.

I also notice that my puppies aren't making a peep.

"I can't believe my dogs aren't barking at you," I say, quite astounded. "They are usually crazy when they see anyone that isn't in our family."

"Yeah, my dog is pretty crazy too. Her name is Lovely . . . but I didn't want to name her that."

Once we start talking, it is hard to stop.

I soon feel like Riley is part of our family.

When we arrive at our destination, Mom, Dad, Kayley, and my pups begin their walk around the 3.2-mile loop. Tasha follows them on her little, black bike. Since she absolutely hates walking, Mom is letting her ride instead.

Riley and I sit stretching for a few minutes. And then, I stand to my feet.

Riley follows suit.

We start to walk, side by side, following after my family.

After a few seconds, I break the silence. "Do you want to start running or just walk?"

We both laugh and take off down the trail.

From the start, I can tell that we are running pretty fast.

When we pass my family, Tasha leaves them behind and follows after us on her little bike. Earlier, I heard Kayley telling her to spy on us.

We continue to pick up the pace as we charge up the hills and through the wooded turns.

I look over at Riley and notice that his face is bright red. It is pretty hot outside.

"Do you want to stop at two miles?" I gasp to him.

He doesn't say a word.

He pulls a step ahead, so I respond by pulling a step ahead.

We are racing now.

This is what always happens when we run together.

Again, I gasp, "Do you want to stop at two miles?"

I don't usually ask to stop, but I am exhausted and overheating. And I am not sure how much longer I can keep up this pace.

When we finally reach the two-mile mark, I ask once more, "Do you want to stop?"

"Sure."

We roll to a halt and both lean over, placing our hands on our knees. I look over at Riley, and his face is glowing. He is just as tired as I am.

"Do you want to walk the rest of the way or run again in a little bit?"

"I'm fine with walking," he responds, with a tired grin.

We walk in silence for a while, but when our energy returns, we begin to talk.

Tasha just stares at us with a goofy grin on her face.

"So, did you know I once hit a chipmunk with my bike on this trail?" I turn and ask him when we are approaching the scene of my past crime.

"Really? You killed a chipmunk?"

"Not on purpose! It crossed in front of my bike, and I actually slowed down so I wouldn't hit it. However, once I thought it was safe to speed back up, the dumb thing doubled back and ran right through my wheel. It was horrible! It just laid there, convulsing, so my dad stepped on it to put it out of its misery." I try to give him a better picture of what happened with wild motions. He just laughs. "It was so sad. I rode off bawling, and my family buried it on the side of the trail. They even made a cross out of sticks."

"Wow. That is kind of funny."

"It was NOT funny! I felt terrible. I don't even like killing ants."

"I ran over a snake with my bike once, but that wasn't so bad. It was on one of the other paths."

"Snakes are gross. But chipmunks are so cute!" I pause. "I'm not sure I'd even care if I hit a snake."

"Oh, you would," Riley smiles, as he raises an eyebrow flirtatiously.

"Well, maybe."

"So, did I ever tell you about the time our phone fell into the Coyote River?" Riley inquires.

"Nope."

"Oh man, it was crazy. My little sister, Milly, was messing around with it at the same time she was playing with Lovely. She bumped into the dog and the phone went flying right into the water. My mom was so mad."

"Isn't she like only five years old?"

"Yep. She can have such a bad temper though . . . and can be so violent. Once she dumped flour all over the kitchen floor."

"I bet your mom loved that."

"No, she didn't. She was pretty mad."

"Yeah, my sister, Kayley, can be violent too. Once, when we were younger, I was reading a book in the apple tree, and she came up to me and bit me. Then, she ran into the house to tell my mom that I bit her!! It was ridiculous!!"

"She doesn't seem like she would be violent."

"Oh, she can be!" I assure him.

We continue walking and talking for the remainder of the loop. Tasha just rides behind us quietly, giving me silly faces every now and then. I am sure she is storing up ammunition to use on me later.

When we are done stretching and the rest of my family completes the loop, we hop back in the van.

Riley and I talk the entire way home.

"Oh man, have you ever seen the movie, *Jumanji*?" Riley questions.

"Yep."

"The part with the spiders always creeps me out."

"Me too! I remember watching it at Jillian Mills' house when I was younger and not even being able to sleep."

"I watched it at Johnny's house. We were all pretty freaked out."

"Spiders are creepy . . . but what is even creepier is my closet!"

"Are you serious?"

"Yeah! I used to think an old woman lived in there."

"ARE YOU SERIOUS??" he says again, more emphatically this time.

"Yes." I laugh. "I once woke up and thought I saw her standing by my bed. I just closed my eyes and hid under my blanket, sure she was going to stab me."

"Wow."

"I think it might have just been Kayley's blanket hanging down from her bed though." I giggle and then clarify. "We have a bunk bed."

"Janey likes to write in her notebook too," Tasha suddenly pipes up from the back.

Oh, dear. Where did THAT come from?

I turn a light shade of red and laugh nonchalantly. "That's what you do in a notebook, Tasha."

I sure hope that shuts her up. I do not want her to say anything more about my assignment notebook, as that is what she is referring to. I may or may not write about Riley in there, and I do not want him to know. That would be awkward.

When we finally reach the Gray residence, my heart sinks just a little.

My fun "date" with Riley is almost done. I will have to wait until practice tomorrow to run with him again. It is less than twenty-four hours from now, but it seems so far away.

"Thank you for inviting me!" he says excitedly, as he hops out of the van.

"Bye!" I give him a huge smile as I wave good-bye.

"Bye!"

I look over my shoulder as we drive away. Mr. Gray waves farewell, and Riley just stands there, grinning from ear to ear.

In this moment, I don't even care that Kayley and Tasha will probably tease me for at least a week.

I like my running buddy, and my running buddy likes me.

How can it get any more wonderful than that?

Into the Darkness

"Hey, guys! We are supposed to walk AROUND the gym." I raise my voice so that the members of the track team can hear. We have just finished another day of practice, and I am reminded of Mrs. Murky's announcement beforehand. The drama kids are practicing for this year's spring play in the gymnasium and need to be free of disturbances.

"Does it really matter?" Someone sounds aggravated.

"Yeah. Mrs. Murky told us to walk around at the start of practice."

I watch as half of the kids ignore my words and continue right on through the darkened gym.

"But Mrs. Murky said . . ."

"Just let them go," Johnny states calmly. "They can get in trouble if they want to."

We are all about to take the detour when I hear a voice calling out my name.

"Jaaaa-ney!" It is Josie Jamison.

Why on earth would she be talking to me?

Jessica Donner emerges out of the inky blackness to stand beside her.

"Mrs. Powers told us to tell your team that you can walk through the gym now." Josie is quite authoritative with her words.

I gaze over at Riley and Johnny, and they both shrug their shoulders.

"Mrs. Murky told us we couldn't." I am hesitant to believe.

"Well, we are done practicing, so it is okay now." Jessica is wearing a slightly ominous smirk. Maybe her face is just stuck like that.

"Come on, Janey," Riley beckons me forward.

"Are you sure?"

"They said it's okay."

I think about it for another second before deciding it is okay.

I surge into the darkness, following after Riley and Johnny, very aware that I am very unaware of my surroundings.

It isn't until I faintly see a shadow in front of me that I realize I should not have come this way.

However, before I can even comprehend what that shadow might be or even think about slowing down, I am flying through the air.

In under a second, my face is connecting with a colossal wooden corner.

"THWACK!!"

It is as if I have fallen inside of an enormous upside-down table.

"Owww, owww, owww . . ." I moan like a puppy that just had its foot run over by a truck.

Holding my head, I crumple into the fetal position on the gym floor.

In the inky blackness, I see the shadow of Riley swinging around and turning back towards me.

"Janey, are you okay?" I can't see his facial expression, but I know it is one of concern.

"Yeah. I think so."

I actually don't think so, but I am not sure what else to say. I also don't want Riley to think I'm a wimpy girl.

"Are you sure?"

"Yeah. I'm sure."

I slowly stand up, still holding my head, and walk in an almost drugged state to the door.

Riley walks alongside me until he knows I'm not going to keel over and die.

"See you tomorrow, Janey. I hope you are okay."

"Bye, Riley . . . and thanks."

I open the door and head from the gloomy gym into the bright hallway. I turn to the right and make a quick left into the locker room. At the end of the corridor, a full-length mirror throws my reflection right back at me.

I gasp and increase my speed as to get a closer look.

There is a huge, purple goose egg forming over my right eye and another huge, purple goose egg to the right of my right eye. My forehead and nose are also bloody, and there are red streaks dripping down my face.

"Oh my word! JANEY!!" I make out Corina Whitson's reflection in the mirror beside me, and her mouth is gaping. "You need to go to the nurse!"

"No. I need to take the late bus home."

"JANEY ELLER." She is emphatic. "You are going to go to the nurse IMMEDIATELY."

"But . . ."

"But nothing. Come on!" She grabs my arm and pulls me out of the locker room.

"How am I going to get home?"

"Call your parents. I'm sure they are willing to pick you up."

I am not in the mood to fight the stubborn Corina Whitson, so I reluctantly follow her where she leads.

Ahead, I can see through the office window, and both of my track coaches are inside.

Oh boy.

"Well, Janey, I have to catch my bus." Corina releases my arm. "Are you going to be okay?"

"Yeah, I'm okay," I lie again. I don't really want to face my coaches looking like this.

I take a step through the door.

"Eller, did you get into a fight?" Mr. Jacobs tries to suppress a chuckle as I round the corner into the main office.

Mrs. Murky, on the other hand, is not so amused.

"Janey! What happened?" She rushes to my side.

"I smashed my face on a table." I am still somewhat stunned.

"A table? A table did THAT to you? Are you sure it wasn't the Parkville girl? We could tell everyone you got into a fist fight with her. That would make for a much better story."

Haha. Mr. Jacobs is a major jokester.

"Noooooo," I giggle through my pain. The Parkville girl, whose name is Erica Maves, is my arch rival in both track and cross country. "She may beat me in every race, but she would never literally BEAT me."

"How did your face run into a table? I mean, I know your legs do a lot of running, but your face runs too?"

Oh man. Mr. J. is on a roll!

"Well . . ." I start slowly because I'm not sure how to tell Mr. J. and Mrs. Murky that I had somewhat gone against something they had told us to do. "You know how we were told to walk AROUND the gym after we were done with track practice?"

"Yeah. We told everyone that at the start of practice," Mrs. Murky recalls.

"Well, I remembered you had told us to do that. I was actually the one reminding everyone to not walk through the gym."

"Good. At least someone listens to something I say."

"But then, right as I was about to take the detour, some of the drama kids—I think Jessica Donner and Josie Jamison—told us just to come through the gym. They said they were done practicing, and it was okay. They even said Mrs. Powers told them to tell us it was okay. I was hesitant to listen, especially since they are generally mean to me, but they assured me it was okay. So, Riley, Johnny, and the rest of us headed into the darkness. It was pitch-black, and I didn't notice the upside-down table or box or whatever it was until I was tripping over it. My face hit the corner, and, now," I pause for effect, "I look like this. I was going to just take the late bus home, but Corina insisted I go to the nurse instead."

"You were just going to go home?" Murkdog, which is our nickname for her, shakes her head. "You don't always have to be so tough, Janey." She proceeds to lead me into a back room, which is apparently the nurse's office, and cleans up my wounds. The hydrogen peroxide hurts a bunch, but at least there isn't blood dripping down my face anymore.

Once I am no longer so freaky looking, my dad comes to school to pick me up since I have missed the late bus. This day has been quite the adventure.

The next morning, I am rather nervous about attending the high school for my Algebra 2 class. I am already a naïve, little eighth grader; I do NOT need to be a naïve, little, hideous eighth grader. I pretend to fix my bangs as I walk down the hallway in order to cover my bruises in the stealthiest way I can think of. I don't want anyone to think I am some kind of rebellious troublemaker.

I make it to Mr. Reader's class with only a few odd stares and dramatic double takes. I feel a bit of relief.

Once in the safety of the four walls of the classroom, I stop "fixing my bangs" and just allow my face to be seen.

"Janey! What happened to you?" I am asked this more times than I would like to count, but I enjoy telling my story. I am like my dad in that way. We both thrive on storytelling.

It isn't until I am back at the middle school that I receive the biggest reactions and revelations.

And they involve Jessica and Josie, the two angels of darkness.

I am swerving through the crowds of people when the two of them intersect my path.

"Janey???" They stop dead in their tracks. Gasping, they slowly cover their mouths. The color drains from their faces.

I slow for a second, confused by their concern, and then continue on my way to Mrs. Richards' class. As I turn into the room, I see the pale duo still looking my way.

What is up with those two?

"Birthday twin!! What happened to you?" Ray Devine gawks at me as he too finds his seat.

I retell my tale of woe.

In response, he pulls up one of his pant legs to reveal a gash at least a foot long.

"I ran into the table too."

"Oh, wow."

"I heard a few other kids got hurt as well."

"Really?"

"Yeah, and do you want to know what I heard? I heard that two of the drama girls placed that table purposely in the middle of that dark gym to WATCH people get hurt."

Jessica and Josie. It HAD to be their idea.

"Are you kidding me?"

"No, I am totally serious!"

Now it all makes sense.

"That is why they were so persistent in having us come through the gym."

"Yep. They are a bunch of jerk faces!"

And, now, they are a couple of pale faces.

"Oh my goodness. They hurt so many people!"

"Yep. Like I said, they are jerk faces."

I try to stomach the fact that I nearly lost my eye due to the stupidity of a couple girls. I think about it all throughout our spelling test and through the rest of the class period.

As the day continues, my head begins to throb. I am sure I have a concussion.

In my seventh hour class, I am on the verge of crying. I just want to lie down on a soft couch and sleep the pain away.

It is when I am feeling the worst that my teacher, Mrs. Powers, comes my way. Her face looks pained, and I am almost positive she is going to ask me if I am okay. I try as hard as I can to smile up at her only to be crushed by an atomic bomb of words.

"I don't feel sorry for you one bit. You knew you weren't supposed to go through that gym."

That is all she says.

And she walks away.

And not only does she walk away, but she heads right for Josie Jamison.

"That was a lovely skit you performed in class yesterday," she encourages her.

I want to vomit now, and, this time, it is not because I am about to run a race.

It is because all is not right in this world.

Running is Pain

"Dad, please stop whistling. It is making me sick." I lean back in the passenger seat and close my eyes.

We are on our way to my first 10k, the Hamilton Milk Run, and I am feeling extremely queasy. Maybe it is because cars make me motion sick, or maybe it is because we are swerving all over the place on this country road. Maybe it is because of the root beer floats we had at midnight after my eighth-grade graduation, or maybe it is just because I will be running this race with Riley. Whatever the reason, and no matter how silly it may seem, even Dad's whistling is making me nauseous.

Dad stops his whistling, but the song he was whistling with is still playing on the radio.

"Dad, please turn the music off. I think I'm going to puke." I cringe and try to think about anything other than the fact that I am in a moving vehicle, on my way to a 6.2-mile race in the ninety-degree heat. I breathe deeply and try to calm my thoughts and my nerves.

"DAD!! I said to turn the music ALL THE WAY OFF!!"

No more than a second after I take this authoritative tone, my breakfast of cinnamon toast and orange juice projects from my mouth in its new and uglier form.

"JANEY!!!" Dad's eyes nearly pop out of his balding head as he swings the car to the side of the road. "Why didn't you tell me to pull over???"

"I told you to turn the music off," I whisper weakly, disgusted at myself. There is puke all over my hands and my seat and the floor beneath my feet.

Dad is still shaking his head at our luck, but he is chuckling now.

"Janey, what are we going to do with you?"

I watch as Mom, Kayley, and Tasha pull over in the car behind us. They are traveling separately because of Tasha's soccer game.

"What's wrong?!" Kayley shouts out the window. "Why are you guys stopping?"

"Janey threw up all over the car," Dad replies.

"WHAT??!!" Mom throws her hands up in the air. "Why didn't you pull over?"

"There wasn't really any time."

"Ewwww!" Tasha scrunches up her nose. "That's gross!"

Dad uses a water bottle and a random handkerchief to clean up my mess. I just stand there stupidly, of no help to anyone. I wish I was never plagued with this business of puking. Why did God give me such a weak stomach?

When we are finally able to continue our journey to Hamilton, I realize I feel slightly dizzy and quite low on energy. How on earth will I run a 10k on an empty stomach? I have never even run farther than six miles on a content stomach.

I close my eyes for the rest of the trip—exhausted, embarrassed, and nervous about meeting up with Riley.

We make it the rest of the way without incident.

As soon as we step out of our red escort, I see Riley, Milly (Riley's five-year-old sister), and Mr. and Mrs. Gray. They are standing beside two bikes in the grass.

"Hey, Eller family!" Mrs. Gray notices us immediately. She is extremely extroverted and welcoming, an overall awesome lady. "Are both Janey AND Kayley running today?"

"Yeah, this is Kayley's first race!" I say with excitement. "She is running the two mile, and I am running the 10k . . . with Riley." I smile over at my favorite guy friend as he follows shyly after his mom.

"That sounds great!" She looks over at my parents. "Are Mom and Dad excited to watch their two daughters run?"

"Yeah. I just hope Janey has enough energy. She threw up all over the car on the way here."

"DAD!!" I cannot believe he just outed me in front of Riley. I lower my head and try not to make eye contact with him.

"Oh no! Are you sick?" Mrs. Gray asks.

"Did you drink some of that weird Gatorade again?" Riley smirks, remembering back to the cross country season when Mom had given me this weird health drink before one of my races.

"No, she's just nervous," Dad answers for me, patting me on the back.

"Would Mom or Dad like to ride one of the bikes we brought? You could ride alongside Janey on her longer race. Mr. Gray is going to try and do the same with Riley."

"We can do that?"

"Sure! I do it all the time in the 10k our family runs in Louisville each year."

Mom looks over at Dad, and, once he gives her a nod, she responds, "I'll ride it."

"Okay! I also have a helmet you can use."

Once Mom gathers the helmet and the bike, Riley and I walk to the side and talk about the upcoming race. As usual, we walk awkward circles around each other as we talk. My parents are always teasing me about it.

"So, are you ready to run?" he asks me quietly.

"I don't know. It's so hot! And I feel kind of weak."

"Yeah, it is supposed to be ninety-five degrees today."

"Oh man, seriously?" This whole heat thing is scaring me more and more. "I hope this race is mostly in the shade."

"I think only the first two miles are shaded . . . and maybe the last half mile."

"Really?"

"Yeah."

"Well, I'm glad I'm wearing a tank top then!" I look down at the little white shirt I am wearing, the one with the miniature blue flower on the neckline. I haven't really worn this since third grade, but I pulled it out just for a steamy day like today.

"Are you tired from graduation?" Riley wonders.

"Yeah. I was up until midnight. I do not think I got enough sleep!"

"I can't believe you will be in high school next year." Riley looks down at his shoes, slightly disheartened.

"Me neither." I think about life without Riley in the same school as me and add, "It will be sad no longer being on a team with you too."

"Yeah. Who will I compete against?"

We give each other a little grin and then look away. We can't make eye contact for too long.

"Maybe Kayley will run with you." I point to my soon to be sixth-grade sister as she joins our group. She may be young, but she is already pretty fast.

When it is time to make our way to the starting line, Kayley heads to the front, and Riley and I find spots in about the third or fourth row of people. We cannot start too fast if we are running 6.2 miles.

In a matter of minutes, the gun is sounding, and our herd is stampeding forward.

Kayley darts out like a sprinter, but Riley and I conserve our energy and try not to start too fast.

"Go, Janey!!!!!" my little sister, Tasha, screams in her adorable, high-pitched voice. "You can dooooooo it!!!"

At about the one-mile mark, Riley and I come up on Kayley. She is walking, and I am 100 percent certain it is because of a cramp. "Come on, Kayley! KEEP GOING!!! You are already halfway!"

She gives me a pained look in response and tries to start running again.

I feel some satisfaction in passing my sister, but I feel sad for her too. I wanted her to do well in her first race.

Up until the two-mile mark, Riley and I run side by side.

"14:04!" a man calls out from the side of the street.

Holy cow! I often run that time in my two-mile races.

Did we start too fast?

I realize the answer to that question is a resounding "YES" in just a matter of minutes, as Riley begins to pull ahead and leave me in the dust.

Luckily, Mom joins me on the bike she is borrowing right when I need her most.

"You are doing a good job, Janey!" she exclaims, as she starts to tailgate me.

We are heading into an ugly, treeless section of the course, and it feels like it is 100 degrees.

I can use whatever encouragement she can give me.

I am starting to overheat.

The sun is beating down on me like an angry Gabby Rader on the assault.

At the three-mile hydration stop, I pour water all over my head—downing my shirt, my shorts, and my shoes in the cool liquid.

"23:12!" another man calls out from the grass.

Wow, I have slowed down to nine-minute pace.

I roll up my tank top, tucking it into my sports bra. I don't even care what the spectators think of me.

I am broiling.

Over the course of the next mile, my pace slows to a crawl. I can barely lift my legs, so I shuffle.

I honestly think I am going to pass out.

Can I just lie down in the grass and take a nap?

"Good job, Janey!" My mom is still there, reassuring me. I can't lie down on the job with her watching me.

But even though I feel like a sloth and am running at a snail's pace, I am gaining on Riley. He must really be dying.

We are almost at the four-mile mark when I see him hobble over to the grass. Maybe he read my thoughts on the whole nap idea.

As soon as he reaches the side of the road, he falls to the ground and curls up in the fetal position. And, then, he starts puking all over the place, just like I did earlier in the car.

This is just not our day.

Seeing him lie down is like an invitation to follow his lead. I have already been thinking about lying down, but, now that he is doing it, the urge becomes even greater. It could be quite the bonding experience to die together at the four-mile mark of the Hamilton Milk Run.

So, right there, in the middle of the steaming asphalt, I sprawl myself out on the pavement and close my eyes.

"JANEY!!" Mom sounds frantic as she comes to a halt beside me.

"Number fifty-eight, are you okay?"

A nearby race official runs to my side.

All I can do is look up at him and my mom. I am too sleepy to say much else.

"Can you stand up?" the man asks.

I make a face that says "no."

"Here, you need to stand up."

I look over at Riley, who is still lying in the ditch. Why does he get to lay down all contented-like without anyone bothering him?

"COME ON, JANEY!!!! GET UP!!!"

This time, it is not the official calling out to me or my mom, but it is my gym teacher, Mrs. Pfeiffer, the lady who stood up for me when all the girls in my gym class treated me like dirt. She is still running the out section of the out and back that I am now on my way back on.

"YOU CAN DO THIS, JANEY!!!" she cries.

Her words are just the motivation I need to continue. I am not going to be a quitter.

Lifting myself up from the hot blacktop, I start to walk forward, towards the four-mile mark.

I cross it, still walking but increasing speed with each step.

"36:45!"

My fourth mile was practically the same as my first two miles put together.

I keep walking until Mrs. Pfeiffer's daughter, Maddie, the one she told me about in gym class that one horrible day, comes up alongside me.

"Come on, Janey. Run with me!" I am not sure how she even recognizes me or knows my name, but I am willing to listen to her words.

I start to jog alongside her. We talk about the ridiculous heat and the course in general for about a half mile, until I start to realize that I am actually beginning to feel good again.

When I regain most of my strength, I pull ahead of Maddie and continue pushing forward. I am not sure if Riley has picked himself up from his grassy grave on the side of the road, but I keep pressing on, hoping he is okay.

With about a quarter mile left, I pass Mrs. Gray, Milly, Kayley, Tasha, and my dad on the final turn.

Dad is focusing his video camera right on me, taping me as I plod along.

"Go, Janey!!!!" they all cheer.

"Where is Riley?" Mrs. Gray calls out to me.

"Back there," is all I manage to say, as I point to the stretch of road behind me.

I pick up the pace a little more on the final straightaway, using the last bit of strength I possess.

I never thought I would reach this point of the race, especially not when I was lying flat on the pavement.

As I cross the finish line in *"52:02,"* I feel more accomplished than I have in a long time.

I am wet, sweaty, and disgustingly dirty, but I am done.

It is a wonderful thing.

I shuffle my feet as I head for the shade of a nearby building. There is a table of refreshing water cups there, and it looks as welcoming as an oasis in a desert.

I am DESPERATE for both the shade and the water.

From the cool of my hideaway, I watch as an exhausted Riley crosses the finish line.

"55:45."

I slowly make my way over to my tired friend as he meanders towards the grass where Dad is standing with his video camera. He wants to have as much footage of this day as he can.

Once I catch up to Riley, it is time for the mini interview.

"So, how was it?" Dad asks, focusing in on our faces.

"Horrible," Riley answers for the both of us.

"Horrible" is a great word to use.

But, at the same time, the word "beautiful" might also suffice. Riley and I pushed through vomiting, heat, and pain to reach this finish. We shared in this together.

Running may be pain, but it is a beautiful pain when you are beside the guy that means the most to you.

First Dance

I smooth out the folds in my flowery, blue dress and place my fingers nervously on the yellow piano keys. Patting my bangs quickly into place, I sail into my new favorite song, "Rustle of Spring," written by Christian Sinding. My fingers fly across the keys, and I move my head dramatically with the music in regular "Janey" fashion.

Behind me, in the kitchen, a few of my friends are fussing over their make-up, silky dresses, and made-up hair. Because I really don't want to engage in such frivolous activities, I decide to play a little music.

When no one is looking, I quickly examine my reflection in a nearby mirror. In my size-twelve dress from the kids' department at T.J. Maxx that I have owned since I was ten years old, I hardly look the age of a sophomore in high school. And, with two butterfly clips adorning my untamable mane, anyone can see I have no regard for the latest teenage trend. Keeley tells me I should wear one of her more grown-up, black, slinky dresses, and Nicolette McFadden and Ashley Dolita ask to do my hair, but I refuse their attempts to further beautify me.

Today is homecoming, and I don't really know what to expect. All I know is that I feel as jittery as ever and as if the butterflies in my stomach are ready to make an exit through my throat.

I never imagined I would be in this predicament, not at least until Mrs. Gray shouted out of her car window that one day after cross country practice, "Riley wants to go to homecoming with you!!!!!" Who on earth is asked to a dance by their dream guy's mother? Only someone like me, I guess.

Just as I start repeating "Rustle of Spring," I see an aquamarine vehicle pull into Keeley's driveway. I gulp, smooth my dress and hair, and pretend to practice even more. One by one, boys file out of the car and head towards the back of the house. I take a deep breath as I strain my neck just a little farther. I don't see Riley anywhere.

He must have chickened out. I knew getting asked to a dance by him was merely a fantasy. Maybe his mom only wanted her son to have a date.

That is when Keeley snaps me back to reality.

"Hey! Janey Eller! Riley is wearing the same color shirt as your dress!" She smiles happily as she gazes out her patio windows.

I try not to react to her statement and swing back around towards the old, out-of-tune piano. Inside, I am smiling while simultaneously debating if I should run away from the whole debacle. Mom and Dad don't really even approve of the idea of a school dance.

Soon, the boys are entering the front door. I replay the last few measures nonchalantly and hop up from my safe spot on the bench. I barely lift my feet as I walk towards the entrance of the living room and peak my head around the corner just a few inches. There, in the group of boys, clad in a blue-collared shirt, tie, and khakis, stands Riley, my three-year crush. I pull my head back into its shell and sneak back around the corner. The butterflies start working overtime. I am sure some of them are losing their wings in the chaos. I bravely peak my head back out and watch as Nicolette places her red, sparkly Dorothy-style high heels on her feet and as Keeley slips on her white slippers.

It is at this moment that Ashley notices me. She heads in my direction.

I slink back around the corner.

"Janey, you should put your shoes on now. Go get them."

"Uh . . . uh . . . I can't," I stammer anxiously, as I quickly look over at Riley. "Can you please get them for me?"

I don't know what my problem is. I mean, it is just Riley. It is just the boy I have run with ever since seventh grade. He isn't like a famous celebrity or an all-time favorite Bible character. He is just a freshman boy. And he is actually somewhat nerdy. What power does he hold over me?

Ashley doesn't question my insanity and ambles back to the front door to pick up my shoes. I strap them onto my feet by the piano bench and take a deep breath.

In the other room, pictures are the main event.

I am usually a fast walker, but, right at this moment, I can't even seem to put one foot in front of the other. I slowly step into the living room, and Riley's gaze immediately catches mine. I smirk at him, he smirks at me, and we quickly look away.

"Mom, can you take a picture of Janey and Riley?" Keeley gives me her award-winning smile.

I feel as if the fiery sulfur that rained down on Sodom and Gomorrah has just splashed across my face. I quickly turn away once more.

"Janey, Riley, come over here for a picture." Mrs. Hanes looks a little too excited for this photo shoot.

Riley slowly walks over to me. He scoots ever so close and smiles proudly. I can only squirm and look completely embarrassed.

"Put your arm around her!" cheers Keeley.

I think I am going to die.

Riley carefully lifts his arm and drapes it lovingly over my shoulder.

I close my eyes and almost fall to the floor. I feel the fiery sulfur return to my cheeks.

"Smile, Janey!"

I think I might faint. Riley's arm is actually around me. This almost happened once in eighth grade on the last day of band because of a dare, but now it is actually a reality.

After what seems like an eternity, Keeley's mom turns the flash on and takes a picture.

Out of the corner of my eye, I can see Riley smiling as proudly as if he has just won the state cross country meet.

I squirm around shyly and disappear back into the crowd of people.

All I can hear is the beating of my heart.

When we arrive at the dance, however, I can no longer hear the beating of my heart. All I can hear is the "thump, thump, thump" of the bass.

I suddenly feel as if I am paralyzed.

Why did I come? I can't go in there. I can't dance. And I can't dance with Riley if he asks. My mom and dad don't want me dancing with boys.

I freeze.

Nicolette must notice that I am uncomfortable because she links her arm into mine and asks if I am okay.

"I think so." I gulp down enough oxygen to keep breathing.

"You are going to have sooooo much fun, Janey!" Ashley is quite enthusiastic.

"I hope so," I whisper. No one can hear me over the booming music emanating from the speakers.

We walk into the gym, and it is crowded.

I feel claustrophobic.

I feel out of place.

I look down at my outfit and want to make a run for it.

I am almost positive a nearby group is discussing my ensemble and laughing.

"Let's make a circle and dance!" Nicolette says cheerfully. "Come on, Janey!"

I give her a half-hearted smile.

Everyone around me starts to move back and forth and groove to the music.

How do they even know what to do?

"Come on, Janey! Dance!"

I stand motionless.

"You are at a dance, girl! Come on!" Keeley grabs one of my arms, and Nicolette grabs the other. They swing my limp limbs to and fro as if I am dancing all by myself.

I feel so uncomfortable.

I have to get out of here!

When they let go of my arms, I take a few steps back from the group and debate my next move.

"Janey! Riley told me he is going to ask you to dance soon!" Ashley looks so very happy.

"He is?"

"Yeah."

I nearly passed out when he put his arm around me for the photo shoot; I will probably drop dead if I actually have to dance with him.

That is when I make a run for it. I don't literally run, but I hastily walk into the hallway.

I can breathe a little better out here.

I wander around the hallway for most of the dance.

Every once in a while, I walk back into the gym to look around for Riley, who must think I am a horrible date, but, each time, I quickly backtrack to my safety zone.

I am terrified he will find me.

Everything within me wants to dance with him. I have dreamed of this night. But my paralysis and complete awkwardness is going to prevent it from ever happening.

After about an hour or so, Riley's older sister, Petra, approaches me. She looks concerned.

"Do you want my dad to come and pick you guys up?"

I want to say "no," but I instead say "maybe."

"Okay, well, I will give him a call."

It is after she asks me this question that Riley finds me. His eyes sparkle in the light.

"So, I guess you want to leave?" I can't tell if he is upset with me or not.

"I don't know." I never said I wanted to leave. Maybe I can still get up the nerve to dance.

"Well, my sister is calling my dad to come get us."

"Okay." I can't say much else. I feel like a failure. My dreams are being dashed, and it is every bit my fault. Why can't I just be smooth and cool like everyone else?

After about ten minutes of standing in fairly awkward silence, Petra returns to tell me and Riley that their dad has arrived.

Walking side by side in silence, Riley and I head down the hallway and out of the school.

Once in the car, Mr. Gray swings around, a huge grin on his face. "How was the dance?"

"It was okay," we both say in unison. No one wants to say that it was a total disaster.

We drive for a few minutes before Mr. Gray makes another attempt at conversation. We are stopped at a red light.

"So, Janey, are you coming over for ice cream, or am I driving you home?"

Am I supposed to come over for ice cream?

Does Riley WANT me to come over for ice cream?

I panic for a second.

"I need to know before this light turns green."

I panic a little more.

I look over to see if I can read Riley's reaction to the ice cream idea.

It is too dark to tell.

"Um . . . well . . . I guess you can drive me home." I am kicking myself as I say the words.

Janey, you are an idiot! Why the heck didn't you say "yes?"

Mr. Gray swivels the steering wheel and enters the turn lane so we can turn left. We would have gone straight towards Avery Forest if I had said "yes" to ice cream.

I want to cry.

Why did God make me like this?

I don't know how to dress.

I don't know how to dance.

And I don't even know how to act around the boy I love.

I look down at Riley's hand sitting on the seat between us.

I am now almost positive that my dreams of holding that hand will never come true.

The Stocky One

The sun is winking through the trees, dropping closer and closer to the horizon, as I head to the registration table. In one hour, the Tree to Tree 5k will begin, and I need to pick up my bib number.

"Janey!!!" Kassidy Boyer, one of Petra Gray's best friends, is waiting at the table to greet me. "Are you going to win this race today?"

"I hope so!" I flash a bright smile her way. I love it when Petra's friends talk to me. It makes me feel closer to Riley. I want to tell her my sister isn't running and that is why I actually have a shot, but I don't. No one needs to know why my impending victory will not be as difficult as it should have been.

"So, you pre-registered, right?" She starts to dig through the race bags in a cardboard box on the ground.

"No, we weren't sure if we would be back in time because we were on a bike trip." Bike trips are my family's annual summer vacation where we leave home with little more than our bikes, our tent, and the clothes on our backs. I made sure we rode a few extra miles the last two days just so we could arrive home in time for this race.

"That will be twenty dollars."

I promptly place my money on the table as she hands me a waiver. I sign my name saying I will not sue anyone if I drop dead on the course.

After she writes my name on a bib number, picks out a small tee-shirt (it is actually kind of cute with a smiling tree running across it), and drops both items into the race goody bag to give to me, I jog back over to my family. I scan the forming crowd to see if I can spot Riley anywhere. I don't see him yet. As I strain my eyes and neck to continue searching, my eyes fixate on a familiar silver-haired woman. It is Mrs. Gray, Riley's mom. If she is around, he must be nearby.

"Hey, Eller family!" she calls out to us with a wave.

"Hi," I say somewhat shyly. I love this lady, but she is the mother of my long-time crush, so I always feel a bit nervous around her.

"So, are both of you girls running the race?" She looks to me and then to Kayley.

"I'm running, but Kayley isn't."

"Oh." She looks over at my twiggy sister. "Why aren't you racing?" she asks quizzically.

"Eh. I don't really want to. And it costs money." She looks over at me. "And I want to watch Janey run!"

"It would be exciting to watch the two of you race." Her Kentucky accent is adorable, but the direction this conversation is heading is making me uncomfortable.

All I can do is look over at Kayley and cringe. I don't EVER want to race her head to head because I know FOR SURE I would lose. She ran a 5:25 mile this year as a seventh grader for goodness' sake! And last year, she was the first sixth grader to cross the line in the cross country state meet. I DO NOT want to race her. I am glad she is choosing not to run because if she DID run, I would just look like a fool.

"It's okay. We don't need to race." Kayley looks just as uncomfortable.

"Well, I still think it would be exciting!"

No, it would not.

"Riley is around here somewhere, but I'm not sure where he went." She too scans the crowd. I am sure she knows that I want to know where he is. It may sound weird, but I am almost positive her son shows her all the notes that I write to him.

"Oh." That is all I can say. I don't want to make it sound like I am too desperate to see him.

"He saw you guys ride past our house yesterday on your bikes and ran into the house shouting, 'MOM!! The Eller's are home from their trip!' He seemed excited that you would be here for the race."

Oh, really?

"So, Kayley, are you going to be on the high school team this year?" She looks back to Kayley.

"Oh, no," she chuckles. "I'm still in junior high for one more year."

"Oh, this is funny." She looks back to me. "One of the moms didn't know the difference between the two of you. She thought you were the same person."

"Yeah?"

"Yeah. I cleared up the confusion for her though. I told her, 'Janey is the stocky one, and Kayley is the skinny one.'"

I scrunch up my face, completely taken aback by the comment.

"Oh." I have to say something to acknowledge that she has spoken, but, if I say anything else, it probably won't be nice.

Did she just imply that I'm FAT?

She just called me STOCKY, and, in my mind, STOCKY is synonymous with chunky, husky, or big-boned. And I don't think I am any of those.

I KNOW I am not as fast as Kayley, even though I work harder than anyone in Waveland High School, and I KNOW I am not as skinny as Kayley, even though I am thinner than most everyone in my grade, so why does everyone else have to always bring it up? I HATE being compared to Kayley. She is practically perfect in every arena, and I hate that I feel like I have to be this perfect person to live up to all that she has accomplished in her thirteen years of life. Whether it is how fast we run, how high we score on standardized tests, how well we write, or how thin we are, we are ALWAYS compared. And I don't like it. The first question anyone asks us when they meet us is this: "Sooooo, who is faster?" And I can't even count the amount of times I have been asked this question at school: "So, why is your seventh-grade sister so much faster than you? Shouldn't you be faster than her?" It make me want to swing my fist and land a punch in the middle of their faces.

"Well, girls, I better get back to work! I am in charge of this thing this year!" And with that, Mrs. Gray interrupts my angry thoughts and leaves us with a parting smile.

"Bye!" we say at the same time.

I know that she could be my future mother-in-law, at least in my most favorable of dreams, but she has no right to call me "stocky."

I choose to start my warm-up at this time and jog off down the hilly street, her words still fresh in my mind.

Janey is the stocky one, and Kayley is the skinny one.

I don't think people realize how much power their words can have.

Basketball Blues

I can see the white sheet of paper glistening on the wall as I close in on my fate. In less than five seconds, I will know if I have made the varsity girls' basketball team.

There are several girls mulling around the list when I arrive. They are scanning the names, and each smiles when she finds her own.

The list is in alphabetical order.

"Karolyn Anderson, Liliana Bays, Nikki Birkle, Reina Blink, Lidiya Bobrov, Amie Devereux, Shannon Fritz, Jenny Lawrence . . ."

Hang on . . . where is my name?

Where is *"Janey Eller?"*

I anxiously read back through the names I have already read.

And then, I read the rest of the list.

"Raquel Palacios, Trisha Rink, Gwen Roberts, Corina Whitson, Maggie Williams."

Where is MY name?

I read back through the list once more.

My name isn't there.

I stare at the list blankly for only a couple more seconds . . . and then I burst into an uncontrollable fit of tears.

I am the ONLY person that didn't make the team . . . well at least the only person that didn't make the team that actually came to tryouts each day.

There are thirteen people without me.

Why couldn't there have been FOURTEEN?

Isn't an EVEN number of players better for drills?

At one of the summer league games, Coach Dobbs said he needed ALL of us on the team this season. ALL OF US. Was I not included in that ALL?

My world is a monsoon as I make my way through the hallway. I can barely see where I am going.

I stare at my feet the entire way to Honors U.S. History. I don't want anyone to see me in this state . . . especially not someone like Riley.

Coach Dobbs must think I am terrible at basketball.

He must think I am the suckiest player of all time to be the ONLY person cut from the team.

And to think I believed that garbage written in the packet he handed us before tryouts.

"In order to be a member of the Waveland Rays basketball team, each player must give 100 percent at practice. A lack of effort is unacceptable and will not be rewarded."

If that was true, how did Trisha make the team and I didn't? She was thrown out of tryouts for slacking and being disrespectful. (And I'm sure you can remember how she treated me at recess back in fifth grade.)

Why do I even try?

Why did I even go to EVERY SINGLE summer league game?

And why did I have my mom buy me a brand new pair of basketball shoes? What will I use them for now?

Yesterday, at tryouts, we shot three pointers at the end of the day. And you know who made the most threes? I DID!!

Did it even matter how I performed at tryouts?

I mean, I guess I could have done a better job on the box-out drill, but I was paired with none other than Lidiya Bobrov, the Ukrainian freight train/body builder. Her butt is seriously made of steel. With the thirty plus pounds she has on my small frame, there is no way I was ever going to dominate her in that drill.

I bet he was never going to put my name on that list in the first place.

I am a natural distance runner, not a natural basketball player.

I will never be cool enough, coordinated enough, or suave enough to ever fit with that team.

Once I reach class, I avoid looking at Mr. Kerry and find my seat.

I remember not to slouch, as slouching is NEVER allowed in his class, but I do lower my head. I hate when people see me cry.

A few runaway tears fall to my desk, and I quickly wipe them away. I don't want Mr. Kerry to call me out in front of the class.

"Aww, Janey, are you okay?" Nikki Birkle's voice awakens me from my fog. She is one of the thirteen that actually made the cut.

"No, not really." I brush the tears from my eyes, but it is useless. They only continue to rush down my face like a waterfall. "I'm the only person that didn't make the team," I mutter.

"Oh no! Really? I'm so sorry, girl." She pats my shoulder. "I have no idea why you didn't make the team. You hustle more than anyone else."

"Yeah," I whisper. It isn't like I'm trying to brag, but I know I work hard. Everyone knows it. Last year, at practice, Mr. Olaf actually stopped the drill we were doing to point out how I was the only person that always hustled, that always ran back to the line, and that always gave 100 percent. It was kind of embarrassing but meant a whole lot to me. Someone had actually recognized the effort I put in each and every day.

"Well, did you talk to Coach Dobbs about his decision?"

"Should I?"

"Yes, you should. You deserve to know why you didn't make it."

I sit there silently for a few moments. Talking to Coach Dobbs sounds like the scariest thing in the world right about now. At tryouts, he basically said that crying was forbidden. And there is no way I can go about talking to him and NOT cry.

But I want to know why I didn't make the team . . . and if, by chance, he made a mistake.

I improved SO MUCH at the end of sophomore year. I was to the point where I played half of each game. Mr. Olaf had finally rewarded my hard work, and I was actually not as nervous out on the court as I once was.

But I guess that never mattered in the eyes of Mr. Dobbs.

"I guess I will do that," I mutter hesitantly.

"Good. And remember, Janey, I'm here for you."

I sit through the rest of class with a moist set of eyes, and all throughout the rest of the morning, I randomly break out into tears. It is ridiculous.

During study hall, however, I break up the nerve to talk to Mr. Dobbs.

We walk to a set of stairs in the hallway and each take a seat.

"Janey," he pauses and then continues, "I think I made a mistake cutting you from the team."

And there it is.

"You were the best defensive player we had."

"Why did you cut me off the team then?" I ask quietly.

"I'm not sure. I had your name on the list, and, then, for some reason, I went back and took it off before I went to bed."

Okaaaaayyyyy . . .

"I'm not sure why, but that is what I did."

My mom's words float around in my head as he repeats the part of not being sure why he cut me. *"We prayed for you at Mom's In Touch, Jenny. We prayed that you would only make the basketball team if God wanted you to."*

Hmmmmmm. It kind of seems like God didn't want me on this team if Mr. Dobbs doesn't even know why he deleted me from the list.

"I have never actually cut a player from the team before."

Well, that makes me feel a whole lot better.

"I always gave the girls the option of staying on the team with the knowledge that they just wouldn't compete in the games." He pauses and seems to contemplate what he will say next. "And that is what I should have done with you—given you the option of being a practice player." He pauses once more and then adds, "I have never before had a girl that hustles as much as you do."

"I don't care if I play in the games. I just want to practice," I whisper.

"Basketball practice keeps me in shape."

"Mr. Olaf told me that. He was actually pretty upset I cut you. He said, 'She may not be the best in a game, but she helps a lot at practice.'"

I always knew I loved Mr. Olaf. He was and is my all-time favorite basketball coach.

"Even Mr. Willer was upset. He told me, 'You will never find someone who works harder and is more determined than Janey Eller.'"

I can't help but smile at that statement. I knew my cross country coach always had my back.

"Could I just be on the team and not play in the games?" I meekly inquire.

"Well, it is too late now, I think. I already cut you. But you can be a manager if you want."

"No, that is okay." I pause. "I will probably just focus more on my running if I can't play."

If I don't have to go to basketball practice every day, then maybe I can actually train with Melanie and Nicolette in the winter. That could be fun. And, unlike most of the basketball girls, they always include me.

"I'm sorry, Janey. You can always try out again next year."

"I guess."

I am not sure I want to go through this all over again.

We sit there in silence for a few moments.

Then Mr. Dobbs stands to his feet.

"Well, I better go, Janey."

"Okay."

"Bye, Janey."

"Bye."

As Coach Dobbs turns and walks towards his classroom, I decide that I am going to train harder for this upcoming track season than ever before. If I can't be on the team, I will use my time wisely. If I can't play basketball, I will make improvements in my running.

I am not about to let this rejection and this setback bring me down.

God didn't want me to make the team for a reason, and, even though it hurts, I know it must be for the best.

Sweat is dripping down my face as I make my way around the track.

The temperature is soaring at ninety-two degrees, and wearing sweatpants and a long sleeve shirt isn't exactly helping keep me cool.

It is our last home track meet of the season, my last chance to try and break the 800-meter school record while fresh. Come Sectionals, I will have to run three or four races and will be less likely to run a personal best.

I finish up the second lap of my fourth warm-up (yeah, I'm pretty stir crazy) and sprawl out beneath the shade of a tree.

"It is SO HOT," I state.

"Yeah, it is," Melanie replies. "I'm so glad I don't have to run the two mile today."

"Maybe you shouldn't be wearing all your sweats, Janey." Lena Champion chuckles as she pokes me. "That would probably help."

"But I have to stay loose," I argue.

"I think you will be loose enough in this heat, girl."

The school record right now is 2:27.1.

I ran a 2:27.7 at conference and took third place. That was after already running the 4 x 800 though, in which I had a split of 2:28. I should be able to run sub 2:27 when fresh, right?

The hard part is that I will have absolutely NO competition today. There are literally less than ten girls that showed up from the other team. Who knows how many of them will even run the open 800.

But I guess I don't need competition. Some of my best runs are at practice when I am all by myself.

I have trained hard since November, and I can do this. Because I didn't play basketball, I was able to build up more endurance, and it is definitely paying off this track season.

The meet passes by rather rapidly, and, soon, the 800 is upon me. I chuck my sweats onto the infield and make my way to the starting line.

For some reason, I feel super weak.

Sweat pours down my face, my neck, and my back in torrents.

Maybe I ran too many warm-ups.

It is too hot to warm up five different times.

And maybe I shouldn't have kept my sweats on for so long.

I think I am going to be sick.

Once at the starting line, I realize there are only five other girls in this race, only one of them being from the other team.

I really will have to do this all by myself.

When the gun sounds, I shoot out from the line, fast and strong. There is no time to feel weak now.

I can hear footsteps behind me for the first 200, but they soon disappear. It is just me and the open track now.

I push through the first 400, sun beating down on me, and cross the line in 1:11.

That seems a tad slow. I wanted to be at a 1:10 or slightly under.

But I guess a 1:11 is okay.

I just need to blaze through this second lap.

"Go, Janey, go!"

"You can do this, girl!!"

I surge through the 500 mark and then through the 600, using every bit of energy that I possess.

When I hit the final turn, I make sure to stay in lane one.

Usually, I swerve to the right and end up in lane six or something crazy like that. In my head, it makes me feel faster, but, mathematically, it only makes me run farther, which should correlate to a slower time.

I need every tenth of a second I can get today.

As I work the last straightaway, my legs begin to wobble.

"You can do this, girl!!" Lena screams.

With thirty meters left, my legs nearly buckle.

"Go, Janey, go!!!"

"Run, Janey, RUN!!!!"

"You're going to get it, girl!!!!!"

With ten meters left, my legs nearly give way again.

"COME ON, JANEY!!!!!!!"

I charge all the way through the finish and then collapse as I hear the time being called out.

"2:26.3!"

"Oh my gosh, Janey!! YOU DID IT!!!" Lena shouts.

Yes, I did it.

I broke the school record AND matched Kayley's best 800 time.

Now, I just want to sleep . . . and possibly hide beneath a massive shade tree.

My heart is racing like mad as I sprawl out in the grassy infield. Asha Brainerd and Lola Slone kneel down beside me, telling me I should stand up, but I cannot.

I broke the school record on the hottest day of the year thus far.

And I did it all alone.

The next finisher, Lynnea Rend, is twelve seconds behind with a 2:38.

My heart continues to race for the next ten minutes, up until it is time for the 1600, which I am supposed to run.

I can barely bring myself to my feet, but I do.

Dragging my legs, I make my way over to my coach and give him the hard facts.

"Mr. Willer," I groan, "I don't think I can run the mile. I'm still feeling awful. And my heart is racing. It has only been ten minutes since the 800."

That is the biggest issue with competing against small teams. There is no time to rest.

Mr. Willer furrows his brows and crosses his arms.

Oh, great. He doesn't look happy at all.

"Jane, if you don't run the mile, it won't even matter to me that you ran the school record."

Ouch. Mr. Willer is in one of THOSE moods today.

"But, Mr. Willer, I feel like I'm going to pass out."

And I do. I used up every bit of energy I had to run that time.

And why do I have to run three races? Everyone else only has to run one or two today. This is supposed to be a FUN meet.

"It doesn't matter if you feel terrible. You should still be able to run."

Mr. Willer puts his hand to my wrist in order to feel my heartbeat.

"Your pulse is only 180."

ONLY 180?? It has been over ten minutes since I finished racing. It should at least be back down to under 100.

And, with that, Mr. Willer walks away in a huff.

I just stand there—exhausted, dumbfounded, and hurt.

I gave my ALL in that last race, and it doesn't even matter to him?

During the 1600, Mr. Faraway approaches me.

"Eller, why aren't you out there racing?"

"I don't feel good. I still feel like I'm going to pass out."

Mr. Faraway just shakes his head.

"You should still be able to run the race."

I can't believe these coaches. I ran the best time of my life, and all they seem to care about is that I can't handle running the mile.

Incredible.

Once the 4 x 400 rolls around, I feel my energy returning.

I think I can handle a one-lap race.

I make my way over to Mr. Willer.

"I think I should be able to run the 4 x 400 now," I tell him.

Crossing his arms once more, he looks me over and shakes his head.

"If you can't run the mile, you don't deserve to run the 4 x 400."

"But I don't feel so bad after a little more rest," I insist.

"You should have run the mile. Your heart rate was only 180 when the gun went off."

ONLY 180?? Why does he keep saying that like it's a good thing?

And, with that, he walks away once again, leaving me appalled and infuriated.

Isn't anything I ever do GOOD ENOUGH for these people?

At every other meet, I fight through four races . . . FOUR RACES.

Very few people have to do that.

You'd think, just this once, these coaches would cut me some slack.

But no, Janey Eller has to be perfect.

Janey Eller has to be able to race even when she is knocking on death's door.

I lower my head as I begin to cry.

Today was supposed to be a happy day, but, instead, it is the opposite.

Pudding in Time

"That is the time I usually run for two and a half miles!" I excitedly exclaim after I find out how quickly I ran the 2.7-mile time trial. The results have just been posted, and we are all scanning the list to find out our times and our group placement for the week. I am in group number seven. Kayley, my speed-demon sister, is in group number six. As usual, she has finished ahead of me, but I am unusually close to her this time.

"That's awesome, Janey!" Annie Basil is all smiles. "I hope that someday I can run as fast as you and Kayley!" Annie is a twiggy incoming freshman, like my sister, but isn't exactly quick. She is in group twelve.

"You just need to keep practicing, Annie! If you do, we could have a really fast team this season."

We are at a fairly prestigious cross country camp in the upper woods of Wisconsin, and my hope is that our whole team can improve so that we can actually make it to sectionals this year.

Once we find out that Sammie Panzer is in group ten, Lila Maloney is in group twelve with Annie, and Wendy James, Annie's cousin, is in group fifteen, we decide to go to dinner. After running, food is a favorite of mine.

"I can't wait to see what kind of workouts we do this week!" I am still bubbling over with excitement as we make our way to the dining hall.

"I can't wait to see what the dances are like," Sammie sighs, her blue eyes becoming all puppy-dog-like.

"I bet there are some really cute running guys!" Annie adds happily.

These girls are seriously boy-crazy, especially Sammie.

"I'm sure there will be a lot of hotties!" Sammie responds.

Oh brother. If there is one thing I could care less about, it is dances. I never want to go to one of those again.

"Why do they assume all runners want to go to a dance?" Kayley says exactly what I am thinking.

"Because dances are FUN," Wendy explains, her eyes twinkling. Doesn't she know that Kayley will never buy that?

"They aren't fun. They are lame. I went to the eighth-grade graduation dance, and it was so borrrrrring."

"I thought so too," I pipe up and say. "They told me there would be games, and there were NO GAMES. So, I just ate food the whole time."

"Same here," Kayley mutters.

"You guys need to just live a little." Wendy playfully nudges me. "I bet if Riley was here, you would be all over that dance." She gives me a wink.

As if she can read my mind, Kayley speed walks ahead of the group, and I follow after her. Food has to be better than this conversation.

When I finally arrive in the cafeteria and pick up a tray, a whole slew of amazingness awaits my salivating chops. There are huge pieces of fresh pineapple, large chunks of red watermelon, steaming slices of deep-dish pizza, a colorful garden salad with a whole bunch of toppings, and creamy chocolate pudding. I am in food heaven. I fill up my tray and head over to an empty table. Soon, Kayley and the rest of the crew join me.

"This food is SOOOO good!" I tell anyone who will listen. My mind is no longer on the senselessness of dances but only on this delectable sustenance. "Yum!"

"I know! I LOVE food!" Annie's eyes are bugging out excitedly. She likes food almost more than I do, even though it is impossible to tell by her tiny frame. Her lifelong goal is to actually cross the 100-pound barrier. She says she will have a party the day it happens.

"I like the pizza," Kayley murmurs, as she nibbles on the crust. She always eats her food in tiny bites.

"The pizza is delicious, but I don't really like the pudding." Sammie pushes her cup of chocolaty goodness aside.

"How can you not like the pudding? It is amazing!"

"It has a weird taste." Sammie picks up her neglected cup. "Do you want it?"

"Sure!" I am always the human garbage disposal in the school cafeteria, so I might as well keep fulfilling that role here.

I dip my spoon into the glass and indulge in my second helping of dessert.

As I scoop up the last bit of chocolate goop, I watch as Wendy pushes her own pudding aside. "I don't really like it either." She turns up her nose. "I'm going to throw it away."

"NO!! Don't throw it out! You can't waste food, especially when it's good." My mom always taught us to clean our plates.

"Do you want it?" Wendy eyes her pudding and then eyes me.

"Um, sure." I am a bit less enthusiastic this time but not reluctant. Pudding is still pudding.

When Lila echoes the sentiment of Sammie and Wendy, I almost let her throw her dessert away, but I stop her at the last second.

"Here, give it to me. I'll eat the pudding."

Once I have finished my four helpings of chocolate delight, I feel a bit nauseous.

"You didn't have to eat all that pudding." Lila can tell I'm not feeling all that great.

"Oh, it's fine. I need all the energy I can get for the workouts this week!" And, with that, I pick up my empty tray and bring it to the disposal area. I have never once felt bad about myself for eating a lot, and I am not going to start now. Food is my fuel, and the more I eat, the farther I will be able to go.

Running Low

"My little cousin is going to ask Riley to homecoming! Isn't that so adorable?"

All I have to hear is the name Riley, and I am all ears.

I swivel around in my seat and tune in to Wendy's conversation with Jillian Mills. They are a few rows back, but I can clearly make out what they are saying. Wendy is radiant, all smiles, but Jillian looks a tad concerned.

"Is Janey okay with that?" Jillian doesn't sound as excited as I think Wendy hopes she will be.

"Why does that matter? She isn't dating him or anything." Wendy rolls her eyes.

"Yeah, but that would really hurt her. She still likes him an awful lot you know." Jillian and I aren't as close as we once were in sixth grade, but it is nice to know she still stands up for me.

"Yeah, but shouldn't Annie be happy too?" Wendy obviously doesn't care about how I feel.

"Yeah, but aren't there OTHER boys she can ask? Like FRESHMAN boys?"

"I guess. But Riley is really sweet. And it is JUST a dance. It isn't like she is going to marry him. If Janey wanted to go with him that badly, she would ask him herself." Wendy is verging on defensive.

"Janey would never ask a guy to a dance. You know that."

"Well, you snooze, you lose." I REALLY do not like this side of Wendy.

"Well, you and Annie can do whatever you want, but you might want to think about your decision a little more before you destroy your friendship with Janey." Jillian looks slightly aggravated and turns to face the window.

Before they can tell I heard any of their conversation, I swivel back around in my seat.

I am hurt, and I am angry.

My heart sinks just a little more as I sink down in my seat.

That Wendy James. Who does she think she is? How can she act like she is my friend and then go and set up her cousin with the guy she knows I have liked since seventh grade?

I am furious.

When we reach the park where the race will be held, I grab my spike bag and backpack and glumly head off the bus. I am not in any mood to run a race.

"Janey!!!" Annie runs up alongside me. "Are you excited to run???" She is in a super peppy mood today.

"Not really." Is she acting super sweet just so I will give her my personal blessing to go with Riley to the dance? "I'm not feeling all that great."

"Aww. I'm sorry, Janey. Are you sick?"

"No. I just don't think I will run very well today."

"Well, you've got to have a better attitude than that."

"I know. I'm just not having the best day, and I keep running slower and slower at every meet."

"Well, I hope today goes better for you!"

"Thanks."

Once we walk the course and run somewhat of a warm-up, it is time for the race.

"Have you thrown up yet, Janey?" Bradley Whitson thinks he is being humorous.

"No, and please don't talk about it."

"Why? Do you feel like you are going to puke?"

"Kind of."

I walk away from the talk of vomiting and head to the starting line. I really am feeling nauseous.

I only make it a few meters before I begin to retch. I put my hands on my knees and just let it happen.

"Ewwwww!" a girl from another team shrieks.

Once I am finished, I complete my walk to the dreaded starting line. All my energy is gone.

From the moment the gun sounds, I can tell I am going to have one of my worst races on record. My legs are just dead. I feel like I am jogging, but I cannot do anything about it.

I turn to look behind me at each and every flag, at each and every turn. I have no hope of passing anyone ahead of me, so I choose to focus on who is coming after me.

Sammie passes me first. She hasn't yet beat me this season, but she will today. She is improving a lot, and, although it hurts my pride to have her pass me, it isn't the worst thing that could happen.

"Jane! We need you. We need you to GET UP THERE!!" Mr. Willer sounds a little desperate when Sammie blows by me. He has seen me run like this before, so it should be no surprise that it is happening again. This happens to me EVERY YEAR. I start off each season wonderfully, looking like I will have a promising year, but, then, I progressively fall apart.

"Eller! BREATHE!! You're not breathing!" Mr. Faraway is bellowing at me now. I'm surprised he isn't blowing his whistle to put a little pep in my step.

Even though I feel like I am running super slowly, I am our third runner for most of the race. Kayley, my younger sister, blew past me at 800 meters, and she has long since become a tiny speck in the distance.

It is when Annie passes me, with only 400 meters to go, that I fall apart.

"Come on, Janey. You can do it!" she says supportively, as she bounds past me like a gazelle.

Not Annie. Not today.

"Come on, Janey. Stay with me." She makes a little hand motion for me to keep up with her.

I desperately want to pass her back or at least stay up with her, but I am out of energy. I am probably running close to nine-minute pace now.

When I cross the finish line, I crumble to the ground.

The clock reads *"23:58."*

It's my worst 5k ever . . . up until this point at least.

Mr. Willer shakes his head in defeat.

I know what he is thinking.

It is the same thing he is always thinking.

Jane, it's all in your head.

Second-Chance Dance

"Janey! It's for you!" Dad calls out my name as he emerges from Gramma's room.

Startled from my thoughts of U.S. presidents and their impacts on society, I jump up from the couch.

"It is?"

Who could be calling me? The only person who ever calls me is Keeley when she forgets her math book at school.

When I reach the phone, my dad has an odd twinkle in his eye.

"Here she is," he tells the unknown listener.

"Hi!" I give my usual cheery greeting, the one where people mistake me for a five-year-old.

My dad closes the door behind him as I hear the words, "Hey, Janey."

Holy moly. It's Riley. He barely even talks to me anymore, and, now, he's calling me?

"Hi," I repeat, much quieter this time.

"So, how has track been going?" he asks. His voice is deeper than it used to be, but his Wisconsin accent is as strong as ever.

"It's been okay, but not as good as last year. I have barely been able to break six minutes in the mile." I pause. "How is tennis?"

"Good. I get to play first singles."

"Awesome!" I am excited for him but still a little confused as to where this conversation is headed.

"So, Janey, this is why I'm actually calling." Here it comes. "Do you want to go to prom . . . with me?"

Did I just space out, or did I hear him correctly?

Riley wants to go to prom WITH ME?

Doesn't he know what happened last time we went to dance together?

Doesn't he remember that I am utterly terrified to dance in public?

"Um . . . um . . . hmmm . . . I don't know." My voice is practically inaudible now.

I have been dreaming of this day since seventh grade, and, now that it is actually happening, my mouth is undergoing temporary paralysis.

"I'm sorry. What did you say?"

I said YES! YES! Everything within me says YES!

"I'm not sure."

I am a chicken. Plus, I don't even know if my parents will let me go. They let me go to homecoming, but this is PROM. This is a whole different ball game.

"You don't want to go?"

"Oh, I didn't say that. I just don't know if my parents will let me go. They are kind of anti-dancing."

"Well, it isn't a big deal. We don't HAVE to go. It is only if you really WANT to go. It is your decision. No one is going to be mad at you if you say 'no.'"

"I want to go. I want to go . . . with you." I wonder if he even heard me. My voice is shaky and faint.

"Well, Janey. You would have to dance . . . and dress up all nice . . . and stay up late . . . and be around a bunch of people."

"I know."

I would have to dance. Crud. I couldn't do it last time, so how am I going to do it this time?

But I would have one more chance to dance with him . . . with Riley.

"And there would be slow dances."

"I know," I say even quieter this time. "I just don't even really know how to dance. I mean, it just makes me feel so weird. I sometimes pretend to be a ballerina . . . but that is when barely anyone is watching."

He laughs, easing some of the tension.

"Well, it wouldn't be worth it if we just stood on the side."

"Yeah, I know." It is like I am a broken record.

I want to puke.

Why does something so mysteriously exciting seem so nauseating at the same time?

"Do you want to just think it over?" I am almost positive Riley can hear the war going on inside my head.

"Yeah." I pause and muster up the courage to ask him a question that is pressing on my mind. "Riley, if I don't go, will you ask someone else?" My fear of saying "no" is that some other girl will end up living out my dream.

"Probably not."

Phew. "Oh, okay." I am somewhat relieved. "Well, I guess I just need some time to think about it."

"Okay! Just let me know when you've made a decision. I need to buy the tickets soon if we end up going."

"I will."

"Bye, Janey."

"Bye."

With a click, I hang up the phone.

The last time I talked to Riley on the phone was in the summer after eighth grade, four years ago, when he called me to go running with him before the Waveland 10k. I never thought he was still interested. He was always gabbing with Kitty Farnsworth, Summer Lochen, and Eva Raison in band and at lunch. I thought I was ancient history.

I am giddy, yet scared to leave the room. I must prepare for the inevitable teasing from my sisters. I sit by the phone for another minute before I can cook up the nerve to exit.

"Who was on the phone, Janey?" Tasha is waiting right outside the door for me, wearing this ridiculous, toothy grin.

"It was nobody."

"Is 'nobody' your new nickname for Riley?" Kayley yells out from the living room.

"Shut up!"

"Janey, don't talk to your sister like that," Dad chides.

"What did he want?" My mom's curiosity pulls her from the living room and into the kitchen.

"Nothing."

"So 'nobody' wants 'nothing,'" Kayley summarizes.

"I guess we will just have to read about it in your assignment notebook," Tasha says slyly.

"Janey, we KNOW Riley called you, so why did he call?"

"How do you know?" I am just trying to be difficult now.

"Dad answered the phone. Duh." Kayley states the obvious.

"Did he ask you to another dance?" Tasha pokes me.

"I don't know."

"Did he ask you to prom?" she continues.

I will just let Tasha do all the work of figuring it out.

"Yeah."

"Ooooooooooh! Janey has a BOYFRIEND!"

"I do NOT. Riley is just my friend."

"That must be why you always write 'Janey Lynn Gray' all over your assignment notebooks."

"I DO NOT, Tasha!!" I lunge at her, and she races away, giggling.

"So, what did you tell him? Did you say 'yes'?"

"I . . . I told him I wasn't sure."

"Yeah, right. She said 'yes.'"

"No, Kayley. I told him I wasn't sure. I don't think Mom and Dad really want me to go."

"Well, we don't really like dances, but we won't stop you. You went to homecoming with him."

"I didn't even dance though," I mumble.

"It's up to you, Janey. You always make good decisions."

Over the next few days, I mull over what to do. I don't want Mom and Dad to be disappointed in me if I go, but I don't want to pass up on this opportunity either.

After much thought, I decide to say "no." I don't want to, but it is what I am going to do.

Friday comes, and I decide to catch him as he walks to tennis practice. We have a meet at Morrison, so I wait by the double doors for the bus . . . and for Riley to walk past me. After five minutes, I see him coming. I must be brave.

I clear my throat. "Hey, Riley." I stop him in his tracks.

"Hey, Janey."

Here goes nothing.

"I think it is better if we don't go to prom."

I expect him to be upset, but he appears unscathed. "Okay, Janey. That's fine." He continues walking down the hallway, out the door, and into the April sunshine.

What did I do?

Setting my backpack on the floor, I glumly slide down the wall and wait for the rest of the track girls to arrive.

When we finally file onto the bus, I sit near the front and gaze out the window. I think I see Riley on the tennis courts, looking my way as he bounces a ball with his racket.

"Hey, Janey!" My Crazy Twin, Lena Champion, sits down beside me. "What's up, chica?"

"Hey," I say, a little less enthusiastically.

"What's the matter, hun?"

"Well . . . I told Riley I didn't want to go to prom with him."

"WHAT??!!" Lena practically falls out of the seat. "But you totally want to go! You've been pining after this kid ever since I first met you. How could you possibly tell me you don't want to go with him?" She is outraged. "We even practiced slow dancing at the lock-in, girl!"

"I DO want to go with him."

"Then why did you tell him you DON'T want to go? You are crazy, my Crazy Twin!"

"Well, it is too late now. I already told him 'no.'"

"Do you have his number?" Lena unzips her backpack and pulls out her cell phone.

"I know his home phone number."

"What is it then?"

"He isn't home right now. He's over there at practice."

The bus starts to pull away.

"Then I will talk to his mom. Here, what is his number?"

I rattle off the digits from memory. The only other numbers I know by heart my own (obviously) and Keeley's and Jillian's, from back in our days as "The Three Musketeers."

Lena quickly punches the numbers into her phone and puts it to her ear. "I'll take care of you, girl," she whispers.

"Hello. Is this Mrs. Gray?"

Silence. I feel slightly nauseous, and it isn't because we are on a school bus.

"This is Lena Champion, and I want to talk to Riley."

Silence. I am so glad I am not the one on the phone right now.

"Yes, I know he is at tennis practice right now, but I want to know if I can talk to him when he gets home."

Silence.

"You could just have him call me on my cell phone."

Silence.

"Oh, you mean I can just call his cell phone? What's the number?" Lena gives me a thumbs-up. She scrambles to find a pen and paper in her backpack. She listens as the number is rattled off and writes it down. "Thank you so much, Mrs. Gray. Have a great day."

"I have his number!" She waves the paper around happily. "Do you want me to call it right now?"

"He is probably practicing."

"Maybe. But we could at least try it. We did just leave, and it looked like they were all standing around."

"Oh, okay. I guess you can try."

Lena picks up her phone and starts dialing the digits, one by one. She holds it up to her ear and waits. My stomach does a nosedive.

"Hello? Riley?"

Silence. I feel as if he can see me through her phone. I need to hide.

"This is Lena Champion."

Silence. He is probably wondering why on earth he is getting this phone call.

"So, Janey apparently told you she didn't want to go to prom with you a few minutes ago. Well, she totally does want to go with you. I am here with her now, and what she wanted to say to you in the hallway was 'yes.'"

Silence. How is he going to respond to that?

"Yeah, I think she was just a little nervous because she was talking to you." She winks at me. I don't know if I should hug her or kick her.

Silence.

"Do you want to talk to her?"

No. Say "no." Please, say "no."

"Here she is."

I carefully take the cell phone from Lena's hands.

"Hello?" I speak quietly so that the rest of the girls on the bus can't hear this conversation.

"Hey, Janey. So, I hear from Lena that you actually DO want to go to prom?"

"Yeah, I do."

"Are you positive about this? I need to know so I can buy the tickets."

"Yeah. I'm positive."

"Okay, as long as you are sure."

"Yep."

"Okay. Well, I will talk to you later then."

"Bye."

I breathe a sigh of relief and hand the phone back to a super ecstatic Lena.

"You are going to PROM!!! WITH RILEY!!! I'm so excited for you, Janey!" She gives me a huge hug, unable to contain her happiness. It is like she just won a lifetime supply of my mom's famous cookies. She bounces around like a giddy schoolgirl.

"Champion!" Mr. Willer, chomping on an apple, turns around in his seat. "Did you just say that ELLER is going to prom?"

"Yup! She is going with RILEY!" She winks at me as she says this.

"Alright, Jane!" Mr. Willer raises his hand as if to give me a high five. "That Riley has been sweet on you for like five whole years now."

I just sink in my seat, an embarrassed, happy, terrified mess.

I, Janey Eller, am going to prom with Riley Gray.

*****

When the day of prom arrives, my friends whisk me away to Ashley Dolita's house. They demand that I let them straighten my hair and do my make-up. I cave on the hair part but NOT on the make-up. I will not be a clown for anyone, not even for Riley.

Before they begin the straightening process, they tell me to put on my dress. I head into the bathroom to undress and zip myself into Annie's eighth-grade graduation dress. It is dark pink, floor length, and sparkly, with a high neck line that isn't at all provocative. Annie is letting me borrow it for the night, and I, for one, can barely believe I can fit into something stick-thin Annie once wore.

I take a deep breath before I exit the bathroom. I am unsure what the reaction of the girls will be to this dress.

"JANEY!!" Keeley is the first to exclaim. "You look gorgeous!"

"Yeah, wow! Janey, you look great!" Ellie Dorolek is also astounded.

That dress makes you look awesome!" Laurel Bloom adds.

I smirk.

"You are such a skinny-mini," Ashley remarks, eyeing my waist-line.

"I am not. Kayley is the skinny-mini."

"Well, you are too." Keeley pokes me. "Here, sit down so we can straighten your hair."

I plop down in the swivel chair, and the four girls try to make sense of my thick, frizzy hair. They brush it, comb it, and start to run a few different straighteners through it. My head feels like it is on fire.

"Your hair is beautiful, Janey." Ashley smiles as she runs a straightener through my wavy locks.

"Really?" I don't think I have ever heard anyone tell me that before. I glance over into the mirror.

"Yeah. A lot of girls would die to have hair like yours."

"I can barely do anything with my hair," Keeley says, also looking into the mirror. "It is so thin and straight, and curls don't hold very well in it."

"You are lucky, Janey." Laurel is full of compliments too.

Lucky? Me? This wild mane of hair has been the source of so much name-calling. How could I be lucky?

The girls run three different straighteners through my hair at once. Even still, it takes nearly an hour for them to finish. Once they finish, they twist the hair on the top of my head into little cornrows, making sure not to touch my bangs. I cannot believe how light my hair feels. It is like it is nonexistent.

"Riley isn't going to know what to think when he sees you, Janey!" Keeley grins from ear to ear. "I wish I could go to prom just to see his face!"

After Keeley drives me home, I await the arrival of Riley. I stare out the window with excitement and a bit of fear. My memories of the homecoming disaster are still fresh in my mind, and I can't help but feel a little anxious about a repeat in events.

When the aquamarine minivan finally pulls into my driveway, I am unsure of what to do. Should I just wait inside nonchalantly or run out the door as if I have been anticipating this moment all day?

I choose to wait inside.

"Janey! Riley's here!" Tasha won't let me be nonchalant for very long.

"Oh, okay." I try not to blush as I pick up the boutonniere from the table and slowly make my way onto the front porch. I reach down to pick up the pink one-inch heels Annie lent me and put one on each foot. They are like my Cinderella slippers.

When I finally muster up the courage to actually look out the porch windows, I see Riley walking up the little path of stones that leads to our front door. Dressed in a fancy black tux, he is grinning sheepishly.

I take another deep breath, open the door, and step outside.

"Hi, Riley." I try not to look him straight in the eye.

"Your dress is really pretty, Janey."

"Thanks." I am blushing for sure now.

"Here, I got this for you." He carefully opens a clear plastic box with a sweet-smelling corsage inside. It is made up of tiny, pink flowers and a little, pink bow. The words *"Lady Fair"* are engraved on the shiny metal band holding the flowers in place.

"You put it on your arm."

He hands it to me, and I slide it over my hand and into its proper position. I have never worn a flower on my arm before. It is kind of weird.

"I got this for you too." I pull the pink-flowered boutonniere out of its box. I hand it to him, unsure of what to do.

"Pin it on him, Janey." I look over to see Mrs. Gray stepping out of the jeep. Since Riley doesn't yet have his license, his mom and his sister, Petra, are driving us to the high school, where the coach buses that will take us to prom are parked.

I look her way and freeze.

Riley places the boutonniere back into my hand.

By now, Tasha, Kayley, my mom, and my dad are ALL watching.

I clumsily undo the safety pin on the back of the flower and glance up at Riley. Here goes nothing. I reach for his jacket and shakily attach the boutonniere. Luckily, I do not jab him with the pin. I am starting to sweat from the stress of it all though.

"Okay, now it's time for pictures!" Mrs. Gray is happier than a child on Christmas. "Put your arm around her, Riley."

It is homecoming all over again.

I stand in place and try not to make a face as Riley wraps his arm around my waist. It makes me feel safe and loved to be in his one-armed embrace, but it also terrifies me. I try not to look at Tasha because I know she is scrunching up her nose and giggling like any ten-year-old sister would do.

"Smile!" Mrs. Gray says cheerily. She snaps at least a dozen pictures, and Dad manages to take a few too.

When the very awkward photo shoot is finished, I quietly follow him through the grass to his car. I try not to trip because of the shoes I am wearing. He opens one of the doors for me, like a true gentleman, and, once I step up into the vehicle, he lightly shuts the door.

"You look so pretty, Janey!" Petra turns to look at me and smiles brightly. "I love your dress!"

"Thanks, Petra. Annie let me borrow it."

Once Riley is seated beside me, we pull out of the driveway.

The journey to prom has begun.

*****

"Janey, you are so pretty!!!"

"Wow! You are beautiful, Janey!"

"Janey, can I take a picture with you?"

"Oh my goodness! Janey Eller, I hardly recognized you!"

"We need to take a picture together!"

"You are SOOOOOO pretty, Janey!"

"Ow! Ow! JANEY!!"

"Can I get a picture with the prettiest girl at the prom???"

From the time we arrive at the high school to the time we leave on the coach buses to head to the country club, I am all the rage. Heads turn and jaws drop just at the sight of me. I even have my own paparazzi. Everyone can't seem to get over how "pretty" I am.

It is all very surreal.

I swear I must be dreaming.

*****

"You are beautiful, no matter what they say. Words can't bring you down, oh no." Christina Aguilera's soft, yet powerful, voice wafts through the ballroom as Riley looks over at me.

"Do you want to dance?"

It is the moment of reckoning.

"Yes," I whisper in return.

I am not running and hiding this time.

Riley gently leads me out onto the dance floor as the butterflies in my stomach begin to take flight. This is really happening. My palms suddenly feel very sweaty. When we are in the middle of the crowd, he turns back in my direction, locks eyes with me, and places his arms around my waist. In response, I put my hands on his shoulders as we begin to sway back and forth.

"You are beautiful in every single way. Yes, words can't bring you down, oh no. So don't you bring me down today."

I close my eyes and sail off on a euphoric sunset. Riley is holding me close, and all is right with the world.

*****

"Rileeeeeeey, let's play a game." Eva Raison links arms with Riley as she flirtatiously pulls him into a nearby room.

"Yeah, Riley," Kitty Farnsworth laughs, as she links arms with Eva and pulls a board game from the shelf.

Sitting stoically on the sofa, all I can do is watch.

See, the plan had been for Petra and Riley to drop me off at home after the prom . . . until Riley mentioned something about Eva and Kitty inviting him over for a little get-together after the main event. Feeling jealous, I asked if I could go too. I mean, Riley went to prom with ME, not with Eva and Kitty.

Now, only a couple hours later, I am regretting my decision to attend this little shindig. My only purpose here is to be a wallflower—a lame, speechless, defeated wallflower.

Eva and Kitty are all over Riley—tickling him, putting their heads on his shoulders, and giggling like total idiots.

It is enough to make me vomit.

Why isn't Riley talking to ME?? He asked me to prom and dreamily danced with me to every slow song. Didn't that mean anything to him? And why did these girls invite him over here? Eva had her own date to the prom, and Kitty didn't even go to the dance. Do they both have crushes on MY Riley?

Suddenly, all is wrong with the world.

I curl up on the couch and pray that morning comes quickly.

Graduation from high school comes and goes. I barely remember any of it because all I can do is cry.

"What is wrong with her?" Gramma asks my dad. "Graduation is a happy time."

No, graduation is NOT a happy time. I will be leaving Mom, Dad, Kayley, Tasha, Lena, Keeley . . . and Riley. I can barely stomach watching him play his trumpet during "Pomp and Circumstance," and, after the ceremony, I nervously wait outside the school so that I can give him a hug before I leave.

"Bye, Riley," I say through tears, as I give him a timid embrace.

"Bye, Janey."

Everyone around me is smiling, laughing, enthusiastically twirling their caps, and taking their final photos together.

As for me, I can't even smile. A chapter of my life is coming to a close, and it isn't a chapter I will be able to re-read.

I sit down at my computer and open up AOL Instant Messenger. It is so cool actually having the internet at my disposal at college. We never had it at home. I notice that Riley is online. I haven't talked to him since the summer, so I strike up a conversation.

>Energizereller: "Hi, Riley! How are you??? I never get to see you anymore."
>XCrunnerRG: "I'm good."
>Energizereller: "How is cross country going? I wish I could still be there with you guys!"
>XCrunnerRG: "It's okay. How's college?"
>Energizereller: "It is so much fun! My team is awesome, and we do so many fun things together! Oh, and I ran a 5:30 at training camp! It was my best mile time ever!"
>XCrunnerRG: "Nice."
>Energizereller: "I haven't been running as well lately though."
>XCrunnerRG: "☹"
>Energizereller: "I just feel so tired all the time."

It is partway through this chat that I decide to ask him the question—the question that has been pressing on my mind since ninth grade.

>Energizereller: "So, Riley. Can I ask you something? It is something I have wanted to ask you for a while."
>XCrunnerRG: "What?"
>Energizereller: "Well, it might be weird."
>XCrunnerRG: "What is it?"

AHHHH!! Why am I doing this? I shouldn't ask him this question. I just shouldn't. I am not sure I am going to like the answer.
But I NEED to know.

>Energizereller: "Do you still like me?"

There, I said it. I stand up from my chair and pace around the room. I do not want to read his response.

But I HAVE to know.

I walk back to my seat and stare at the screen.

I do not at all like the words I see glaring back at me.

XCrunnerRG: "As a friend."

I feel as if a vortex has just sucked all the oxygen from my lungs.

Energizereller: "Oh."

I feel something horribly raw start to well up within me.

Maybe I should just call it a night. Maybe I should go for my eight-mile run now. Maybe I should close the AOL chat box before things go downhill.

But I NEED to know more.

Energizereller: "Why?"
XCrunnerRG: "Well, to be honest, Janey, it just got kind of boring. You never wanted to do anything fun."

BORING??!! How dare he say that!

Energizereller: "How can you say that? We had a lot of fun together."
XCrunnerRG: "Well, it got old. It was always the same thing."

I know I should stop before this gets any uglier, but I press on.

Energizereller: "How long have you felt this way?"
XCrunnerRG: "Since like ninth grade."

Whatever was welling up within me is now cascading from my eyes.

Energizereller: "Okay. So, if you didn't like me and thought I was boring, why did you ask me to homecoming and to prom?"
XCrunnerRG: "Well, let's see here. I was bribed to ask you to

homecoming, and I was blackmailed to ask you to prom."

That must be why HIS MOM asked me to homecoming. She was the one that wanted us to go together.

And I knew him asking me to prom was too good to be true.

The cascade erupting from my eyes turns into a torrent. I can barely even make out the words on the computer anymore.

What a jerk!!! What a mean, horrible, cruel jerk!! And to think I spent a third of my life, which is six whole years, dreaming of him, writing to him, pining after him, falling for him.

Energizereller: "How can you even say anything so mean?"

XCrunnerRG: "I'm sorry, Janey. I never wanted to hurt you."

Energizereller: "Well, you did. I can't even believe I thought you were my friend."

XCrunnerRG: "I AM your friend."

Energizereller: Well, you are being really mean. It meant so much for me to go to prom with you, but now I see it was all a lie. You never even cared."

XCrunnerRG: "Don't be like that, Janey."

Energizereller: "Riley, I need to go running."

XCrunnerRG: "Okay. Bye, Janey."

Energizereller: "Bye."

Slamming my hands down on the keyboard, I close the chat box with as much force as I can muster. Jumping up from my seat, I storm over to the door, slip on my running shoes, sprint down the hallway, rush down the steps, and head out into the darkness.

I am in the mood for a long, hard run.

"C'mon, Janey! Get up there!" The shout cuts through the crisp October breeze, and, once again, Daniel Swan gives me a discouraged look.

Trudging up the long, green hill, following after the sea of colorful jerseys, I thoroughly have lost all joy of racing. There go Bella, Aris, and Tara, I think to myself, as three more girls from my team pass by and move forward into the sea of color.

"Seven minutes!" A voice booms out at the mile mark.

Seven minutes? That is slower than I started the Hamilton Milk Run 10k with Riley in eighth grade.

I am kicking myself for starting at such a leisurely pace, and I am also kicking myself for letting any thought of Riley come into my mind. That kid broke my heart, and, now, running is doing another number on my heart.

Although I have started out with a terrible first mile time-wise, I feel as if I have just run a six flat. My legs feel like lead, my heart is pounding, and I continue decelerating past the never-ending row of spectators. I am so glad my parents didn't come to this race.

We circle around a post and re-enter the grassy straightaway near the starting line. I feel like I am going nowhere.

As we pass through a patch of sand at the end of the straightaway, I hear familiar breathing coming up from behind me. It is Jeannette. She too is passing me.

"C'mon, Janey!" Now, Coach McDevitt is yelling. "Get up there!"

What the heck is wrong with me? If I keep this up, Corina will pass me.

I am now jogging slower than a granny. My arms swing sporadically, and my vision is hazing.

I have to stop.

Slowing a little more, my legs suddenly give out, and I fall to the ground. I close my eyes as I just lay there, motionless.

"Can you get up?"

I just lie there, dead to the world.

"Are you okay?"

I just need to rest.

Suddenly, I am being pulled up off the ground by a couple of grown men. My legs woozily wobble like a newborn fawn. They want to see if I can stand, but I just want to lie back down on the soft grass.

I am so tired.

I really thought today would be different. I thought I had done everything right. But, thinking back to the warm-up, I realize that this was bound to happen. I had used all of my energy just to complete the two-mile jog, and, even then, I couldn't keep up with the team.

In a few minutes, they are strapping me into a stretcher and lifting me up into an ambulance.

Oh, brother.

What is Coach McDevitt going to think of me now? I am an epic failure as a freshman.

A man takes my blood pressure.

"140 over 60."

For some reason, those numbers sound just a little odd to me.

"You from Lazarus University?" The man hovering over me asks.

I nod slowly as I squint up at him.

"I'm a Christian too," he says.

Soon, Coach and his mustache are standing by the ambulance door, thoughtfully gazing up at my tired body. I give him a weak smile.

"Coach, I don't need to be in this ambulance," I softly mutter.

His face seems to say otherwise.

The doors close, and Coach is no longer in my line of sight.

The vehicle begins to jostle back and forth as we drive across the sand and the grassy fields, heading towards the finish line. Ironically, I am still finishing this race.

Eventually, I am allowed to leave the containment of the stretcher.

I tiredly take the timing chip off my shoe (it was pointless to even put it on), and drop it into the bin.

Quitter, I think, but I know I am being too hard on myself. Running is not supposed to be torture, but that is what it has become—pure and utter torture. I felt so amazing at summer camp, up in Michigan, but every practice and race since then has become progressively worse. Early in the season, I ran up with Arika and Carmella, the two fastest girls on the team. But, now, I have faded to the slowest runner.

I see Judy, our team manager, approach me.

"Janey, are you okay?" She looks extremely concerned.

"I think so," I half-heartedly mutter.

I am such a loser.

I leave Judy and head to the starting line to search for my sweats. Once my arms are filled, I head to the tent, our purple fortress of rest.

I lie down as soon as I reach the purple tarp. I just want to sleep.

"Janey, what happened?" Carmella sits down beside me, ready to offer her comfort.

"JANEY!!! Are you okay??" Arika's blue eyes are enormous pools of worry.

Okay, so I guess I won't be able to sleep, not just yet.

Everyone huddles around me, asking me how I am and what the heck happened to me. By now, everyone has heard about my ambulance escapade.

"Here, you should eat something." Erin Snelling hands me a juicy, green apple.

I am not the biggest fan of green apples, but I am willing to eat whatever it takes to regain my strength. I munch on the crunchy sphere of fruit, and, in my dazed stupor, I eat the whole thing—seeds, stem, and all.

Everyone is amused.

"Geeze, Janey. You ate that apple like it was a piece of pizza," Arika giggles, and I am reminded of our pizza eating contest earlier in the season.

I grin somewhat stupidly, still pretty out of it.

"Janey, come here." Coach McDevitt is motioning for me to leave the warmth of the tent.

I sluggishly walk over to his side.

"What?"

"We need to get you a blood test as soon as possible. I am almost positive you are iron deficient."

"Okay." I am willing to do anything, even resort to being stabbed with needles, to figure out what is wrong with me.

"So, on Monday, instead of coming to practice, Coach Washer is going to take you to the doctor. I am pretty sure they will insist on you having your ferritin tested."

Washer grins, showing all of his teeth, as he joins our little powwow. He looks hyper, as usual.

"But shouldn't I come to practice?"

"No. I don't even want you to THINK about running until we figure out the problem."

"But . . ."

"No buts. No running. Last time you went running, you ended up in an ambulance. We do not want that to happen again."

"Janey, we want you to be healthy." Washer tousles my braid.

"Yeah, I know." I smile, and, for the first time, I feel like there might be a light at the end of the tunnel.

*****

"What is the name of your spouse?"

"Wait, what?" I think I heard what she said, but I'm sure I heard wrong.

"What is the name of your spouse? He is your husband, right?" The secretary points over at Washer.

I am completely taken off guard.

"What? EWWWW!!!! I DO NOT have a husband!!" Most people think I am a junior higher. How could I be married . . . to a balding man? "He's my COACH!!"

I am appalled, but Washer can only chuckle.

We are in the waiting room of the doctor's office, and I am already wishing I could be back at practice.

"Oh, I'm sorry." The secretary looks slightly flustered by her mistake. "You can have a seat and wait for the nurse to call you in."

I hurriedly find a seat and pick up the nearest magazine. I don't want to look Washer in the eye, not after THAT.

"Janey Eller?"

I never even have a chance to open the magazine.

I jump up from my seat, still averting Washer's eyes, and follow after the nurse. Washer follows after me.

She leads me into a little room and asks me about my issues. After hearing my story, she decides a blood test is definitely in order.

"We are going to do a routine blood test but also check your ferritin."

Ferritin. Coach mentioned that.

"What is ferritin?"

"It is the protein that stores, deposits, and transfers your iron. If it is low, you will experience fatigue, dizziness, weakness, headaches, leg pain, shortness of breath, and sometimes even irritability."

Washer can't help but laugh out loud.

I send him a look without making direct eye contact.

"That must be why I always have such horrible headaches . . . and why I can barely pick up my legs when I run . . . and why I can barely make it up the stairs going to class . . . and why I am exhausted every morning when I try to get out of bed." I am rambling for my own benefit now. It is all starting to make sense. My ferritin HAS to be low.

"Okay, well the only way we can know for sure is to take your blood."

Yippee. I can't wait. (Note the sarcasm.)

"This isn't even going to hurt," she says, as she clambers through her drawers.

Oh, sure. That is what they all say. I immediately close my eyes because I know what is coming next.

"Here, hold this." I slowly open one eye to see her handing me a cute teddy bear. She must be able to read my fear.

"Okay." I look over at Washer and find he is still chuckling. Oh, brother. First, the secretary thinks I am old enough to be married, and, now, the nurse thinks I am a baby.

I slowly take the stuffed animal, trying to make it look as if I really don't need it.

I close my eyes once more and wait for the needle to make its entrance.

"You need to relax."

I know I am extremely tense, but how can I not be when I am about to be stabbed with this nurse's weapon of choice?

I clutch the teddy bear a little tighter as I simultaneously try to relax.

I wince as soon as I feel the prick.

I try to breathe but am pretty sure I am holding my breath the entire time.

"Okay, you are allllllll done!"

I open my eyes when she finishes and watch as she places a puffy cotton ball and Band-Aid on my arm. I glance to my right and see four vials of my dark red blood on a tray. I should probably keep my eyes shut.

Once everything is finished, the nurse escorts us from the room.

"We will call you as soon as we have your results," she says.

We head outside, and Washer gives me a playful nudge.

I, for the first time since the secretary asked me the awkward question, choose to make eye contact with the man. He is smirking down at me.

"So, I look young enough to be your husband?"

I don't want to, but I can't help but giggle.

"HA-HA."

*****

Coach McDevitt calls me the next morning with the news.

"You aren't just iron deficient. You are severely anemic."

"Really?"

"Yeah, really. The doctor said that he has never seen such a low ferritin level before, not in an athlete at least."

"Wow. How low was it?"

"It was a TWO."

"A TWO??" I am astounded. In the little internet research I have been doing, I found that, for girls, ferritin should be in the range of 18 to 160.

"Yes, a two."

"Holy moly!"

"Yeah, that is the reason why you were running so slow and feeling so awful."

"And probably the reason I always got slower and slower throughout every season of high school," I mutter, more to myself than to him.

"Yep."

Everything is starting to make sense now.

"The doctor said that we need to get you on iron pills right away. He wants you to take three a day—one at breakfast, one at lunch, and one at dinner. They are non-prescription, so I can pick them up at the store for you and bring them to practice."

"Oh, so I can run today?" I am hopeful.

"Absolutely not."

"Why not?" I send him a frown through the phone.

"We need to nip this in the bud as soon as possible, and the only way to do that is to let you build your iron up BEFORE you start running again."

"Can I at least go for a walk?" I need to do SOMETHING. I feel jittery just thinking about not running for a week.

"Nope. I just want you to come on down to practice and sit with Washer and I while the girls run."

"But how will I stay in shape?"

"Trust me, you won't lose anything in one week. You will only lose something if you DO run."

"Oh . . . okay."

"Trust me on this, Janey. You are going to surprise a whole lot of people after we get you healthy."

The air is chilly, biting even, as I head to the starting line of another race. It is exactly one month since I took my weeklong break, and I am feeling super energetic.

I see my parents standing nearby and wave. They came all the way to Iowa to watch me run, and I can't wait to surprise them.

"Janey, girl, you can win this thing," Samara, my short Brazilian buddy, whispers my way as we do our first run out.

"Yeah right. I'm not going to win."

"I think you can."

"I was fourth on the time trial last week."

"That was last week. This week you are even stronger. Believe me, you can win." Samara is adamant.

Can I? The last cross country race I won was a triangular meet against Stevens and Lakeland North junior year of high school. Yes, I felt great in that meet, but I'm not even positive the Stevens girls were trying that day. This is REGIONALS . . . in COLLEGE. There is no way I will win.

After we huddle up to do our little cheer (*"Feel the rhythm. Feel the rhyme. Come on girls, it's running time!"*), Coach McDevitt pulls me aside.

"Okay, Janey. This is what I want you to do. Go out with Samara. Just stay right with her, and if you feel like you can go faster, just GO."

"Okay, Coach! I'm ready for this!"

Usually, I am terrified to race, but, today, I am excited. In the past two weeks, I have re-discovered my love of running, and, today, I am ready to see what I can do. I haven't felt this good since this summer at cross country camp.

"It is SOOOO cold!" Arika squeals at the starting line.

"I know!" Samara jumps up and down. The cold weather is not her friend. She usually comes to practice in a puffy parka whenever it drops below forty degrees.

Minutes before arriving at the race, I had seen a sign saying it was nineteen degrees, so it is definitely a brisk day.

"I wish Coach let us wear long spandex," Tara chatters.

"I KNOW!!" Arika squeals again.

"Well, at least he lets us wear something with long sleeves." Carmella is always an optimist.

Luckily, for me, I don't mind running in the cold. Hot weather is my enemy.

When the gun finally sounds, I dart from the start and settle in behind Arika, Carmella, and a couple of girls in yellow and blue jerseys. Samara is about a half-step behind me.

I am following Coach's plan, I tell myself, even though I am not exactly right next to Samara.

We surge across the frosted plain, gunning for recently-harvested corn fields.

The Newsboys song, "Spirit Thing," pops into my head. I guess this will be my anthem for this race. I never really choose what will be my theme song for a particular race. It kind of just comes to me. Whatever it is, it has to be better than "The NEW and IMPROVED Bunny Song."

"It's not a family trait, it's nothing that I ate, and it didn't come from skating with holy rollers."

When we reach about a half mile, we turn to the left and descend a hill that runs along the side of the farm fields.

I use the downhill to reel in Arika and Carmella, the two leaders of the race. By the time I reach the bottom of the hill, I am neck and neck with my two teammates, running right between them.

Could this really be happening? I mean, I know we still have over two miles left in the race, but I am feeling better than I ever have before. I am feeling even better than I did at cross country camp when I ran the 5:30 mile, better than when I took fifth place at Sectionals in the 800-meter run, better than that triangular meet where I beat everyone by forty seconds, better than when I won cross country conference back in seventh grade.

I run alongside the two for another half mile, strong and relaxed.

"5:47!" The split of our first mile comes as a shock to me. That used to be the time I'd run for one mile, all out, in high school, and, now, it feels like a cake walk.

It is at this point that I make a decision. I am going to take the lead.

"It's just a Spirit thing. It's just a holy nudge. It's like a circuit judge in the brain."

Still strong and relaxed, I pull one meter ahead . . . then two . . . then three. Soon, I have a fifty-meter lead. I know because of the crazy cheers of my family.

"GO, JANEY!!!!!" Kayley has a look of shock on her face as she screams at the top of her lungs.

"THAT'S MY SISTER!!!!" Tasha shrieks. She too looks shocked.

"You have about fifty meters on them, Janey!! You can WIN THIS THING!!!" Dad wears a ridiculous grin.

"You look AWESOME, Janey!!!!!!" Mom is jumping up and down, ecstatic. I am pretty sure she is crying.

I can't believe this is happening. I can't believe it at all. I am pretty sure

I am wearing my own ridiculous grin.

"Twelve minutes!" I pull through the two mile with a HUGE PR. My previous personal record was a 13:16, and that was for exactly two miles, not for a split in a 5k.

"Thank you, Jesus! Thank you, Jesus!" I whisper through methodical breaths, as I fly across another frosted field. "Thank you, Jesus! Thank you, Jesus!" This has now become my anthem. It is all because of Him that I am able to run like this anyways.

At one point, I pull to a 100-meter lead, but, in the last half mile, one of the runners starts to make her move. It is Carmella, our team kicker.

"GO, JANEY!!!!" My whole family, the whole guys' team, and my two coaches are all cheering for me. Some are jumping up and down. "GO, JANEY, GO!!!!"

I keep pressing on, squeezing out every last bit of speed that I possess. Even with iron, I will never have a kick.

I want to look back, but I don't. I am never looking back again.

I cross the finish line in first, six seconds ahead of Carmella, the second place runner.

"*19:19,*" the red letters of the clock read.

Carmella doesn't stop sprinting until she reaches me in the chute.

"JANEY!!! Oh, girl, I am so proud of you!" She is just as happy as I am, and I can tell by the way she wraps me in a bear hug and lifts me off the ground. She doesn't seem to care at all that she has taken second place.

I am mauled by the rest of the crowd as soon as I exit the chute.

"JANEY!! I am so proud of you!!!" My mom gives me a huge hug. "We couldn't believe that was YOU out there."

"Yeah, when you rounded the corner in FIRST PLACE, we couldn't believe our eyes! We thought for sure you would die out, like you used to do in high school, but you didn't. And your quads were just rippling each time you took a step. I have never EVER seen you look that strong. You were like a Clydesdale horse!" My dad's eyes are huge.

"Oh, Dad," I laugh, as he gives me an enormous hug.

"I told you that God would reward you one day for your hard work."

My dad often told me this in high school, when I had struggle after struggle, all obviously due to iron deficiency. Back then, I never really believed it, but, now, I can see what he told me coming to fruition.

"Janey! THAT WAS YOUR BEST RACE EVER!!!!"

"Yeah, we couldn't believe that was OUR sister!" Kayley and Tasha join in the happy festivities.

"WOW, someone ate their Wheaties this morning." Bobby Etters just shakes his head with a smile as he walks past our little group.

Nope, I had my iron, I think to myself.

"Nice job, Janey!!!" Lyle Rego calls out.

"Wow, great job, Janey!" Daniel adds.

"Janey, Janey, Janey." Washer shakes his head as he runs up to me, wearing his biggest smile yet. "WOW!" He joins in on the hug fest.

That is when Coach McDevitt arrives on the scene. Pulling a "Washer," he chuckles and shakes his head. "Janey, Janey, Janey. That was one of the most exciting races I have EVER watched. WOW." Looking over at my family, he continues. "I tell her to go out with Samara, and she goes out and takes the whole thing. WOW." He wraps me in a warm embrace that lasts for several seconds. "This kiddo is the runner of the year."

"All her coaches in high school always told her it was all in her head," Dad tells him.

"Really?"

"Yep! They told me that all the time." I freely answer his question because I have firsthand experience.

My dad continues. "We had Kayley, our middle daughter, tested, and she too is iron deficient, not nearly as bad as Janey but still pretty bad. Unluckily, for her, she only had one week of her season left when she found out the news."

"It is all because of YOU that our daughters will now be able to run like this." My mom starts to cry. "Janey would have never found this out if it hadn't been for you. Thank you so much."

"We are very lucky to work with your daughter, Mrs. Eller. It is our pleasure."

"JANEY!! I knew you could do it!" Samara is soon at my side as well, wrapping me in another hug. I am pretty sure I have never been hugged so much in all my life. "Didn't I tell you that you would win?"

I think back to her seemingly prophetic words before the start of the race. How did she know?

"Yeah, you did tell me that. I didn't believe you, but you apparently believed it. Why did you think I would win?"

"I have SEEN you run, Janey. I KNEW you could do it."

Coach told me one month back that I would surprise some people, but I never thought the surprise would be this big.

"Thank you, Jesus," I whisper just one more time. "Thank you SO MUCH!"

The Donut Queen

"How many donuts have YOU had tonight, Janey?" Samara gives me a wink.

"Uh, I don't know. I think two."

We are all gathered in Erin Snelling's apartment for one of our many track team get-togethers, and the dessert on the menu tonight is homemade cinnamon-sugar donuts.

"Ohhhhhhh. I had three." Samara gives me another mischievous wink. "I'm beating you, Janey." She lightly pokes me as she chuckles in her adorable Samara way.

"We're not having a contest are we?"

"I don't know, are we?" There is a twinkle in her eyes. On our cross country team, we are the two energizer bunnies. We both keep going and going and going. And while this is good when it applies to running, it isn't as good when it applies to eating.

I don't have any desire to eat any more donuts. I'm not even a huge donut fan. But if this is a competition, I can't let Samara win. I won our pizza-eating contest on the way home from our second cross country meet of the season, and I will win this contest as well.

I jump up and head to the kitchen. I grab two, still warm, cinnamon-sugar-covered donuts and prance back into the living room. When I know Samara is watching me, I devour each sugary orbit in a matter of bites.

She emphatically places her hands on her hips and waltzes back into the kitchen. When she returns, she holds up five fingers defiantly.

But I don't want any more donuts, I think to myself.

"Janey, Samara is beating you!" Arika catches on quickly to what is happening. "Maybe I should just get me some of my own donuts." She swaggers into the kitchen with a goofy grin on her face.

Without saying anything, I jump back up and jog into the kitchen after her. Reluctantly, I pick up two more, now lukewarm, donuts.

I eat them a little slower this time, but I still eat them.

As I finish my last bite, Samara stands up once more and walks into the kitchen. She is gone for a while, and when she returns, she is licking her lips.

"Yum. I just LOVE donuts!" she says rather dramatically.

"How many have you had?" I ask nonchalantly.

"Oh, just seven."

"Oh."

"How many have you had, Janey?"

Without answering, I race back into the kitchen. Grabbing two more, now cold, donuts, I bring them back into the living room. Once I have eaten, I give Samara my answer.

"I've had eight!"

"Well, I guess you win again, Janey. I'm too full to have any more." Samara pats her stomach in surrender. She looks over at Arika and laughs.

"Wait. Why are you laughing?"

The only response they can give me is more laughter.

"What is SO funny??"

After the giggle fit ends, Samara tries to make a serious face.

"Well, Janey, you see, I only had three donuts."

"WHAT???" Why on earth did I make myself eat eight?

"Yep."

"Why did you tell me you had SEVEN???"

"I thought it was funny," she chuckles. "All I did was walk into the kitchen, stand there for a while, and pretend I was eating donuts."

I cross my arms and stare her down for about ten seconds.

"You are so gullible, Janey," Arika laughs.

"And soooooooo competitive," Samara states.

I guess both of those statements are true, but I am going to be on my toes from here on out. I am not falling for any more so-called eating contests with my little energizer buddy or with anyone else. If there is anything I am always willing to do it is to eat MORE FOOD, and I don't want them to take advantage of that willingness anymore.

Bangs 'n Fangs

"Why don't you grow out your bangs?" Judy looks at me curiously as she leans forward on the couch.

We are having another girls' track team get-together, but, this time, we are at Coach McDevitt's house. And, this time, I almost wish we were talking about donuts again. Instead, we are talking about my hair. UGH.

"Yeah, why don't you?" Half the girls on the track team chime in, asking the dreaded question one more time.

Oh great, now this is a team affair.

"Um, I don't want to. I like how my bangs look." I furrow my brow with a bit of resentment. I expect this question from everyone else on the planet but not from these girls. They should know better. They are supposed to be my friends.

"Yeah, but you would look sooooooooooo pretty if you grew out your bangs." Melody, one of our newest additions to the team, flashes me her winning smile, as if to disguise the jab.

What on earth does THAT mean? Is she saying I'm ugly? Everyone thought I was pretty at prom in high school, and I had bangs back then too.

"Well, I don't want to. I like my hair the way it is." I am not easily swayed, especially when digs are being thrown my way.

"Come on, Janey. You should just try it."

"Yeah, you never know what you will look like until you give it a chance!"

"Yeah, but I don't want to!" Good grief, do I ever tell them how to wear their hair or how to dress? Did I ever even ask them for advice on the matter?

"Why are you so stubborn, Janey? Geeze." Melody is bordering on frustration now.

That's it. I came here to have fun, not to be insulted by the fashion police.

"I can have bangs if I want to have bangs! It is MY hair, and I LIKE the way it looks." I stand firm, clinging to the fact that I have the right to do what I want with the dead cells cascading from my own head.

"Well, we are the ones that have to look at you."

Silence sweeps across the room as I look at Judy in near horror.

I feel the wet droplets fighting their way to the surface as I stand up and make my exit.

There goes my night of fun and relaxation with the girls.

Dessert Desertion

"For the next three days, I want you to keep track of how many calories you consume. I want you to pay attention to WHAT you eat and HOW MUCH of it you eat. You can read labels or estimate. Include beverages and snacks—EVERYTHING. I want us to all take a good look at what we are eating so that we can make some goals for ourselves."

Sitting in nutrition class, I wonder why on earth I need to be here. I am active. I am fit. And I know how to take care of myself. Why do I need this class? Maybe back in fourth grade I needed this class—back when I lived to eat dairy, dairy, and MORE dairy—but not now. I'm a runner. What in my diet needs to change?

Once Mrs. Windsor, or whatever her name is, finishes handing out the charts she would like us to use for counting our calories, I speed out of that class. Don't get me wrong. It is an easy class. It is just the same old thing I have been hearing since seventh-grade health class. Eat healthy. Exercise every day. Blah, blah, blah, blah, blah. I KNOW ALREADY!!

For the next three days, I count my calories like a pro. I am between 2,800 and 3,100 for each day. I know it is higher than most of my female counterparts, but I am a runner—a fit, healthy, runner.

When I find myself back in class, our skinny, little, bespectacled professor, Mrs. Windsor, is set on us making our goals. She is sort of a health nut.

"If you have found that you are eating a few too many calories, you can cut back on your overall food intake. If you have found you eat a few too many desserts, you can cut back on those. If you have realized that all you eat is from the dairy group, you can eat a little less of that and maybe throw in some more vegetables. If you have found you eat way too many fatty foods, change that immediately. Find SOMETHING that is wrong with your diet, and change it."

I look down at my charts. Nothing is really standing out to me.

I mean, she did say women—even active women—shouldn't really eat much more than 2,200 calories or so a day, but I don't fit into that group. I am not a normal woman. I am not even a normal, active woman. I am a distance runner. And while I am at it, I don't actually even like that word—woman.

What if there is NOTHING I want to change?

I scan my charts once more and focus on the amount of desserts I eat. I eat two cookies each day at lunch and ice cream each night at dinner. She did say we could cut back on that as a goal.

Maybe I can just eat dessert once a day instead?

I mean, I guess it wouldn't KILL me to trade in my cookies for some carrots.

I leave the class, unsure if I really want to follow through on ANY of these goals, but I decide I will try it. This is school, and I need to do something to earn a good grade on this unit.

For the next week, I say no to the cookies. And it isn't even really that hard. I actually think I feel a teensy-weensy-tiny bit better because of it.

And then, Mrs. Windsor, our little drill sergeant, cracks down even more with her "goal" assignment.

"For the next week, I want you to make an even harder goal for yourself. Look back through your charts, and see what else you can change. Or, maybe, use the same goal you already had and tweak it a little."

I think about my dessert goal. Could I make it stricter? I mean, I don't really want to eat less than I already do, but if it is for a grade . . .

For the next week, I decide to only eat dessert every other day.

It doesn't really bother me. I just replace my ice cream with a little more salad or a little more soup.

I meet my goal without a struggle.

Luckily, Mrs. Windsor stops with the whole "goal craze." She doesn't tell us to make our goals harder or tweak them one last time. Other than having our class write several reflections on the experience, she doesn't really mention the goals again.

But even if she doesn't mention the goals anymore, they don't really leave my mind. They are still there—pressed down, ironed on, and STUCK.

Even though I can, I don't go back to eating my cookies or even eating dessert every day. Instead, I start eating it even less.

Mrs. Windsor may not have meant to, but she has engrained herself into my head, spectacles and all, and even if I don't really want to be the healthiest runner on the street, I am starting to care just a little bit more about what I put into my body.

And it may not be a good thing.

I am NOT a Pig

"Janey! You've only eaten one roll. Have another." Lori, my eight-year-old cousin, is staring me down suspiciously.

"Oh, no, that's okay." I shrug her off and try to turn the conversation in another direction.

"So, what game do you guys want to play after dinner? We could play Mafia!"

Lori is not easily deterred.

"Come on, Janey! You used to always have like five or six rolls. You ALWAYS eat like a pig, remember?" She rolls her eyes and oinks.

Now, I'm the one staring her down.

"It's really okay. I'm full." And then I add, "And I am NOT a pig." I cross my arms in slight disdain.

We are all together as an extended family, eating dinner at Aunt Kat and Uncle Kevin's house. Their nine kids are all surrounding me at the kiddy table, which I still sit at even though I am nineteen years old, and they are all trying to coerce me to eat more.

"Come on, Janey. Just have one more roll!!!"

"Yeah, Janey. Even Caroline had three. You can't let Caroline beat you."

"Yeah, you don't want to lose. It's a contest, you know."

"What about another piece of lasagna? You could have another piece of that."

I awake from the verbal attack coming from the little people to find that Aunt Kat is hovering over me.

She is dishing out another piece of pasta and is about to put it on my plate.

"No," I state rather firmly, "I don't want any more."

It is like I am invisible. She doesn't even hear me.

The lasagna slides onto my plate, and I just stare at it.

"I need to get rid of it, and I know you will always eat more," Aunt Kat says with her usual smile.

"But I said I didn't want it," I mutter under my breath.

I am infuriated.

She is FORCING me to eat more.

She is FORCING me to get fat.

I am healthy, and I eat when I want to eat and what I want to eat.

I am the one in control of my own food intake.

She is not.

But the damage is done. The lasagna is already on my plate, and I will always clear my plate, even with these new goals of mine.

I rip apart the fleshy pasta with a bit more force than needed and scan my surroundings to make sure that no one else is about to plop something else on my plate.

"Is something wrong, Janey?" Tasha asks, a quizzical look on her face.

"No." I don't mean it, but I say it anyways. We are in a room filled with extremely quizzical relatives, and I need to just pretend everything is okay.

"Janey, you are such a pig!" Lori oinks again. That girl just doesn't know when to stop.

Kayley raises her hand as if she is going to pelt her but lowers it before she does something dumb. She, being quite observant, can definitely tell that I am not in the mood for name-calling.

I, in response, stand up and head to the bathroom.

No one can see me cry in there.

Dropping Seconds by the Pound

"17:38!!!" The time is called out by an ecstatic Coach McDevitt. He sprints my way with arms outstretched. Washer isn't far behind him.

Yes, I have just been outkicked by two top-notch runners in the last twenty meters of the race, moving from first to third place in the blink of an eye, but I have run a HUGE PR. My previous personal record on a track was an 18:26. I don't think anyone can actually even believe what is happening. I, for one, can barely believe it.

"HOLY COW, Janey!!!! That was AMAZING!!!!" Little Kerin, my adorable roommate, sprints to my side. "17:38!!! I am so proud of you, roomie!" If she could pick me up, she probably would.

Soon, Beth, Arika, Carmella, Kate, Ashley, Sherry, and all my friends are congratulating me on my run.

This is our first outdoor meet of the season, and, if it is any prediction of what is to come, I can't wait to reach the end of the season.

During indoor, I tore down every single one of my PR's, all except for my 800 (I never ran it) and my 400 split in the 1600-meter relay.

3:04 on the 1000 meter run.

3:43 on my 1200 meter split in the distance medley relay.

5:08 on the mile run.

10:15 and a huge first place on the 3000 meter run.

I am on a roll.

And, the thing is, I am never tired anymore. I feel amazing every day of every week, every rep of every interval workout.

My iron is up, my dessert intake is down, my fat intake is dissipating, and I think I am a little lighter than I used to be.

I doubt anyone would mistake me for being "stocky" now.

"Janey!" Coach, still shaking his head in near disbelief, returns to my side. "I bet you could easily break 17:10 by the end of the season if you keep this up."

"Really??" I often question Coach's high hopes, but this one I may be able to buy into.

"Yep. I wouldn't say it if I didn't think it was possible. You are ready to run with the BIG dogs!"

17:10. Wow. I can't even imagine.

Well, here goes nothing.

Hide 'n Seek

A lovely melody begins to play, and I sit mesmerized. The tune is eerily beautiful, but the words are what hold me spellbound.

I am in chapel, surrounded by at least 2,000 students, and we are listening to Scott Phillips sing a couple of his songs as he strums along on his guitar. Right now, he is performing the song "Hide and Seek." He isn't a well-known artist, yet his lyrics, especially in this particular song, are gripping.

"I am the champion of hide and seek
No one ever finds me
Many have tried
And I've found to keep the perfect hiding place
The secret's not to give away
What happens inside

Then you will be the only one who knows
You'll think you've got control
But it's not the way it goes

And I don't want it to be this way anymore
And I don't want it to be this way anymore
My thoughts are running away with my head
They're thinking me instead
And it's out of my control

Here's hope . . . I've found it in a flag of white
Lifted up into the sky
Surrendered myself

The more control you try to gain
The more control you lose
Till what you've done to get control
Is now controlling you

And I don't want it to be this way anymore
And I don't want it to be this way anymore
My thoughts are running away with my head
They're thinking me instead
And it's out of my control

> *The problem with this hiding place is*
> *I've been here so many days and*
> *I can't seem to find my way back home*
> *So I will send a signal flare*
> *Attach it to a simple prayer*
> *And hope to find someone who cares to help*
> *To save me from myself."*

The person he is singing about is ME . . . and he doesn't even know it. He doesn't even know who I am, for that matter, but I KNOW who I am. I am this "champion of hide and seek." I am not letting anyone into my little world of food, and the food that I once looked to as a means to propel me along is now starting to take over my life. I was in control, but now I am losing control. And like the song says, "I don't want it to be this way anymore." I want someone to save me from myself. But will I ever be able to "find my way back home?" Will I ever be able to hold up the "flag of white" and "surrender myself?"

I feel a very real sense of sorrow as the song ends and Dr. Rowling dismisses us.

My heart is starting to soften and ache in a very real way, and I know what I need to do.

BUT, at the same time, I don't think I am willing to do it, not yet at least. I am not yet willing to sacrifice my newfound prowess on the track all because of a little conviction from a beautiful song.

The little bit of softening that has occurred immediately reverses as I walk out of the building.

I am going to just let my heart keep on deceiving me.

All is still well in my world.

"We should all weigh ourselves!" Tasha runs into the bathroom to pull out the scale. As usual, she wants to see how our annual summer bike trip has affected us. "I'll go first." She steps onto the scale and grins. "I lost three pounds." She pumps her fist in the air.

Dad goes next. "175, baby."

Then, it is my turn. I step on the scale, unafraid. I know I am at a healthy weight.

When the scale calibrates, the number that I see doesn't seem to register.

Is this scale broken?

"What does it say?" Tasha asks.

"Ummm . . ." Should I tell them? They might freak out. Well, Mom might freak out.

"Janey?" Tasha is waiting.

"Ninety-eight pounds," I practically whisper.

"Ninety-eight POUNDS!!!!" Mom reacts just how I thought she would. She is staring at me, horrified.

Inside, I also feel a little horrified. I never meant to reach the double digits. I mean, I broke the 100-pound barrier in sixth grade, and I was at least three inches shorter back then. In all honesty, I was always happy in my usual weight range of 115 to 120.

"Janey, you are WAY too skinny!!" Mom's eyes are practically bugging out of her head. "You need to gain some weight!"

"It's just because we just finished a bike trip," I say, trying to brush it off, even though, inside, I am panicking. If the numbers on the scale are accurate, I NEED to gain weight. BUT, if I gain weight, I might slow down. I had a faster track season than ever before, and I am still flying on all of my runs. Yes, I did feel a little more lightheaded than usual on this year's bike trip, but I am still extremely fit.

Kayley and Mom both go on to weigh themselves, but I don't really hear a word they say. I am stuck in my thoughts, and I am stuck in a sticky situation. And I am not sure how I will ever rip myself from it.

"Trust in the LORD with all your heart and lean not on your own understanding; in all your ways acknowledge him, and he will make your paths straight. Do not be wise in your own eyes; fear the LORD and shun evil. This will bring health to your body and nourishment to your bones." –Proverbs 3:5-8

I stare at the words in my Bible and freeze.

I read the last two verses again.

"Do not be wise in your own eyes; fear the Lord and shun evil. This will bring health to your body and nourishment to your bones."

It is like someone has hit me over the head with a frying pan.

If God ever wanted to smack me with a verse, this is the one.

I am trying so hard to be this healthy person but am going about it in the completely wrong way.

How can I truly expect to be healthy when I am being wise in my own eyes? How can I truly expect to be healthy when I don't listen to the advice of anyone else? Everyone keeps telling me I am too skinny, and I KNOW I am too skinny. Everyone keeps telling me I need to gain weight, and I KNOW I need to gain weight. Even though I am still running well, I haven't functioned as a woman in nearly a year, and I KNOW that is not healthy.

How can my bones be nourished?

How can my body truly be healthy?

I have lost all control of myself, and I need to give that control back over to God.

I NEED to fear the Lord.

I close my Bible and mull over the words in my head as I drift off to sleep.

The fact that I weighed ninety-eight pounds didn't really drive me to the point of wanting to change, but maybe this will.

The question is, am I ready?

The Hot List

"Morgan is at the top of the boys' list."

"Yeah, Autumn and Ashley are in their top three as well."

"I think Kate, Addy, Beth, and Carmella were all listed too."

Okay, so I admit my attention has been peaked.

I pause outside of our cabin door and inquire, "What are you guys talking about?"

I may be chilly, but I can wait to grab my sweatshirt.

"Well, the guys made a top-ten hottest girls' list of our cross country team." Arika shakes her head with disgust as she plops down beside me on the front step of the cabin.

"Oh." I scrunch up my nose at the thought.

"Yeah, doesn't it make you mad?" Tara adds.

"Kind of." I feel a bit deflated. I didn't know our boys were like that, at least not Kaden or Carter Connors. Yes, we all know that Morgan is curvy and lovely, with cute, little curls and a smile that borders on divine. And yes, we are all aware that Autumn has gorgeous hair, a sexy smile, and is easily the most flirtatious girl on the team. And yes, we are not blind to the fact that Ashley has eyes like pools of turquoise. We all know all of this. So WHY do the boys have to drive that point home? And WHY do they think I'm not pretty enough or good enough to be on their list? I am thin, fit, fast, energetic, and have an innocent smile. And, even better, I can keep up with our fastest guys on distance runs and even hold conversations along the way.

"It is just dumb," I quickly conclude, as I inspect my wiry body.

It doesn't matter if I weigh 118 pounds or 98 pounds. The boys are never really going to notice me or see me as pretty.

Milkshakes, Anyone?

"Go Beth! Go Carmella!" I cheer on my teammates as they push through the last part of the race. Oh, how I wish I was out there running with my girls. "Go, Samara! Go, Arika!"

We are at our first cross country invitational of the season, and I am resigned to the role of team cheerleader. The tendonitis in my knee that first popped up at summer camp is still aggravating me, and Coach wants me to rest. I keep taking a day off here and there, jumping back in for the hard workouts, but that hasn't worked out too well so far. It still hurts to even lift my knee.

After cheering on all of my teammates and congratulating them at the finish, I head back over to where Dad is standing.

"I wish you were out there running!" Dad wraps me in a warm embrace.

"I know! My knee just hurts too much." I frown as I lightly move my right knee in little circles. "I've tried to stretch it out a bunch, but it just won't get any looser."

"Well, I'm glad I could come even if you aren't running. We all miss you at home." He gives me another side hug.

That makes me smile. I always love to see my family members.

"Is Kayley running in her meet tomorrow?" I ask. She was in a boot most of the summer because of a stress fracture.

"Yep. She is still trying to get back in shape, but she will be racing. You know how competitive she is."

Oh, I know. Kayley is a beast. I mean, she ran unknowingly on a stress fracture for most of track season and persevered even though she was in tremendous pain.

"Mr. Eller!" Coach McDevitt walks up beside us. "It's good to see you here!" He gives my dad a firm handshake and a warm smile. "We hope to have your daughter running out there soon." He pats me on the back. "She is ready to have a good season . . . if we can get her healthy."

"Yeah, we all want her healthy," my dad responds.

I feel as if their words have a double meaning.

"We need her to start drinking some milkshakes." Coach's brow furrows with concern. "She needs some meat on those bones." The double meaning is now made apparent.

I feel like they are talking about me behind my back . . . only right in front of me.

I used to love when people would make comments about my

newfound skinniness, but now I am starting to hate it. It is like I have become a circus sideshow.

When Coach leaves, I ask some more about Kayley and her running, Tasha and her basketball, and Mom and her hilarious ways. I want to completely take his mind off the fact that I might be a little too skinny . . . or way too skinny.

I am still not ready to give up control.

I lift my hands to my face anxiously.

"Somebody shoot me now!"

We are all preparing to run the second race of the season, and I actually have the chance to run this time. But, now that I can run, I wish I wasn't running. Racing will always make me sick to my stomach.

"Oh, Janey," Morgan giggles. "You crack me up!"

"I hate racing!" The only way I can keep myself from becoming overly nervous is by being a little negative. It may sound weird, but it seems to work for me.

Once we all steady ourselves on the long, white line, the starter lifts his arm to the sky and pulls the trigger.

I blast from the line at the sight of the smoke.

"BANNGGG!!" The gun echoes across the entirety of Championship Park.

I feel like I am in the high school state meet, and, suddenly, I become excited.

I focus on the end of the first 600-meter straightaway, and I move like a gazelle across the field, working the gradual downhill. Beth is to my right, and Carmella is to my left. My legs feel amazing, and I am right where I need to be.

I float along with my two buddies for the first 800 meters.

It is when we reach the first incline that my energy suddenly evaporates, like water on a hot day.

I have hit an invisible wall.

"Come on, Janey!" Carmella tries to beckon me along, like she did at cross country camp when I started dying on this monstrous dirt hill. "Stay up with us!"

"Come on, Janey! You can do it!" Beth also tries her hand at encouraging me.

I try as hard as I can to stay up with my friends, but I am merely flailing. Their motivating words may have helped at camp, but they do nothing for me today.

I just can't move.

It is like I am iron deficient all over again.

But I know that I am not.

I helplessly watch as the two of them blaze off into the shadows.

Soon, Arika, Samara, Tara, and Sherry blow past me as well.

"Come on, Janey!"

And then, I watch in horror as Morgan, Ashley, and Addy pass me.

I try once more to push my legs just a little faster, but it is useless.

I am practically crawling throughout the entire back loop.

As I emerge into the front loop once more, my roomie, Kerin, passes me.

"Janey! Let's go!"

I just want to cry.

Nearly everyone on our team has passed me, and I am on the verge of collapsing.

My body is as wobbly as a jello jiggler.

In the distance, I see Coach McDevitt staring me down. He has an extremely stern look on his face.

I feel so ashamed.

I swear I must be running nine-minute pace right about now, and there is nothing I can do about it.

As I pass Coach, I feel a firm grip on my left arm, and, right there, at 1.75 miles, he yanks me from the race. He is my angel of mercy sent to rescue me from my torture. But I don't think he is a happy angel.

I stumble off to the side, his hand still firmly gripping my arm.

"You are an anorexic!" he yells angrily, jostling me just a bit.

I am startled, angered, and embarrassed all at once.

Doesn't he know that people can hear him?

"You have to start eating more!" He is firm and looks me right in the eye. "You are not going to run well until you do."

He stands by my pitiful side for a while longer, not saying a whole lot, and then he heads off to the finish line.

I should be crying, but something in his tone has awoken me from my year of fog.

I am an anorexic.

No one else has vocalized the fact, but Coach has finally broken the silence.

And, even though it hurts, his words are what I need to hear.

I have known what I must do for quite some time, but now I am ready to actually do it.

I HAVE to give over control.

If I don't, who knows where my road will take me.

*****

"This food is delicious!" I exclaim, as I dig into Mrs. McCraken's home-cooked morsels.

"Woah, slow down there, girl," Arika giggles.

We are on our way home from the meet, and Beth's parents have graciously agreed to host us for a post-race dinner. And, so far, every bite has been incredible.

Once I finish my first plate, I head up the stairs for seconds.

"Keep filling up that plate!" Coach says with a wink, as I scoop up some more lasagna and the tasty-looking banana pudding.

We both seem to have a special understanding now.

In a matter of hours, I have turned from a girl who carried a heavy burden on her shoulders to a girl that is joyful and free.

I think everyone can see it.

And, in large part, I have Coach to thank for it.

He wasn't afraid to speak the truth even when it was hard . . . even when it may have appeared cruel.

"This pudding is amazing!" I declare when I am back at the table.

"Have you tried any of Mrs. McCracken's famous chocolate chip cookies?" Sherry asks excitedly.

"Not yet, but I definitely will!" I give her a huge smile and continue to eat. I am ready to try anything that will help me regain my energy.

As we were watching the guys' race, I talked quite a bit to Coach McDevitt. He told me he wanted me to take the weekend off of running and just work on upping my calories. He also said he wanted me to start meeting with the trainer on Tuesday. I am willing to try all of it, but, for now, my main goal is just to work on eating more.

*****

I peak my head into the training room, somewhat unsure of myself. I am supposed to talk to this lady named Becky Fate at 9:30 am.

It is 9:25.

Maybe I shouldn't have arrived early.

I see a lady with blonde hair sitting at a desk in the back. She notices me standing there and motions for me to enter.

"Janey Eller?"

"Yeah, I'm Janey." Still unsure of myself and feeling quite awkward, I make my way over to where she is sitting.

"Have a seat, Janey."

After sitting down, she gives me a huge smile.

"So, how are you doing, Janey?"

"Oh, good."

Does she want me to go into detail about the whole ordeal right now?

"Coach McDevitt told me that you needed to meet with me, and I'm assuming you know why he wanted us to talk?"

"Yeah, I know why."

"Okay, good." Becky looks over at me a little more intently. "To start with, I want you to know that I am here to help you. I want to get you back to being healthy and strong, not just so that you can run faster but so that you can enjoy life." She pauses and then continues. "I want you to also know that NO ONE is mad at you, not at all, and I won't think less of you because you are here."

I give her a shy smile. I think I am going to feel quite comfortable with this lady.

"So, I would like to start by weighing you and then testing your body fat. Follow me."

First, she has me stand on the scale. I sure hope I am back in the triple digits.

"*102.*"

I feel a slight relief as I see the numbers before my eyes.

Maybe this is why Annie had a party when she crossed the 100-pound barrier.

"How do you feel about this weight?" Becky asks, somewhat intrigued.

"Well, it is better than it was this summer. I was down to ninety-eight pounds then, and that was NOT good."

"What would you like to see yourself at?"

"Hmmm. I think I should be more than 110 pounds."

"Okay, that is a start. What were you before you lost all this weight?"

"I was 115 when I started college."

"Okay. Well, I would like you to be back at 115 pounds. For your height, 120 would actually be better, but let's make 115 your goal."

"Okay."

"How do you feel about that?"

"It's fine." I look down at my feet. "It's just kind of scary, I guess."

"Why?"

"Because," I try to figure out how to best express my fears, "I dropped so much time when I lost weight . . . and I don't want to lose all the ground I gained."

"That is an understandable fear, Janey."

"It is just that I ran all my best times last track season at around 105 pounds."

"Here's what I think Janey. I think you will be able to run JUST as fast with the extra weight."

"Yeah?"

"Yes, I do. You will have extra energy and be able to regain some of that muscle that you probably lost." She picks up something that looks like metal tweezers. "Here, I actually want to test your body fat. That will give us a better understanding of how you are doing."

After pinching the skin on my stomach and the skin on my thigh, she gives me my reading.

"Your body fat is at nine percent."

"NINE PERCENT??" I am astounded. "I was at sixteen freshman year."

"Yeah, that is very low, Janey." She looks slightly worried, although she is masking it quite well. "To be healthy and to function as a woman, you need to be at twelve percent. And that is just the lowest end of the spectrum. Guys only need five percent body fat, but we girls need more."

"I never wanted to lose that much weight . . . or body fat," I tell her. "All I wanted to do was to eat healthier because of my nutrition teacher."

"Yeah?"

"Yeah. She told us to make goals, and I didn't really want to make them because I thought I ate healthy enough. But . . . she said we needed to. So, I started to eat dessert once a day instead of twice a day. And then, when she said to make a harder goal, I started eating dessert twice a week instead of every day. After that, I just kind of started to cut all sorts of fat out of my diet, not because of a goal but because it just seemed like it made me feel better. I stopped eating cheese. I stopped dipping my veggies into ranch dressing. I stopped drinking milk at lunch. I stopped eating crackers or any sort of processed food. If I ever had a snack, I only had a piece of fruit. That was it. And I only ate when I was actually hungry."

"Well, it is definitely a step that you are willing to talk about this."

"It took my coach pulling me from a race to see that I had to give over control. I just couldn't do it on my own anymore."

"Well, Janey, here is what you need to do if you are really willing to turn this weight issue around. It may seem hard at first, but I need you to make it your goal to eat between 4,000 and 5,000 calories each day."

"Seriously?"

"Yes. Seriously."

"My nutrition teacher sophomore year said I shouldn't eat more than 2,200."

"Did she know you were a distance runner?"

"Yes."

"Well, she was wrong. With your running and overall active lifestyle, you probably need more like 3,000 calories each day to MAINTAIN weight."

"I thought what she said wasn't true, but I thought since she was a professor she knew what she was talking about."

"She didn't. So, in order to gain back this weight and take in all these calories, this is what I need you to do. I want you to supplement your snacks with peanut butter and yogurt. I also want you to splurge each day and eat dessert. With the amount of miles you run, you need it. Fat is NOT a bad thing, not at all. Twenty to thirty percent of your diet should actually come from fat."

"I didn't know that."

"You will find that if you supplement your diet in the right way, it shouldn't be all that hard to add the calories. You will feel full and maybe slightly uncomfortable at first, but that is normal. You probably shrunk your stomach, and we just need to expand it."

"What if I start eating that much food and gain back too much weight? Like, what if I get used to eating 4,000 calories a day and can't stop, even when I am back to being healthy?"

"You won't. I will be working closely with you and will keep meeting with you several times a week. We will work together to get you back on the right path. So, can you do this for me? For the next three days, I want you to keep track of all that you eat. And then, I want you to come to my office again."

"That is what my nutrition teacher made us do."

"Yeah, but this is different. The purpose of this isn't to see what you can cut from your diet but to see what you can add."

"Okay, I can do that."

"Good. Janey, I want to thank you for meeting with me. I can tell you are headed in the right direction." She gives me a warm grin and walks me out of the office.

As I walk back to my dorm, I thoroughly hope that I am headed in the right direction too.

*****

That night, at dinner, Carter inquires of my session with Becky.

"So, Janey, how was your meeting with the trainer?"

"Oh, it went pretty well. I found out that my body fat is NINE PERCENT though. That kind of scared me."

"That is pretty low. What does she want you to do about it?"

"She wants me to eat 4,000 to 5,000 calories every day. I'm not sure how I am going to do that, but I will try." I pause and then add. "I just really hope I don't slow down because of it." I feel comfortable enough around Carter to share this fear. In only the month I have known him, he has become like a brother to me.

"Do you know that I struggled with low body fat before too?" Carter looks up at me as he shovels in a huge plate of pasta. Not only is he our fastest runner, but he also eats like it's his job.

"Really? I never knew guys struggled with that."

"Yeah, my body fat dropped to two percent a couple years ago, and my running suffered BIG TIME because of it."

"Did you feel really tired and like you didn't have any energy?"

"Yeah, I did. I started running TERRIBLY, and it was not fun at all. And, like you, I was told to eat a bunch of calories every day to increase my body fat."

"How was that?"

"Oh, it was hard. I felt like I was force-feeding myself. My stomach just felt huge." He pats his nonexistent belly and makes a face.

"But you felt better because of it?"

"Definitely. Once I gained some weight and increased my body fat, I ran faster than I ever had before."

"Really?"

"Yeah. It didn't slow me down at all. It only made me a much stronger runner."

"Hmmm."

Suddenly, I don't feel as wary of the plan I have been asked to follow.

"Some people, like you and me, Janey, have fast metabolisms, and we need to eat more than others. That is the reason I eat three or four plates of food every night at dinner. I NEED all that energy to keep running well. I don't want my body fat to drop that low again."

I've always wondered how the boy ate so much food at every meal. He is like a bottomless pit.

"Well, I better go get some dessert!" I jump up from my seat with a smile. Carter has both assured me and inspired me.

Ready or not, food here I come!

Build Up

I look into the mirror as I brush my teeth and see something in my reflection I haven't seen in quite a while.

JOY.

My no longer sunken-in cheeks are rosy, and the few pounds I have gained thus far have only added to my beauty.

I give myself a smile after I spit into the sink.

I am on the right track.

We are running our annual five-mile time trial today, and, although I am slightly nervous, I am excited. I have only been eating more for about a week, but I have already felt a huge burst of energy. I would compare it to the way I felt when I started taking iron.

I jog over to the track, and both of the coaches are there waiting. We still have twenty minutes before we leave, but I am always early to practice. Those who are tardy have to run a 400 for every minute they are late, and I do not want to be one of them.

"Janey!" Washer looks down at his watch in playful horror. "You are late!"

"SURE I am." I roll my eyes with a smile. Washer is always joking with me.

"Do you think you are feeling good enough to try this time trial?" Coach McDevitt asks, giving me a pat on the back.

"I think so. I feel like I have so much more energy!" I am practically jumping up and down.

"Good. Remember though, if you start to feel bad, back off."

"Okay! I will."

"I want to make sure we build you back up before you push yourself too hard again. I don't want a repeat of Tuesday."

Tuesday was the day I met with Becky, and we had a workout on the track. I was only able to complete seven of the ten 300s, all the while feeling like I was running at high altitude. Although I was gung-ho about increasing my calories, I obviously was still nowhere near 100 percent.

Once the team arrives, we stretch for a while and then head out to Ivy Creek. My legs feel super bouncy and light. My stomach, however, is in tumult. This is the one downside to gaining back this weight. I practically sprint to the awaiting outhouse when we reach the park.

After all the girls have arrived, Coach gives us five more minutes to stretch. Then, it is time for our out and back run. The boys have already left on their seven-mile time trial, so it is only us girls now.

"Ready, go!" Coach McDevitt shouts, as we all take off down the trail.

I start off fast and steady, right with Beth and Carmella.

"Good job, Janey! You look strong! Keep it up, Beth and Carmella!" Coach McDevitt and Washer fly by us on their bikes as they send encouragement our way.

After about 800 meters, I pull ahead of my two buddies.

"Go, Janey! You look awesome!" I can tell that Beth is excited I am feeling good again.

I am not sure if I will feel this good for the full five miles, but I feel incredible right now, so I push the pace.

And to think I have only been eating more for about a week.

My surge of energy starts to fade, however, around the two-mile mark, but I keep pushing until we reach the turning point. Hitting the wall at two miles is a lot better than hitting the wall at 800 meters.

"14:50!" Coach McDevitt yells at the 2.5 mile mark.

Wow. That is a pretty good time. It is right under six-minute pace.

Leaning over, with my hands on my knees, I take a breather. I remember Coach's advice to back off if I am not feeling 100 percent, and I am going to listen to it.

"Hey, Coach. I think I'm just going to take it easy on the way back," I manage to say through my borderline spastic breathing.

"That is fine, Janey. You ran great for 2.5 miles, and that is a start. You are smart to not push it any farther."

I stand beside Coach, cheering along my teammates, until I see Kate Huff coming. She is running about 7:30 pace. I decide to run back to the start with her.

"Good job, Kate!" She may not be our fastest runner, but her dedication and perseverance is inspiring.

As she turns around, I start to run alongside her.

"Are you going to run with me, Janey?" she asks, her blue eyes twinkling and her mane of curls bobbing.

"Yep!"

"Aww! That is so fun!"

The competitive side of me feels guilty for not pushing as hard as I can for the full five miles, but I can tell Kate appreciates having me run with her. And, to be honest, I kind of enjoy not stressing over a time for once.

The only problem is that my stomach is still churning.

With about an 800 to go, Carter tears past us, blazing through his seven miles.

"Good job, Carter!" we both cheer.

"Good job, girls!" he responds.

Once we cross the finish line, I don't stop running. I head straight for the bathroom.

After I do what needs to be done, I trudge back to where the team is waiting.

I just can't seem to shake this queasy, tumultuous feeling.

"Are you feeling okay, Janey?" Carter asks, reading the pained look on my face.

"My stomach just feels horrible."

"Yeah, that'll happen. I remember feeling the same way. You will feel better in time though."

"Thanks, Carter."

"How was the time trial for you?"

"Well, I ran the first 2.5 miles pretty well, in 14:50."

"That's a great time!" He lifts his hand to give me a high five.

"Yeah, I was running with Beth and Carmella . . . but then I kind of hit a wall. That is why I stopped at 2.5 miles and took it easy on the way back."

"Well, that was smart of you. Just keep doing what you need to do, and soon you won't be hitting any wall."

I give him a huge smile, even though I am still quite nauseous. Beth is sure lucky to have won the affections of such a great guy.

"Are you excited for this weekend?"

"Yep!" Our whole team will be heading up to the Connors' house in Santana Heights once we have eaten and taken showers. It will be like a mini vacation.

"Hey, Janey. Come talk to me." I look up to see Coach McDevitt motioning my way.

"Well, I will talk to you later, Carter."

"Bye."

I wave good-bye to my friend and jog on over to Coach.

"So, how are you feeling?"

"I am extremely queasy, probably because I have been eating so much more."

"How did you feel running?"

"I felt great for two miles, but then I hit a wall."

"That is definitely an improvement from last week."

"Yeah, I know."

"Well, here is what I want you to do this weekend. I want you to take both Saturday and Sunday off of running."

"Why? I've been eating a lot more and am feeling pretty good."

"You still aren't at 100 percent though, and our goal is to get you there. So, just for this weekend, take some time off."

"Can I bike?"

"Sure. You can ride at a relaxed pace. I just don't want you running or pushing your body harder than you need to."

"Okay." I feel slightly deflated, mostly because I just love to run, but I know he is right.

I am willing to do whatever it takes to build up my body so I can run stronger and faster.

I just have to be willing to give it time.

*****

"GO, GO, GO, GO, GO!!!!" A raggedly dressed man swings his right arm in huge, dramatic circles as he directs us towards a barely-noticeable back entrance to the train station.

My adrenaline races as I sprint alongside Carter Connors, Beth close behind. The three of us are leading the team through the streets of Chicago, on a mad dash to the finish line.

Less than fifteen minutes ago, we were all dining on Giordano's pizza, thoroughly enjoying the cheese-filled slices (of which I had THREE), and now we are participating in an unintended time trial. The goal is to make it to the train before it departs the station, and I am not sure our whole team is going to achieve that goal.

Ryan Graber is practically shuffling, complaining about having to go to the bathroom, and Max is limping through the streets in his air cast. He has a stress fracture and is MOST DEFINITELY not supposed to be running. I know I am not supposed to be running this weekend either, but I have no other choice.

We tear through the glass doors and race full-speed through a hallway filled with little shops and fast food restaurants.

"I hope the rest of them hurry up!" I shout between breaths.

"I know!" Carter yells back at me. "This is the last train out of here tonight!"

We reach an escalator, and I tear up it, taking two steps at a time.

"JANEY!!!! You are going the wrong way!" Beth screams up at me, in a cute, high-pitched voice.

"OH NO!!" I have almost reached the top of the moving staircase, but I turn around and tear back down it. It is rather difficult going down an escalator that is moving up, but I am determined to catch this train.

Once I reach my running buddies, the three of us tear down another hallway. The train yard is dead ahead.

"Check the boards!!! Find out which train we are supposed to get on!!!" Carter sounds somewhat frazzled, possibly because he is our tour guide for the day and feels responsible for all of us.

"There it is! Santana Heights!"

"Okay! Let's go!" Carter takes off sprinting, swerving through the crowd of people.

We take off after our fearless leader and sprint for another 150 meters.

"Let's sit in this car!"

Once we are all seated in the train, we all take a couple moments to catch our breath.

"That was intense!" I exclaim.

We are sitting for no more than a minute when the train starts to move.

"Oh no," Beth whispers.

There is no way all of our teammates made it, especially not Max.

We sit in silence, unsure of what to say or do next.

"Hey, you guys!" Kaden breaks the silence as he enters the train car. A bunch of our teammates trickle in behind him.

"WHERE IS THE BATHROOM??!!" Ryan shouts, his hands awkwardly placed in his back pockets.

We all point down the hallway to a compartment with a silver door.

Ryan tears off in a full sprint.

I can't help but laugh.

Looking back at Kaden, I ask, "Did everyone make it?" I nervously anticipate his answer.

"Yep."

"Are you serious?"

"Uh huh. We definitely cut it VERY close though."

The three of us breathe a huge sigh of relief.

"Even Max made it?" I am stunned.

"I stepped on the train just as it started to move." I swivel my head just as Max steps into the train car.

"Really?"

"Yeah. It was incredibly stressful." Chuckling, Max slides down into a seat, exhausted.

I feel like I am living a scene in a movie.

"That was EPIC," someone says.

"Yes, yes it was."

We eventually find our way to the upper level of the car, but I am still on an adrenaline high from our race to the train. What a rush!

Last weekend, I could barely make it 1.75 miles without collapsing, but, tonight, I feel like I could sprint through those Chicago streets for hours.

Oh what a difference a week and a change of heart can make!

I feel nauseous and somewhat dizzy as we run our easy three miles on Mount Cloud's cross country course. Maybe it is because I wrote "Think Happy Thoughts" cards for each member of the team while on the four-hour bus ride. Or maybe it is because, in a matter of hours, I will give the pre-meet devotional, the one where I will talk about my struggle with food. Or maybe it is because the hill at the mile mark is monstrous. All I know is that I am not feeling very well. And tomorrow is Regionals.

"Are you ready for a three-peat tomorrow, Eller?" Washer, still wearing his awkward American-flag running shorts, runs up alongside me. I am not sure why the guys on our team (and apparently some of the coaches), choose to wear such short shorts.

"I'm just going to run." I don't really want to think about the fact that I haven't yet lost a college cross country regional meet. "I don't want to put any pressure on myself."

"Oh, you want to win though. I know you." He nudges me.

He is right. I DO want to win. And I KNOW I can win too. I have been the fastest runner on the team since mid-October, ever since I gained back the needed weight, so I KNOW it is possible. I just don't want to think too much about it.

"You killed that mile-repeat workout last week, and you will do the same tomorrow, Janey." Washer is probably my biggest fan, and, although I really appreciate it, I don't like the added stress. I actually do better when people don't believe in me.

I KNOW I dominated that workout. It was the annual four by one mile repeat workout on the gravel path at Ivy Creek, and I averaged 5:26 for each mile. No other Lazarus girl had ever averaged that fast of a time on that particular workout, and both the coaches made note of it.

"There is our future All-American!" Coach McDevitt would cheer each and every time I passed him that day.

"Woah, Janey! You are running AWESOME!!" all the boys would cheer.

So, yeah, I know I am ready to bust a fast time, even on a hilly course like this, but I don't like thinking about it.

After we finish our three miles, strides, and stretching, we jump back on the coach bus to head to the hotel.

I really don't think I am ready for the talk.

Luckily, we still have to take showers and eat dinner, so I have some more time to organize my thoughts and relax.

I take a speedy, two-minute shower, which leaves my hotel roomies in awe, and prop myself up on the bed with some pillows. I now have time to organize my thoughts.

I think back through all the things that led me to and through this disordered eating. I write down every situation and circumstance that led me to my point of stick-thinness and every situation, Bible verse, person, and thought that brought me out of it. I want to be open with my team. I want them to know how God has worked in my life and hopefully touch someone through it. God has given me a story for a reason, and I am meant to share it, even it is means feeling a bit queasy.

I really do want to puke now.

How can I tell them?

I mean, I KNOW most of them realize what I went through, but saying it out loud is like making it more real. Saying it out loud is like actually admitting to the world that I had a problem, that I'm not perfect, and that I have weaknesses just like everyone else.

Can I do that?

"Janey! It's time for dinner!" Samara startles me from my thoughts. "FOOD TIME!!"

I jump up from bed and follow her out to the bus.

I cram into a seat with Beth and Carter, the team couple. They have only been dating for like a month, but everyone is positive they will be married in a year or two. We sit together at Fazoli's as well, where we dine on the usual pasta and breadsticks amidst lively conversation. It takes my mind off the talk, at least for a while.

When we return to the hotel, the nauseous feeling returns.

I need to run away.

Where can I hide?

"Team meeting in five minutes!" Washer shouts from down the hall.

If I'm going to run, I need to do it now.

But I can't run. I need to be brave.

I grab my Bible and my little journal, with my handwritten outline inside, take a deep breath, and bulldoze my way to Coach's room. I can't be late to my own devotional.

"Hey, Janey! Are you ready for your talk?" Coach McDevitt asks as soon as I make my presence known.

"Ummmm . . . I don't know. I hope so!" I plop down beside Washer on one of the beds and open up my notebook. I am still not sure what I will and will not say.

"You'll do great," Washer reassures me.

The team starts to file in a couple at a time until the room is packed.

All eyes are on me.

I usually enjoy being the center of attention but not right now.

"So, Janey, do you want to open up our meeting?" Now all eyes are really on me.

"Sure."

Breathe, Janey, BREATHE. My heart is pumping faster than during a mile-rep workout.

What are they going to think about me after this?

"So, I would like to start by reading from Proverbs 3:5-8." I open up my Bible and proceed to read.

"Trust in the LORD with all your heart and lean not on your own understanding; in all your ways acknowledge him, and he will make your paths straight. Do not be wise in your own eyes; fear the LORD and shun evil. This will bring health to your body and nourishment to your bones."

I close my Bible and look out into my audience.

"One year ago, I would have said that I trusted God in many areas of my life—in running, in friendships, and in various other arenas. I would have said that I had given everything in my life over to Him. I would have said I spent a lot of time with Him and had a deep relationship with Him. BUT there was one thing I hadn't completely handed over, and that was my eating habits."

As soon as I start to share, my nerves completely dissipate. I am not sure why I was even so afraid. I think the enemy, the devil, just wanted keep me from sharing by shooting flaming darts of fear my way.

I take the whole team through my yearlong journey, and, once I finish, everyone claps. Beth and Samara both give me a big hug.

"Thanks so much for sharing that, Janey! That took a lot of courage." Coach McDevitt looks like he is on the verge of tears. He was there through the whole struggle, and he knows how it affected me.

I give him a big smile and breathe another deep breath.

Thank you, Jesus, for helping me share.

After Coach gives us some advice on race strategy, he dismisses us so that we can go to sleep.

On my way out of the room, Ryan Graber, one of my favorite guys on the team, pulls me aside.

"Janey, I just wanted to thank you so much for sharing! I know it might have been scary, but it is something I definitely needed to hear. Even if it didn't affect anyone else, it affected me, so I want to thank you for being so brave. God is using you, girl, and he definitely used you tonight." He pats me on the shoulder and heads to his room.

All I can do is smile.

Someone WAS touched.

Someone WAS impacted by the fact I was willing to be open and honest.

I feel as if a huge burden has just been lifted as I turn and skip back to my room.

Thank you, Jesus.

*****

I am running free and fast, leading the whole pack of runners.
The fields and trees are just a blur around me.
I am winning the race.
I have just passed the one-mile mark.
And then, we reach THE HILL—the gigantic, monstrous mountain.
And it is covered in mud—a thick, goopy, soupy mud.
I try to run, but I am going nowhere.
The mud just sucks me into it like an angry vortex.
I fall to my knees and begin to crawl. I crawl in desperation.
For every two feet I gain, I lose one.
Beth passes me. Carmella passes me. Arika passes me.
They don't even seem to notice the mud.
I try to stand up, but I keep falling to the ground.
Samara passes me. Tara passes me. Sherry passes me.
All I can do is crawl through the mud like a helpless, hopeless fool.
Addy passes me. Morgan passes me. Ashley passes me.
All I can see is the murky, slippery MUD. It is all around me.
Kate passes me. Autumn passes me. EVERYONE is passing me.
I am going to take dead last in this race.
When I finally reach the top of the hill, the race restarts.
I am in the front again.
The sea of color follows behind me like an angry mob.
There isn't a goopy drop of mud in sight.
I am a gazelle, a warrior, a winner.
The fields and trees are just a blur around me.
No one is going to rip this lead from my grasp.
I have just passed the one-mile mark.
And then, I lose my way.
I take a wrong turn by the creek.
I can't seem to turn myself around to head back in the right direction.
I am not sure where I am or where I am going.

I just keep running, running, running in the wrong direction.
It is as if my legs have a mind of their own.
I run for ten minutes . . . twenty minutes . . . thirty minutes even.
I run for an hour.
I now know that everyone has finished the race.
But I am still nowhere near the finish.
I have taken dead last.

I wake up from the nightmare in a sweat, stressed out beyond belief. It was all just a dream. I try to go back to sleep, but I can't. I am just so scared that these dreams will come true.

Why do races do this to me?

*****

"JANEY!! SAMARA!! ARIKA!! COME QUICK!!!!"

I am in the middle of picking out a pair of racing socks for the regional race when Sherry tears into the room.

"What's wrong?" I jump up and run to the door, ready for a fire to be sweeping through the hotel.

"Nothing's wrong! Just come on! I've got to show you something!"

I am the first one out the door. Samara and Arika are close behind.

We jog after Sherry to her room.

"Okay, now, get ready!" she says.

We enter the room, and the three of us gasp.

The entire hotel room is filled with flowers—flowers of all colors and all varieties.

"WOAH!!" we all exclaim. "Where did these come from?"

Beth sits on one of the beds with a dreamy grin the size of Texas on her face.

"They're from Carter, for our one-month anniversary!!!!" she cries.

"Are you serious???" My mouth swings open like a trap door.

"Yeah!!! Isn't that so sweet of him?"

I'm not sure if I should be thrilled or freaked out. If this is what he does after one month, what is he going to do after two months? What about after three months?

"They are so beautiful!" Samara says giddily, as she carefully walks around the room, bending down to smell each and every bouquet.

"Awwww! This is just the most romantic thing I have ever seen!" Arika adds.

"How did they get in here without you noticing?" I ask, still dumbfounded by the amount of flowers surrounding me. There are fewer flowers than this at an actual wedding.

"They must have snuck in during the middle of the night!" Beth is radiant. There is no way I will beat her in a race after such an uplifting morning as this. I know how much joyful circumstances like this can improve a person's time.

"Actually, I gave them one of our keys so they could get in," Sherry smirks, as she places her hands on both hips proudly.

"Seriously? Couldn't they get in trouble for going into your room?" I will always be a rule follower, even when it comes to the sweet, the sentimental, and the sappy.

"Oh, Coach knew all about it!" Beth cheers, slugging the air.

"Oh, okay. Good." And then I ask another question on my mind. "Where are you going to put all of these flowers when we have to leave?"

"I'm not sure yet," she chuckles. "I might call my parents and ask if they can come pick them up for me."

After basking in Beth's joy for a few minutes, we head back to our room to finish getting ready for Regionals.

I'm not sure if anything will top that insanely amazing display of affection.

*****

I am running free and fast, leading the whole pack of runners.

The fields and trees are just a blur around me.

I am winning the race.

I have just passed the one-mile mark.

And then, we reach THE HILL—the gigantic, monstrous mountain.

And this time, that hill has NOTHING on me.

This time, I am not dreaming. I am running FOR REAL.

I hit the hill strong and work each and every step until I crest the top of it. I don't think I have ever run uphill so quickly and smoothly. I float on the downhill as it swoops into roller coaster-like bumps.

Alien Ant Farm's "Smooth Criminal," which is quite possibly the last song I heard while riding in Carter's truck with Beth, is propelling me along.

"Annie, are you okay? You okay? You okay, Annie? Annie, are you okay? You okay? You okay, Annie?"

I am unsure of the rest of the words or of their meaning, but the beat is a great one to run to.

I surge through the rest of the roller coaster bumps and back down the lower side of the monster hill. I pass the two-mile mark.

On the loud speaker, "Smooth Criminal" plays. What are the odds?

"Annie, are you okay? You okay? You okay, Annie? Annie, are you okay? You okay? You okay, Annie?"

I run even faster as I push into the last mile of the race.

Ahead of me, the lead "gator" charges forward.

"GO, JANEY!!!!" Washer calls from inside the green go-cart. "Go for a three-peat!"

For the first time since my first regional win, I think I actually smile while racing.

If I ever thought I had a chance at winning, it is now.

I leap across the teeny-tiny creek and swing around the outside of some trees. I am now headed to the last half-mile loop. I press on and on and on and on, around the tennis courts and through a couple zig-zags, quickly approaching the end of the race.

As I blast through the finish, the clock reads "*18:17.*"

I have bested my cross country 5k PR by one second and on a rather difficult course too.

Beth comes in second place with "*18:32.*"
Carmella comes in third place with "*18:47.*"
Samara comes in fourth place with "*19:36.*"
And Sherry comes in fifth place with "*19:47.*"

We have scored fifteen points.

I win Regionals for the third straight year, AND our team scores a perfect point total.

To celebrate our win, I roll down the monstrous hill. I roll and roll and roll and roll until I reach the bottom. When I come to a stop, I am slightly dizzy and partially discombobulated, but I don't even care. I just lay there, arms outstretched, staring up at the cloudy sky.

This weekend is one for the record books, from the sharing of my story for the first time to the record number of flowers, from the three-peat to the team victory.

It doesn't get much better than this . . . not on earth at least!

"WILL JANEY ELLER COME TO THE FRONT DESK? JANEY ELLER, COME TO THE FRONT DESK."

I am in the middle of scooping up another bite of my mixture of soft-serve ice cream and blueberry pie when I hear my name being called on the loud speaker.

I am startled.

"Why do they want me? What did I do?"

"I don't know, Janey. Maybe you should go see." Beth looks like she is trying to mask a smile with confusion.

Kaden and Carter both raise their eyebrows mischievously.

Do they know something I don't know?

I hope I'm not in trouble for wearing shorts to breakfast the other day. That rule is ridiculous.

I jump to my feet and speed through the cafeteria to find out my life sentence.

I am about to ask the lady manning the desk what she wants when I hear I very familiar voice.

"Jaaannney!"

I turn my head to see Ryan Graber grinning at me.

Was he called to the front desk too? I don't think I heard his name on the loud speaker.

"Hey!"

Ryan is one of the most awesome guys on our cross country team, and it is always a delight to run with him, eat with him, talk with him, act silly with him, or just run into him randomly.

"So, Janey, I was just wondering. Do you want to go to the formal with me? You know, the Christmas Banquet?"

I swear my mouth drops to the floor. I am also pretty positive that my eyes light up more than fireworks being shot off on the Fourth of July.

What about Autumn? I was positive Ryan would go with her. They always act like they are dating.

All these people near the front desk are looking at the two of us, smiling.

"Yes!" I don't even have to think twice.

"Good! You are such an amazing girl, and I am lucky to go with you."

"Awww, thanks Graber!"

"Well, I will see you at breakfast tomorrow, Janey! I'm glad you said 'yes!'"

I don't even need to try to smile. I am just overflowing with happiness. I practically skip back into the cafeteria to where Beth, Kaden, and Carter are sitting.

"Sooooo, what did you say?" Kaden grins over at me when I take my seat.

"Huh?"

"What did you tell Graber?"

"How did YOUUUU know?"

"Trust me, I know. I'm his roommate. So, what did you say?"

I don't even blush.

"I told him 'yes!'" I am as springy as a bouncy ball.

"He has been planning to ask you to the banquet for quite a while."

"Really???"

"Yep!"

"What about Autumn? I was sure he would go with her . . . if he was going to go at all."

"All I know is that he wanted to ask you."

I feel like I'm in some incredible dream.

An amazing guy on our cross country team has finally noticed me!

BUT does he like me?

I mean, he must if he chose to ask me and not Autumn.

I keep these thoughts inside as I say good-bye to my cross country buddies and head back to my dorm.

I can't wait to tell my roommate, Kerin!

I practically sprint back to my dorm and storm up the stairs to room 221.

"Kerin! Guess what??!!"

"What?" She can tell something is up because my energy level is high, even for me.

"Ryan Graber asked me to go to the Christmas Banquet!"

"Really?" A smile lights up her face as she gives me her undivided attention.

"Yeah!!" I am practically dancing.

"Awwwwwww! So, how did he ask you?"

"I was called to the front desk while I was in the cafeteria, and he was there waiting for me!"

"That is adorable, Janey! I'm so happy for you!"

I am radiant.

"Graber is such a great guy too," she adds. "You two will be so cute together."

I want to ask her if she thinks he likes me, but I am not that courageous. Maybe I will just ask in a written message on Facebook. Yep, I am a coward when it comes to talking about boys.

I sit down at my computer, ready to spread the news to all my friends.

Ryan Graber asked me to the Christmas Banquet!

Hooray!

*****

The day of the Christmas Banquet is one of anticipation and joy.

Beth comes to my room at 3:30 pm to try and figure out my hair. Neither of us is very gifted in the fashion arena, but she is willing to try her hand at taming my mane. We laugh a whole lot and mess around with different styles. She straightens it a little, curls it a little, and moves some strands of hair here and there. In the end, we both agree it is perfect.

Once she finishes, she musses her own hair around until it is in a cute, little up-do in a matter of minutes. She looks adorable no matter what she does, mostly because she radiates joy, love, and warmth. It is no wonder Carter is madly in love with her.

"Do you want me to put a little make-up on you?" Beth's eyes start to dance.

"No, no, no. I'm fine."

"What about just a teeny-tiny bit of mascara?"

"Uhhhhhh . . ."

"It will make your eyelashes pop ever so slightly."

"I don't need it."

"This is a really special night though." She makes a goofy grin, one that is trying to convince me to give in just this once. "And I bet Ryan would like it!"

"Wellllll . . ."

"No one will know but the two of us. I will never tell ANYONE."

"Hmmmmm . . ."

I really do like Ryan, and, because of that, maybe I am willing to step out on an itsy-bitsy limb just this once. No one will ever even know. It isn't like I will cease to be Janey. It won't make me any weaker. And this is BETH. There is hardly anyone else in the whole entire world that I love more . . . and hardly anyone else I trust more to keep this secret.

"Well, okay," I smile secretively, "but just a LITTLE bit."

She whips out a wand and lightly dabs a tad of the mysterious, moist magic on my eyelashes.

It is like it never even happened.

"Okay, let's put on our dresses, Janey!"

We both slip into our banquet attire, and once Kate and Kerin arrive and finish beautifying themselves, we are ready to go. I am running late for the first time in my life, all because I am chilling with the queen of late arrivals, Beth McCracken, but, for some reason, I don't even care. Yes, I do feel a little antsy and urge the girls to move a little faster, but it is nothing like my usual, hurried self. I feel a very real sense of freedom that is quite uncommon for me.

"You look really nice, Janey," Ryan says, as soon as I reach the lobby.

"Thanks, Ryan! Mandy let me borrow her dress." I twirl just a little as I look him over. "I like your spiffy suit!"

"Thank you kindly, ma'am!"

Ryan is wearing a tan suit coat over a bright orange dress shirt. It definitely clashes with my maroon-colored dress, but it makes him all that more adorable. He is awkward, and I am awkward, so what could be better?

The banquet itself is pretty low-key, but it is still fun. We are placed at table seventy-seven with Kaden and his date, Breanna, and we wait and wait and wait to eat. Ryan and I are hungry, as always, and share his slice of red velvet cake and my slice of "toothpaste cake," as we call it, before dinner is even served. Once we are dismissed to the buffet line, we pile our plates with shrimp, chicken, salad, rolls, and mashed potatoes. The shrimp are especially delicious. As we eat, the mariachi band starts to play. They are clad in sombreros and traditional attire. We are too busy eating to clap or sing, but Ryan isn't too busy to yell out random Spanish phrases.

"Muy bien!" Ryan shouts ecstatically. "La música es muy bella!"

I can only chuckle at his goofiness.

Once dinner is over, Ryan, Kaden, and I find Beth and Carter in the crowd (they are at a different table) and run over to the lobby of McMakin, the dorm in which Beth and I make our residence. I have trouble keeping up, due to the fact that Beth's high heels do not fit my feet, and I am kind of wobbling all over the place. Ryan kindly slows down to stay with me and lends me his slightly-retro jacket until we reach the shelter of the building. I feel super connected to him while wearing it. A guy has never lent me his jacket before!

"You know what is so cool, Janey? Our number one and two runners both went to the banquet together—Beth and Carter and you and me." He smiles over at me as we hustle across the snowy sidewalk.

"Yeah! You are right!"

Once inside, I chase Beth up the flights of stairs to her room, now hobbling because of my aching feet. She has two jackets, one for her and one for me, and they won't look super weird with our dresses. All that I possess are a Lazarus cross country jacket and a heavy, green winter coat that I have owned for far too long with arms that are far too short. I am pretty sure my mom bought it for me at the start of sixth grade. After grabbing the jackets and kicking Beth's high heels from my feet, we head to my room where I can slip into my comfortable church sandals. I am not a fan of shoes that destroy your arches for the sake of beauty. We also snag Kerin from my room so she can join in the rest of the night's fun.

After reuniting with the boys in the lobby, we pile into the Connors' spiffy, red truck and head to the mall where we will watch *The Chronicles of Narnia: The Lion, the Witch, and the Wardrobe*. We have some time to kill once we reach our destination, so Beth, Kerin, Carter, and I indulge in a quart of Gold Medal ice cream while Ryan and Kaden play around in a kiddy car, the kind that bounces all around when you put a quarter in it. Those two are seriously little kids at heart. With their 8:30 bedtime, I'm surprised they are even in college!

After the boys tire of being children, they join us on the benches, hyper and happy. We have an interesting conversation, discussing the differences between state schools and small Christian schools like Lazarus. The truth comes out that Kerin thought Ryan was a partier back in the day and that Ryan thought Beth was a partier back at cross country camp. Both are obviously not true, but they lead to quite a lot of laughter. Beth? A PARTIER??!! Yeah right!

When it is finally time for the movie, Ryan sits smack dab between me and Kaden. Even if it seems silly, I am excited just to sit next to him. He startles me during the previews, just to see me jump, but he makes up for it by sharing Kaden's peanut butter M & M's with me. It is an amazing movie and does a fantastic job of contrasting the freedom, love, and life that is in Christ with the bondage, deception, and death that surrounds Satan and his minions. I think all of us like it. I do have moments of slight confusion, as I usually do in movies, but Ryan happily answers each question.

Once the movie is over, the boys head outside to grab the truck and pick up us girls. They are always very gentlemanlike. Beth and I, both shivering, snuggle together in the front seat. The heat takes a while to turn on, but we are warmed by Ryan and Kaden's high-pitched singing. All I can do is smile gleefully over at them in the back seat.

"Wow, you must really like our singing!" Kaden comments with a wink.

That or maybe I just really like Ryan.

I haven't felt this way about a guy since Riley.

The night has nearly come to a close, but there are still two last things on my to-do list. The first is for me and Beth to deliver our hand-crafted picture frames, made out of Popsicle sticks, to Ryan and Carter. The second is for me to play a song for Ryan on the piano. It is an incredibly fast and difficult prelude, but I want to impress him with the tricky serenade.

The picture frames are a big hit. They love the photographs we have chosen and the little notes we have written on the back of each frame. In their opinion, we are both incredibly creative.

"Wow! These are awesome!" Graber exclaims. He especially loves the picture of him and his petite pumpkin friend.

The song is also a big hit. My hands and legs are shaking the entire time, due to the fact my adrenaline is flowing and I am super nervous, but I play it better than I ever have before. I surprise myself and my listeners.

"Wow! Janey, I never knew you were so good! I'm seriously impressed. I bet you could become famous someday!" Graber knows how to butter me up without even meaning to.

I blush a little and thank him.

"Well, I better get back to my dorm before curfew, Janey! I had so much fun tonight! I really enjoyed it!"

"I did too."

He reaches down to give me a warm parting hug.

"Well, I'll see you tomorrow, possibly at lunch!"

"Bye, Graber!"

"Bye!"

I watch as he leaves and then skip up to my room.

My heart is pitter-pattering a happy tune of light staccato notes.

I don't think I will stop smiling for at least a week.

Christmas Crushed

"Riiiiiiing!"

I jump up from my bed, where I am engrossed in reading the book of Genesis, and reach for the phone.

"Hi!" I greet my unknown listener.

"Hi . . . Janey?" It's a guy's voice, possibly Ryan's.

"Yep, this is Janey!"

"Hey! It's Ryan."

Ooooooh. So it IS Ryan.

"Hey! What's up, Ryan!"

Kerin twists around to give me a quizzical look.

I shrug my shoulders back at her.

"I was just wondering if you have a lot to do tonight."

Does he want to hang out with me? If he does, I am TOTALLY free.

"No, not really. I'm done with all my homework already."

"Okay, good. Could you possible meet me in the Red Room in like fifty minutes? I want to talk to you about something." His voice is very serious-sounding, which is odd for Ryan. He is naturally light-hearted, giddy, and carefree.

"Yeah . . . sure." I feel something sink in the pit of my stomach. I don't think this is going to be good.

"Okay, sweet! Well, I will see you in fifty minutes, Janey."

"Bye, Ryan."

I hang up the phone.

I just sit there, emotionless and still.

"What did he say?" Kerin is definitely interested.

"He wants me to meet him in the Red Room to talk."

"Hmmm. What does he want to talk about?"

"I'm not sure." I feel like I am going to hurl.

"Well, tell me how it goes."

"I will."

After slowly trudging back over to my bed, I flop down and just lay there.

Fifty minutes is far too long to let this uncertainty hang over my head. I could run at least seven miles in the time I have to wait.

I could watch nearly a whole episode of *Smallville*. That would take up time and prepare me for the inevitable.

I KNOW what Ryan is going to tell me. I just KNOW. And I don't WANT to know. I just want to keep pretending he likes me more than just a really good friend, but, in fifty minutes, I won't be able to pretend any longer.

Just like Clark never ends up with Lana, I will never end up with Ryan.

Why did I ever get my hopes up??

My stomach starts to churn.

I tear at one of my fingernails with my teeth.

I shake my foot just a little bit.

I stare at my picture from Coach's surprise fiftieth birthday party, the one where Ryan and I are standing side by side, and almost lose it.

I don't want to go to this meeting.

I pick up my journal and decide to write down my thoughts. It is the only way I can feel a little more at ease.

When forty minutes have passed, I sigh, slip into my Nike's, and begin my journey to the Red Room.

Red Room.

Sound like "Red Rum."

Ryan says that "Red Rum" backwards is "murder."

Ugh.

This talk is going to be the death of me.

I don't know for sure what he will say. I mean, he COULD say he IS interested in me. He did seem really happy with me at the banquet.

But I doubt it.

With the way my life seems to work out, this is not going to end how I want it to.

When I arrive at our meeting place, Ryan isn't there. I have arrived early, due to my restlessness, so I sit down at a booth and wait.

Breathe, Janey. Just BREATHE.

And then, there he is, Ryan Graber.

He smiles with slight seriousness. Usually, with Ryan, he flashes his HUGE happy-go-lucky grin, but not tonight.

"Hey, Janey."

"Hey."

"Thanks for meeting me here. I was hoping we could talk."

"Yeah." I am not sure why I am saying "yeah." I am pretty sure I do not want to have this talk.

"So, Janey. I want you to know this first and foremost. I totally respect you as a friend and think you are an awesome girl."

I am positive I know where this is heading now. He is starting out with the positive to ease into the negative.

"But I do not have the kind of feelings for you that would make me pursue a relationship with you."

"Oh." I am as quiet as a feather falling to the earth.

"I know I should have told you this before the dance, but I didn't."

By "dance," he means banquet.

"I didn't want to lead you on or hurt you, but I'm afraid I may have. And I'm sorry about that. Like I said, you are an amazing friend, and I truly value your friendship. I wouldn't want to lose that."

"Oh." I am a feather that is still falling, falling.

"I'm not in a spot to pursue a relationship with anyone right now . . . not even with Autumn."

"Oh." I am falling, falling, falling . . .

"Do you have anything you want to say, Janey? I know I kind of dumped a lot on you right there."

"Uhhhhhh . . ." I don't have words. Falling feathers are just silent wisps, drifting in the wind, not sure of where they will land.

I feel like an idiot. There is so much I want to say, but I am not sure how to say it.

"I'm not sure."

"Okay, well if you ever need to ask me anything, just ask."

"Okay."

"Well, I better go check my mail."

"Okay, yeah, I better go practice the piano."

We both stand up and head our separate ways.

It's over.

I walk with a whole lot less pep in my step than usual. I kind of just drag my feet.

I slowly look over my shoulder and watch as Ryan disappears.

When I reach the piano practice room, I am no longer a silent feather. And I am no longer falling. I have landed in a pool of boiling lava, and that pool is scalding. It is painful. I start to cry as soon as my fingers touch the keys. I pound out the notes to one of my favorite preludes, the one I played for Ryan after the Christmas Banquet. My vision is blurry, but it doesn't matter because I have this song memorized. I don't even try to stop the salty tears from dripping on the keys. No one can see me crying while my back is turned to the rest of the world inside my cage of glass.

Why didn't I say anything?

After an hour of emotional stress relief, I dry my eyes, and head back to my dorm room.

"So, what did he say?" Kerin blurts out the question as soon as I make my entrance.

All I do is look at her.

I don't have to say anything.

"I'm so sorry, Janey."

A single tear slides down my cheek.

"Aww, don't cry, Janey. I love you, girl!"

I want to give her a hug or thank her for always being so sweet to me, but, if I speak, I will burst like a breached dam. All I can do is give her a reluctant look of appreciation and sit down at my computer.

I have to tell Ryan how I REALLY feel about that talk. If I don't, I will feel guilty forever.

As I type, a wave of relief washes over me.

Maybe this will be okay.

I mean, Ryan is still a great guy. He is still a great friend. He didn't string me along or treat me like just another girl. He treated me with respect, and I can appreciate that. He did what a noble guy would do, what a gentleman would do.

When I finish typing, I am still sad, but I am content.

Ryan will never be my boyfriend, but he will always be my friend.

At least I still have that.

Running on a Prayer

"Janey, is there anything you need prayer for?"

The silence of the run is broken as Samara looks over at me with an inquiring grin. It is a lovely January day, warmer than usual, and the two of us are on an eight miler to Ivy Creek and back.

"Yeah, actually there is."

"Yeah?"

My little Brazilian "chaplain" looks excited.

"Yeah. I really feel like I am supposed to go on a mission trip, but nothing seems to be working out. Every trip I look at is at the wrong time or for the wrong age group. I thought this one to Jamaica, to work with orphans, would work, but I am too old for it."

"What made you want to go on a mission trip?" She looks even more intrigued now.

"It was when they were talking about it in chapel that one day, during the missions' conference. I just felt, for the first time, like it was something I was supposed to do. Ever since I gave over control of my eating, I have just felt my fears disappearing. You know, when I was little, I said I would never go on an airplane and never be a missionary, but, now, I'm not saying that anymore."

"That is so great, Janey. God is good."

"Yeah, it's exciting . . . but, like I said, nothing seems to be working out. I sent an inquiry to several organizations like a month ago, and no one has responded."

"Well, we can pray about it."

"Okay."

With her eyes open, Samara lifts up my predicament to the Lord.

I am so glad I have a friend like her.

When the run is over, stretching is complete, and dinner is eaten, I head back to my room. After taking my nightly shower, I sit down at my computer, ready to start my homework. But, first, I have to check my email.

I open my yahoo account, and, there, at the top of my unread messages, is a message from Adventures in Missions.

Could this be what I think it is?

I open the message, and my jaw nearly drops.

"Hey Janey,

Let me ask you a question: What is God challenging you with? Is there something he asked of you to do beyond yourself?

At Adventures in Missions (AIM) we believe God still speaks today and is moving all around the world. That is why our motto is 'Follow God; Reach our World.'

AIM's goal is to help you fulfill this calling to reach the world. We offer several incredible trips to different countries all around the world.

One such trip is Beat the Drum—Zambia. Over 600,000 children have been orphaned by AIDS in Zambia. 84% of those infected with HIV/AIDS are between the ages of 20-29 years old. This means we have to reach the people prior to that time. That is why BTD targets high school students.

Imagine joining together with hundreds of other COLLEGE-AGED volunteers from several different countries for one purpose—to share a message of abstinence and the love of Jesus Christ under the banner of an HIV/AIDS educational campaign in high schools throughout Zambia.

Beat the Drum is one of the most prolific mission movements of our generation. Each team that enters a high school will be multi-national, multi-ethnic, multi-lingual, and have mixed genders.

The Zambian government is allowing complete freedom to share openly of Jesus Christ and the Gospel. Zambia is the third country to receive the Beat the Drum campaign, and each year this campaign has grown in number.

This is your chance to join the movement and make a difference in the lives of hundreds of Zambians!

To sign up, click here:

http://www.adventures.org/a/trips/level3.asp?id=1702

The deadline is February 10th so hurry!"

I finish reading the email and almost laugh. I pray for a trip, and one drops right into my lap.

And, boy, does God have a sense of humor.

This trip is to AFRICA, which is a whole ocean away and is filled with diseases like Malaria and Ebola and animals like lions and black mambas.

And this trip is to talk to HIGH SCHOOL KIDS about ABSTINENCE.

Some people mistake me for a junior higher.

And did anyone see how awkward I was in health class back in the day?

How can this trip be for me?

But it is.

There is just something about the perfect timing of this email that couldn't be any more perfect.

I reach for the phone to call Samara.

And then, once I've talked to my overjoyed friend, I click on the link to begin the application for the trip.

Where God is leading, I will go.

Just Dance

"When forces of evil draw me in, when darkness surrounds me, I begin, to feel the despair and lonely fear, but that's when a stronger voice I hear. It rings from a cross, it reigns through time; it echoes the truth in this heart of mine. The music resounds with healing rain. The rhythm brings freedom from our pain."

The "Beat the Drum" song hits the speakers, and, immediately, all the Zambian children start to dance like it is what they were born to do. They can't seem to help themselves. Rhythm runs through their veins.

I am in the midst of the crowd as the music begins, so I take a chance. I start to dance. Grabbing the hands of the little girl beside me, I begin twirling her in circles as she smiles in wide-eyed bliss.

"Let the new day dawn. Let the Healer come. To the sound of His heart, I will beat the drum. To the song of His grace, see the children run. To the groove of His love, I will beat the drum."

As the group of wildly enthusiastic children begins closing in around me, I let go of the hands of my little friend and start busting out all the moves I've never before attempted in public. The kids giggle gleefully and mimic what I do.

"There's music that's placed within my soul, a song of the love that makes me whole. There's more to this life than it would seem. There's hope for tomorrow; we can dream. We dream of a future in the sun. We know that the healing has begun. We shatter the silence of our day. We speak of the truth, the life, the way."

There is a buzz of something in the air. It is the buzz of JOY.

We dance all around the dusty field and become a mini tornado, the dirt swirling around us with a frenetic fury.

In this moment, there is no place on earth I would rather be.

About a year ago, I would never have been willing to go to Africa, but now, I don't think I ever want to leave.

The kids are beautiful, the people are intensely generous, the waterfalls and trees are breathtaking, there is freedom in the air, and I am uninhibited when it comes to sharing the good news of the gospel.

In all my twenty-one years of life, I don't think I've really ever felt like I belong. But here, I feel it. I feel like this is where I am meant to be. I feel as if this is where I am truly free.

Enough is Enough

"Janey, why don't you let us take you shopping sometime?"

"I hate shopping. It gives me a headache." It is true. I'd rather cut grass with scissors than go shopping for anything other than ice cream or a good book.

"But we could buy you some CUTE clothes. Please, Janey? It would be so much fun!"

"I have enough clothes. Some people in Africa only own ONE shirt and ONE pair of shorts, and I have a whole closet of clothes. I have MORE than enough!"

"Sure, you have enough clothes, but we could go with you to find some more stylish outfits, some outfits that would make the guys say, 'ow, ow!'"

Okay, that was just weird.

"But I don't want to wear different clothes. I like what I have. Arika and Samara gave me a few nice shirts, some skirts, and two pairs of jeans just last year, and I don't need anything else."

"How is a guy ever going to notice you?" Melody is back at it. "You have to present yourself in such a way that a guy will WANT to spend time getting to know you."

I love receiving such shallow advice.

"If a guy really wants to get to know me, he will like me regardless of what I'm wearing." I know what is true, and I am sticking to it.

"Yeah, but he needs to NOTICE you first. He will never notice you if you don't attempt to appeal to him in some way."

She thinks she can persuade me, but she cannot.

"Okay, well, I don't want some shallow guy to like me anyways."

"Come on, Janey. You need to show you care about your looks for ANY guy to show interest."

"I DO care. I don't dress like a slob. I just don't spend my whole life putting on make-up and going shopping for clothes I don't need. If God wanted to create me with make-up on my face, He would have made me like that in the first place."

"Janey, Janey, Janey . . . we are just trying to help you, and you never let us. We tell you to grow out your bangs, and you won't. We ask you to go with us to buy some new clothes, and you won't do that either." Melody pouts, sticking out her lower lip.

"I don't need your help, Melody."

"Don't you ever want to get married?"

I could seriously throw a chair right about now.

"I don't know! Why does it matter?"

"BECAUSE. If you want a guy to pursue you, you need to put yourself out there."

"I am out there. I run through the streets and ride my bike all over town." I amuse myself with my ability to make comments like Amelia Bedelia.

"Seriously, Janey. Listen to us."

"I AM listening to you, but, Melody, I don't agree with you. If God wants to bring a guy into my life, He will do so at the right time. I will never dress a certain way just to impress someone. That is not who I am or who I will ever be."

And, with that, I stand up from the table and make another exit.

I don't think I will ever be understood by American girls.

Listening to the Wrong Voice

"You will definitely be an All-American this time, Janey." Coach laughs as he puts his hand on my shoulder. "There is no doubt about it in my mind." Even his mustache cannot hide his smile. He is so sure of this.

"You really think so?"

"Yep. All you need to do is run like you ran at the last invite, and you will definitely be top six. Let someone else set the pace, and just sit on her shoulder."

"I am definitely not taking the lead this time," I declare emphatically. That is what I did last year, two weeks after having my wisdom teeth pulled. I led for the first two miles, but, when a whole group went around me, I just fell apart. Leading at any sort of national meet, even if it is just NAIA (National Association of Intercollegiate Athletics) indoor, definitely takes its toll.

"You can do this, Janey. Don't think; just run. You are healthy, and you are ready."

Don't THINK? Ha. Does he know who he is talking to right now?

"Okay." I take a deep breath, unsure of all that he has said, and head down the stairs to the holding area.

I want to be All-American SO BADLY.

I want to be listed with the other NAIA greats on our team—Beth, Carmella, Addy, Sherry, Sandra, and the rest.

I don't want to keep feeling like a total nobody because of my amazing ability to choke at meets that matter the most.

The first person I notice when I reach the bottom of the staircase is Petra Pechatnoff, the forty-year-old Russian woman who is twice my age. She has a brown braid and purple uniform, like me, but that is where the similarities end. I don't think I have ever seen this woman, with the witch-like nose and weapon-wielding elbows, ever smile. As she takes off sprinting across the turf, arms pumping with an angry determination, I can tell she is ready to devour the rest of the field.

Breathe, Janey, breathe.

The next person I see is a much friendlier face.

"Janey!"

"Natalie!"

Natalie Santoro, one of the sweetest Cedarland runners, makes her way over to me. Her curly brown ponytail bounces up and down.

"Hey! Are you ready for this?" she asks, grinning. I can tell she is excited to race.

"I think so. I am just really nervous." I swing my arms in large circles and kick out my legs.

"It will be just like the last invite, just without Sara Masterson," she reassures me.

"I hope so."

Sara came in first, I came in second, and Natalie came in third just two weeks ago. We all paced together, up until the last two laps, and it was so much fun.

"Well, I better do some strides!" She gives me another radiant smile and takes off running.

I stand staring at the rest of the girls, scoping out the competition for a few more seconds, and then decide to stride out to the bathroom down the hall.

I sure hope today is different. I sure hope I can break through the barrier of All-American.

But I have too good of a memory to forget the OTHER times I fell short. Let's see if I can recall a few . . . or ALL of these times.

1.) There was freshman indoor when I took second to last in the mile, running nearly thirty seconds slower than I had run all season. The throwing coach told me I just needed to work harder at practice. Excuse me???
2.) Then there was freshman outdoor, when I dropped out of the 5k because I started too fast, began to overheat in the ninety-degree inferno, and couldn't handle the pressure.
3.) Oh, and did I mention sophomore cross country, where I ended up with a kidney infection four days before nationals? Racing on antibiotics, I ran two minutes slower than I had all season and was the last runner on the team to cross the finish line.
4.) Not only that, but, in sophomore indoor, I hit my head on an iron fence the week of the meet, probably giving myself a concussion. It was snowy, and I slipped as we turned the corner. Go figure. I actually didn't run all that awful in the 3k, but I took eighth, which STILL wasn't All-American. If I had only run the time I had run the week before, I would have been fifth.
5.) Outdoor of sophomore year, I ran really well in the 10k and was even told I had finished fifth or sixth place, but, THEN, ten minutes later, I was told I was actually seventh. So close . . . but not close enough.
6.) Do I even want to talk about junior year? I had the cross country season of my life, winning regionals for the third time and leading

the team for practically a month. I ran in the 18:17-18:18 range for three races in a row. BUT THEN, what happened at nationals? I fell apart in the second half of the race and ended up running a 19:36. Coach even yelled out to me, "YOU ARE LETTING THE SAME THING HAPPEN THAT HAPPENED LAST YEAR!!!" Even he could see I was under a sort of curse.

7.) Oh, and then, in indoor of junior year, my wisdom teeth suddenly became infected just two weeks before nationals, and I had to have them surgically removed. And you know how you feel after wisdom teeth surgery? AWFUL!! And, once again, I ran over a minute slower than I had just a couple weeks before.

8.) Outdoor junior year was even worse. Coach didn't even want me to run in the meet because I had been feeling terrible for most of the season. Maybe it was because of the six or seven shots I was given for my trip to Africa, or maybe it was because of my hurt foot, but I felt awful. Even still, I had qualified for nationals, so I was going to run, and I finished second to last. At least I beat someone.

9.) Cross country nationals senior year was better than most of the other national meets. I was even in All-American position with a mile to go. But the fact I don't have a kick left me thirteen places away from achieving my goal when I reached the finish line.

And now, I am ranked third going into my second to last national meet of my career. I CANNOT botch this up.

This is my time.

This is my chance.

But what will Coach think of me if I fail AGAIN?

He will wish he never had me on his team.

He will wish I had gone to Mount Grace, Wheatfield, or ANY other college than Lazarus.

After heading back and forth between the turf and the bathroom more times than I can count (I am incredibly nervous), I feel my energy starting to drain.

And, after I have nearly descended into madness, it is time to make my way out to the track.

Who even created this sport where you run around and around in circles like a gerbil in a cage?

"You suck."

That is when I hear it, the nearly audible voice in my head.

"No, I do not," I mutter.

"You'll never be All-American."

"Shut up, Satan," I whisper under my breath.

I shake off these thoughts as an official leads us onto the track.

"Good luck, Janey," Natalie says cheerfully.

"Thanks. Good luck to you too."

As I toe the line, I remember the plan: I WILL NOT TAKE THE LEAD.

"BAAAAANNNNNNGGG!!!!!"

When the gun sounds, I charge out tentatively, tucking myself in behind the front runner.

I can tell the pace is far too leisurely before we even run halfway around the track.

I WILL NOT TAKE THE LEAD.

I do not want a repeat of last year, so I am following the plan.

I stay in second position as we pass the 400 mark.

"1:36!!"

Oh, no way. That is NOT good. That is WAY too slow.

I WILL NOT TAKE THE . . .

I take the lead. I can't stop myself. If we run this slowly, it is bound to turn into a kickers' race. And that isn't good either . . . not for me.

I drop the pace and pull the group through the 800-meter mark in 3:00.

As the race continues, no one else is willing to take the lead. NO ONE.

I don't like this, not at all. I mean, I love leading in smaller races, but not here, not at nationals.

As we pass through the 1600-meter mark, we are at 5:50, but I feel as if I have run a 5:30. I don't feel like I have any bounce in my step.

"You suck," I hear the disgusting voice whisper again in my head.

I grimace and continue to press forward.

Could someone else PLEASE set the pace?

This was NOT my plan.

I want to be anywhere but here.

When we pass through the 3200, we are at 11:50, and I am still leading. WHY am I still leading??

It only takes a couple of seconds for the group behind me to realize that the pace is far too slow. Once they do, they all decide it's time to stop using me as their pacer. In a matter of moments, six girls have passed me.

I go from first to seventh in less than five seconds.

I have to be sixth to be All-American.

"You'll never be All-American," the putrid voice growls.

I try to speed up, but it is of no use.

GOD, GET ME OUT OF HERE!!!

I just want to escape this present reality.

I panic even more as two more girls move around me.

I try to quicken my stride, but it is only making me slow down.

My mental stress is actually affecting me physically now.

"Stay with them, Janey!!!!" I hear Coach McDevitt yell. He sounds aggravated.

But I can't. I'm trying, but I can't.

"You suck, Janey Eller. You'll never be good enough for him."

I want to cry. My arms and legs don't even seem to know how to work together anymore.

In a quarter mile, I have slowed from six-minute pace to nearly seven-minute pace.

The next quarter mile is even worse.

By now, I don't know if anyone is behind me.

"All you ever do is fail."

I NEED TO GET OUT OF HERE!!!! I am making a total fool of myself!

My breathing quickens, and I'm on the verge of hyperventilating when I pass Coach once more.

"Just get off the track, Janey," he mutters with disgust.

I don't want to quit, but I have to. My mind is going to completely debilitate me if I continue.

So, with that, I pull into the infield, gulping in oxygen as I rest my hands on my knees.

"There is no way you can be All-American now."

I try not to cry, but the tears come out between gasping breaths for air.

"You're a failure."

My heart is broken. I had an amazing chance to do well, and it is now gone. I ate the right food, ran the right workouts, and even went to bed at the right time, but, because I listened to the voice of the enemy, I fell to pieces. What ever happened to those lyrics of the "Beat the Drum" song that had been engrained in my head over the summer? Why am I not listening to the "stronger" voice? Coach will never understand this. He has always been a fighter . . . not a quitter like me.

I lift my head to watch as the leader, who is none other than Petra Pechatnoff, crosses the line.

The finishing time is 17:44.

That is the exact time I ran two weeks ago.

I lower my head in shame.

I am a failure.

"So, Janey, I have an ultimatum for you." Coach saunters over to me, a smirk on his mustached face.

Well, at least he is smiling at me. I thought he would disown me for good after my national-meet performance.

"And what is that?" I am almost afraid to ask.

"You're going to run the marathon at outdoor nationals this year... or else you're off the team."

"Wait, what?" I nearly jump. Did he say something about kicking me off the team?

"I want you to train for the marathon."

My heart starts to quicken, not with fear but with a sort of excited anticipation.

The marathon? The NAIA marathon? The race I've always secretly wanted to run?

I watched Samara nearly die after running the marathon in 3:09:41 last year. (Like seriously, she turned blue after she crossed the finish line and had to be carted off in a stretcher. And THEN, while in the stretcher, she started speaking in tongues . . . or at least a garbled language I had never heard before.) That could be me. I could be the one flopping to the ground like a cold and clammy fish.

But it could also be my chance to run a NEW event, to NOT be that gerbil in the cage.

And THAT is what is making a sort of eagerness well up within me.

I am in a trance with the new possibility when Coach interrupts my thoughts.

"I don't mean this in a bad way or as a criticism, but you think too much."

I lower my head and stare at my Asics.

"Yeahhhhh. I know."

"And that is why you choke at national meets. You just think WAY too much."

"That's me. I'm a thinker." I can admit it. It's true.

"Well, you need to STOP THINKING." He shakes my shoulders with a laugh. "And that is why I'm giving you this opportunity to run a new event."

"I love running new events!" I gleefully exclaim. "I usually run my best the first or second time I try something. After that, I . . . uh . . . yeah, I start thinking too much."

"Well, see? That is why I want you to run it. I've talked to quite a few people, and they all think it's a good idea too."

"I think it's a good idea," Carter chimes in, as he joins our circle. "Janey, you OWN the longer distances. Remember that time you ran with me at camp for part of our long run? Or that time you ran with Graber on his Sunday ten-miler?"

"Yeah, remember that?" Graber jumps into our conversation as well.
How could I forget?

"Yeah."

"You gave me and Jacob a run for our money." Graber grins and shakes his head in a sort of amazement.

"Yeah, Janey, you LOVE to run and can just go forever. The marathon is going to be YOUR event. I just know it." Carter seems as eager as I am.

"You are going to do amazing in it too!" I encourage him. Carter, Kaden, and Richie are already signed up to run the half-marathon qualifier in April.

"So, I guess it is settled. Janey is running the marathon." Coach chuckles one last time and gives me one more pat on the shoulder. "That means you will be running in the half marathon in April as well."

"This is so exciting!" Anabelle Manes squeaks from beside me.

Yes, yes it is.

Just two days ago, I felt like the failure of the universe, but not today.

Today, I have had a challenge placed before me. And when I am given a challenge that is new and different, I am always ready to do whatever it takes to meet that challenge.

BRING ON THE MARATHON!!

Suddenly I See

The smell of rain fills the air as we step out beneath the star-speckled sky.

Today is the day of reckoning.

Today is the day of the marathon.

My stomach is churning as we head into the rental van.

And it isn't just because I am nervous.

It's because I ate WAY too much food last night, including five pieces of thick-crust pizza, bread, salad, and ice cream. I couldn't sleep all night because of my roiling stomach.

I definitely overdid it in the carbo-loading arena.

But it's too late to change that now.

I stare out the window, watching the flower-filled trees and bushes of California pass me by.

KT Tunstall's song, "Suddenly I See," lightly streams from the speakers.

"Her face is a map of the world, is a map of the world. You can see she's a beautiful girl, she's a beautiful girl . . ."

I am not sure what the song is about, but it brightens my mood with its light and cheery sound.

"Suddenly I see, this is what I wanna be. Suddenly I see . . ."

When we reach the track, the stars still stud the sky, but a faint glow of an impending sunrise lines the horizon.

The race will begin in under an hour.

In under an hour, I will be charging into the most challenging three-plus hours of my life thus far.

Just the thought of the race, added to my churning stomach, sends me running for the mobile restrooms. (They are like little trailers and can be found all around the sports complex.)

I run in and out, in and out. How am I ever going to be able to run a marathon feeling like this?

Oh, WHY did I eat so much?

As I jog around between bathroom breaks, I run past Coach. I give him a look of fear.

"How are you feeling?"

"Not so good," I respond.

"You are already psyched out," he replies, shaking his head with a look of frustration.

On normal days, such a reaction would make me cry, but not today. Today, it only fires me up. This race is NOT about pleasing him or anyone else.

This race is about running to please Jesus.

Just you wait, Coach.

As the race approaches, so many thoughts run through my mind. Is my braid tight enough, or will it unravel mid-race? Are my shoes too loose or too snug? Should I really race in a sports bra? What if I start too fast? What if I mentally lose it? What if I am too tired from not sleeping AT ALL last night? What if I ate all the wrong foods? What if the California heat destroys me? (I mean, it IS supposed to be a high of 101 degrees later in the day.) What if my armpits chafe so badly that I can barely move my arms back and forth? What if I can't finish? What if I DON'T get All-American? And most importantly . . . WHAT IF I have to go to the bathroom during the race???

"Therefore, since we are surrounded by such a great cloud of witnesses, let us throw off everything that hinders and the sin that so easily entangles. Let us run with perseverance the race marked out for us. Let us fix our eyes on Jesus . . ."

Amidst my freak-out session, the words of Hebrews 12:1-2 bring encouragement.

I need to "throw off everything that hinders."

I need to STOP worrying.

I need to fix my eyes on Jesus and run for His glory alone.

When it is time to head to the starting line, I throw off the last bit of clothing that may hinder (my shirt) and take a deep breath.

I feel naked.

All that covers my top half is Anita's silky blue and green racing bra.

I rub some Vaseline into my armpits, toss the pebbles out of my shoes, and finally decide I am ready . . . or as ready as I will ever be.

When I reach the group of ninety-one runners lined up on the track, I scope out the field. I am one of the only girls NOT wearing a jersey.

Well, this is awkward.

Beth and Carmella told me ALL THE GIRLS would be racing in sports bras.

I wrap my arms around myself self-consciously and kick out my legs.

I suddenly just want the gun to sound to remove me from this uncomfortable situation.

"BANNNNNGGGG!!!!"

And then it does.

As the sun starts to peak its little head over the horizon, I begin the epic journey, which starts with two laps of the track. Trying to run as steady as I can, I follow after the crowd of boys darting out ahead of me. A few girls, as well as a couple slower guys, form a small pack around me, and we find a perfect rhythm.

Samara's words echo in my mind.

"I have seen you run, and I have seen you race. Today, just RUN."

This is just a long run, and, boy, do I love long runs.

As we exit the track, I feel loose and free. So far, so good.

I run alongside Annie Strum as we head out to the loop we will circle four times. Two other girls, Wendy and Fern, run a step behind. It feels good to be in the lead.

Our little running group chats and laughs to pass the time, but, when silence ensues, music fills my mind.

"I feel like walking the world, like walking the world. You can hear she's a beautiful girl, she's a beautiful girl . . ."

"Suddenly I See" pops into my head as we fly past a row of palm trees.

As the miles pass, I notice that my ankle is starting to ache. I think I tied my one shoe a little too tight.

I back off the pace just a hair, letting Annie, Wendy, and Fern pull ahead.

I want to be able to finish this race, and slowing down a bit now will only help me out later down the road.

Samara's words come to mind again.

"Just WAIT. The race doesn't start until the last six miles."

Last year, Samara had made the mistake of dropping the pace in the middle of the race, and she had to practically walk the last four or so miles because of it.

I have to run smart.

As the heat begins to rise, I make sure to stay hydrated. I gulp down water and Gatorade every time I have the chance. I also learn to treasure the shade which the sun is slowly stealing away.

My fan clubs make an appearance every few miles and encourage me forward.

"You are doing AMAZING, Janey!!"

"Go, Janey, go!"

At the halfway point, a man yells out my time.

"1:27:46!"

That's right around 6:42 pace. I'm doing great!

As the miles continue to pass, the heat continues to rise. I let Isaiah 40:31 become my anthem.

"But those who hope in the Lord will renew their strength. They will soar on wings like eagles; they will run and not grow weary, they will walk and not be faint."

On the third loop, I start to feel a little queasy. The power gel I just inhaled is leaving my stomach in tumult. The little fuel pouches are great for giving added energy, but that is about it.

"The next runner is about sixty meters back," Coach tells me calmly. He isn't trying to worry me; he is just letting me know.

I nod his way and continue to press forward, maintaining both my form and my pace.

I am starting to feel EXTREMELY nauseous though, just like I did before the race began.

I longingly gaze at a porta-potty as I race on by. With the next runner so close behind, there is NO WAY I can stop. And even if she wasn't so close to me, I would never stop anyways. My legs would probably give out if I actually came to a halt. I HAVE to keep going. I am getting All-American this time, and not even a riotous stomach is going to stop me!

"Good job, number twelve!" a random spectator cries.

It is amazing how much cheering can help.

As I continue my jaunt through the beautiful neighborhoods, I come upon a shirtless boy puking on the side of the road. It is Kaden. He looks awful. His girlfriend, Katy, is at his side.

"Good job, Janey! You are rocking this marathon, girl!" Katy cheers.

"Keep it up, Janey," Kaden manages to groan, as he lifts his head to look my way.

"Are you okay?" I call over to Kaden.

"I'm fine, but I think I'm done," he replies glumly. He wanted so badly to run well in this race. "But you can do this, Janey. You are having the race of your life."

Once I pass the two lovebirds, I realize my intestines are now in a full-out war.

This is awful.

I can't stop.

So I let what must happen, happen.

This is just one ugly side effect of long-distance running, and I'm willing to deal with it.

I am just glad the gap with the runner behind me has increased.

As I pass the twenty-mile mark, I remember Samara's words once more.

"The race doesn't start until the last six miles."

I am beyond hot, wet, and sweaty, but I now know I am going to make it. I push just a tad more as I pass beneath the sporadic shade of the stately palm trees.

I am going to be All-American. I just know it.

"Suddenly I see, this is what I wanna be. Suddenly I see, why the [heck] it means so much to me."

With about three miles to go, I pass Mr. Connors. He has a ridiculously huge smile on his face. "You are almost there, Janey!! You have All-American in the bag!!"

I'm surprised he is not waiting at the finish to watch Carter cross the line.

Soon, I am heading out of the loop and back towards the track. There is a whole lot less shade on this stretch, and I am really starting to feel the heat.

About fifty meters ahead, I see a few sprinklers set up on the edge of a yard. Once I reach them, I run as close as I can to the cooling blasts.

Now, THAT feels nice.

Even though my skin has been hydrated, the race is really starting to drag.

Three miles may sound like a short way, but they feel more like ten at the end of a marathon.

"You've got about two and a half miles left!"

"You've got about two and a quarter miles left!"

"You've got about two miles left!"

Ugh, is this never-ending or what?

"But those who hope in the Lord will renew their strength. They will soar on wings like eagles; they will run and not grow weary, they will walk and not be faint."

I make a right, then a left, a right, then a left, then another left, then a right, then a left, then a right, then another right . . .

And that's when I see the track!!!

I dig as deep as I can and pick up my speed even more.

In the distance, I can see *"2:59"* blazing orange on the scoreboard.

Holy moly!

As I enter the track for the last time of my college career, I can feel Coach's joyful gaze. He is beaming.

"Just smile as you run your last lap because you are going to be an All-American!"

No one needs to tell me to smile. I am beyond happy.

"I feel like walking the world, like walking the world, and you can hear she's a beautiful girl, she's a beautiful girl . . ."

The race finishes with a lap and a quarter, and I stay strong the entire way. I am in fourth place, and no one can pass me now.

As I cross the finish, my legs give way.

"*3:01:44,*" the clock reads.

I collapse to the ground and sprawl out under the fiery sun.

"Come on. Let's get you into the shade," a random race official says, as she helps me to my feet.

I wobble my way to the tent and lie back down within the cooler confines.

I never knew my body could ache this badly.

I honestly feel like I've been run over by a truck.

A group of my teammates crowds around the tent to congratulate me. Like Coach, they too are beaming.

"Janey, that was incredible!"

"Janey, you FINISHED!! You're an ALL-AMERICAN!!"

"I am SOOOOOO proud of you, girl!!!"

"WOW. That was the best I've EVER seen you run."

I just lie there, broken, yet bursting with joy.

"I never want to run again," I murmur.

All my teammates can do is laugh.

"Like that is ever going to happen," Carmella chuckles. "Nothing will stop Janey Eller from running."

As I lie there, basking in the pain and the elation, I can't help but think this is a dream.

Races like this rarely happen to chokers like me.

And then, I start to cry.

I am so overcome by emotion that I am practically bawling.

I never before understood tears of joy, but now I do.

Running is pain, but running is also beauty.

Oh, what a way to end my college career.

"I can't believe you have never had a boyfriend." Anastasia Burlington flips her blonde hair over her shoulder as she looks at Elsa Maki, who sits in the desk behind her.

Elsa shrugs and looks down at her map of Washington. She is a sweet, quiet, frizzy-haired girl who could care less about having a guy in her life. Many people think she is my younger sister.

"Don't you want one?" Anastasia continues, her blue eyes wide with interest. She is probably the most boy-crazy girl in my class.

"Anastasia, leave her alone." I come to Elsa's rescue. "No one in here needs to have a boyfriend."

"Miss Eller, most of us are THIRTEEN YEARS OLD. We've had boyfriends since we were in like fifth grade." She seems insulted that I would even think they are too young to be dating.

I can't help but laugh.

"I'm twenty-three, and I've never had a boyfriend."

Anastasia's jaw drops immediately.

"I think Elsa will be fine."

Elsa smiles at me with a look of thanks. The two of us are on the same wavelength.

"Why don't you get one?" Jaclyn Monte questions from the back of the room, suddenly extremely interested in this conversation.

"Why don't I get what?"

"A boyfriend!"

"It isn't like you can buy them at Wal-Mart or something, Jaclyn." I chuckle at my own humor.

"We could give you a makeover, Miss Eller." Jaclyn seems completely serious. "Then the guys would totally notice you."

"Okaaaaaayyyyyy . . . now let's back to our bike trip planning."

I shake my head and begin to walk the room, making sure my students are working for the remaining ten minutes.

I mean, I expect this kind of thing from people my age but NOT from kids ten or more years younger than me. Doesn't this ever end?

As I pass Sally Snyder's desk, she looks up at me.

"Miss Eller, I really like how you brought your sisters to school with you on Monday. That was so fun."

Kayley, now twenty, and Tasha, now sixteen, both came to school with me to put on a bike trip skit for my six classes the other day. I am having my students map out a trip of their own in a state of their choosing, and I thought they would like to have a glimpse into what really happens on such a bike trip before beginning.

"Yeah? Did you like our skit?"

"Yes! It was REALLY funny, especially the part where Kayley flexed. All the boys were so impressed."

I laugh.

"Yeah, my sister is pretty buff."

"Kayley is BEAUTIFUL," Sally grins.

"Aww, thanks, Sally." She is always so complementary.

"And Tasha looks like you."

"Uh, thank you?"

What does THAT mean?

Is she trying to say that Tasha and I are ugly? I mean, I know we don't have straight, perfect hair like Kayley, but we aren't bad looking.

Sally is back to focusing on her map of Arizona, "compliments" already forgotten, but I am now consumed with the ramblings of her twelve-year-old mind.

Why doesn't anyone ever find me beautiful?

Sure, I make it seem like I'm a totally contented 23-year-old, but, really, I'm not.

I want to be the girl someone chooses someday.

I want to be the girl that some guy calls beautiful.

"PAJET."

The letters are scrawled across my yearbook in three different places.

"PAJET?"

What on earth do those letters mean?

I think about it for a while.

It is the third to last day of school, and we are all passing our yearbooks around the room for others to sign. I have purchased one of my own as well because I want to remember all the students I taught this year, even if some nearly drove me up the wall.

"Hey, Sally, come here." I beckon the girl that thinks my sister is most beautiful to my side.

"Do you know what this means?" I point to the five capital letters scrawled across the page.

"Um, I don't know."

"You don't?"

"Um, no." She looks unsure of herself as she says the words.

"Hmmm. Well, I have no idea what it means. I wasn't sure if it was like HAGS (Have A Good Summer) or something like that."

"Yeah, I don't know."

For the rest of the day, I can't get my mind off the five letters.

I come up with as many acronyms as I can.

The best I can come up with is this: *Please Accept Joyfully Every Teenager.*

I ask one student in each class if they have ever before seen this phrase.

It isn't until I question Evan Zimmerman in my ninth-hour class that I have any idea as to what it might mean.

"Ohhhhhh, PAJET. Doesn't that mean like 'People Against Janey Eller Teaching' or something?"

"WHAT??"

"People Against Janey Eller Teaching."

"Did you just make that up?"

"Yep!"

I furrow my brow and think about what he has just said. There is no way someone could come up with an acronym that fast without already having thought about it.

When the final bell rings, I sit in my desk, contemplating what Evan said.

People Against Janey Eller Teaching?

Why would someone write THAT in my yearbook?

"Hey, Miss Eller." Sally quietly makes her way to my desk and has a seat at the computer chair. "So, I actually do know what those letters mean."

"People Against Janey Eller Teaching?"

"Yeah."

"Why didn't you tell me that before, Sally?"

"I didn't want to hurt your feelings."

"Okay, I guess that makes sense." I pause. "Why would three different people write that in my yearbook though?"

"Some kids . . . well . . . they made this Facebook group against you . . . and that is the name of it."

"Seriously??"

"Yeah. It is really stupid because we all think you are a GREAT teacher."

Anita Keppler enters the room as she says this and bounds over to where we are talking.

"Are you talking about PAJET?" she asks, eyes wide with a sort of anger.

"Yeah," Sally responds.

"Ugh. Miss Eller, those kids are just so stupid. You shouldn't even listen to them. You are the best teacher I've EVER had."

"Thanks, Anita." I am thankful for her and for Sally and for the other girls in my corner, but I am feeling a bit sick to my stomach at the knowledge that there is a Facebook group against me.

"Do you guys know who made the group?" I ask tentatively.

"Yeah. It was Wyatt Rollins."

"WYATT??!! WHAT??!!"

"Yeah." Sally looks down at her shoes.

"He is just STUPID," Anita rages adamantly.

"But he is always stopping by to say 'hi!' I thought he liked me."

My heart sinks just a bit. You think you know a person, and, then, THIS happens.

"I don't know, Miss Eller. He probably made the group to be cool."

How is it cool to hurt a person to her core?

"Who else is in the group?" I whisper, wanting to know more but not at the same time.

"I don't know. I don't spend time looking at it because a bunch of losers made it." Anita looks like she wants to fight somebody. "You should talk to Mr. Hart about it, and maybe he can punish them."

"Yeah, maybe." I mull over the idea in my head. "Well, I'm glad you guys told me this."

"Any time, Miss Eller. If you need to know anything else, just ask us."

"Okay, I will."

*****

That night, I immediately head to our computer to try my hand with the Juno dial-up. After about thirty minutes (not even an exaggeration), I am finally logged into Facebook.

"*PAJET, People Against Janey Eller Teaching.*"

I type this into the search bar and wait.

And wait.

And wait.

I swear we are the only family in America that still has dial-up.

When the page finally appears, I see that, like my girls said, Wyatt Rollins is the administrator.

But, other than that, pretty much everything has been deleted from the page.

I do see that Evan Zimmerman is still a part of the group though, along with a couple others who have not been smart enough to abandon ship.

And here I thought Evan liked me as a teacher!

I KNEW he came up with that acronym all too quickly.

After staring at the page for a couple minutes, I send a message to a couple of my friends, copying and pasting the link to the page. I want them to be as mad as I am at this moment.

I mean, I do SOOO much for these kids. I let them come in every day at lunch. I stay late every day after school just to talk to them or help them with their homework. I make them all birthday cards. I write them notes when they are sad. I put their names into all the worksheets. I pray for them. And THIS is what I receive in return?

WHAT IS THE POINT??!!

What is the point of even caring anymore?

*****

The next day, we have a mini assembly during ninth hour where kids can pay to dunk the principal, Mr. Peyton. It is supposed to be a time of laughter and fun. It is supposed to be a time to enjoy the lovely sunshine on this second to last day of school.

But it doesn't end up being any of those things.

Yes, I am surrounded by the girls who adore me—Elsa, Sally, Anita, Alison, and Monique—BUT I am also haunted by the random shouts coming from a group of the "cool kids"—the kids that will never really understand me, no matter how old I am.

"PAJET!" I hear one squirrely boy shout.

He is at the center of this group of guys and girls who are all giggling and whispering. And, all the while, they are looking over at me, the teacher—the one who isn't supposed to be ridiculed anymore.

"PAJET!"

"Just ignore them, Miss Eller," Elsa reassures me. "You know we all love you."

"I know." I give her a weak smile but can't resist giving one last look at the flock of gaggling gawkers.

I guess you can't win them all.

"*Little girl fourteen, flipping through a magazine, says she wants to look that way. But her hair isn't straight, her body isn't fake, and she's always felt overweight. Little girl fourteen, I wish that you could see that beauty is within your heart. You were made with such care, your skin, your body, and your hair are perfect just the way they are.*"

"I love this song!" Ryan Darling, my newest crush, grins over at me from the steering wheel of my car as he turns up the volume. His strawberry-blonde curls lightly dance in the wind.

I am somewhat confused as to why he would be so fond of "More Beautiful You," by Johnny Diaz, mostly because it is more of a song geared towards girls, but I don't question him. I am far too happy to be overly inquisitive.

"I know it's about girls, but I really like its message." He studies my face, seeming to have read my confusion. "God made girls beautiful, and they should realize that." He seems to be reading my soul.

When the song reaches the chorus, Ryan belts out the lyrics, looking over at me every so often. His green eyes, as usual, are mysterious and sparkling.

"*There could never be a more beautiful you. Don't buy the lies, disguises, and hoops they make you jump through. You were made to fill a purpose that only you could do. So there could never be a more beautiful you.*"

As he sings, Ryan grabs the wheel and lightly swerves it back and forth. I know he is trying to put a rise into me, but I just giggle. With any other guy, I would freak out, but not with him.

"*Little girl twenty-one, the things that you've already done, anything to get ahead. And you say you've got a man, but he's got another plan, only wants what you'll do instead.*"

I love the fact he is driving MY car. He looks so comfortable in my usual spot.

"*Little girl twenty-one, you never thought this would come. You starve yourself to play the part. But I can promise you there's a man whose love is true, and he'll treat you like the jewel you are.*"

Is Ryan that man? As he drives, I start to daydream. Things with Riley didn't work, and things with Ryan Graber didn't work. Maybe it was all so that I wouldn't miss out on this amazing guy sitting right beside me. Maybe, just maybe, this will be the guy that chooses to pursue me.

We pull into the 7-Eleven parking lot where Tasha (my sister) and Oscar Domingo (our fun-loving Filipino friend) are waiting for us.

"Let's go get some slushies, guys!" Oscar says cheerfully, as Ryan and I step out of my car.

The four of us played tennis for a couple hours at the park and have now crossed town to grab some cool, icy refreshments. Tasha rode with Oscar, and Ryan rode with me. I couldn't have planned it better.

We sip our sugary glasses of goodness as we sit in the grass in front of the 7-Eleven. Oscar provides the entertainment with silly conversation.

And then, I come to a realization.

"Oh no! Where's my key?" I startle everyone as I scramble around in my drawstring bag. "I can't find it anywhere!"

"Do you have it on a key ring?" Ryan asks.

"Well, I did, but I took it off and put it in the key pocket of my running shorts when we were playing tennis."

"Well, I drove us here with it, so it has to be here somewhere." Ryan rummages through the nearby grass.

"You don't still have it, do you?" I am hoping he never gave it back to me.

"Nope. I gave it back to you."

"Oh no." Ryan's going to think I am senile.

"Janey and her keys." Tasha lowers her head with a shake. She is used to this. I lose my keys like an old person loses his or her teeth . . . or his or her marbles.

I take my socks off and search my shoes. Maybe I have hidden it in a new location.

"What are you doing?" Oscar chuckles.

"I have to find my key!"

After looking in desperation for several minutes, I decide to just enjoy my time in the grass with my friends. I am slightly ill at ease, mostly because Ryan and I are supposed to go hiking after this. If I can't find my key, that isn't likely to happen, and my dreams of chilling alone with him again will be dashed. We have hung out quite a few times this summer. We have gone for hikes, played board games and various sports, and read the Bible together. Just a few weeks ago, Tasha, Ryan, Oscar, and I hung out for twelve hours straight. It was quite the day.

We sit and talk some more, and Oscar keeps hinting at the fact that Ryan and I can leave soon.

"Soooo, maybe we should let the two of you go for your walk now." He is not the best at hinting covertly.

Neither of us says anything. We both kind of just look down at our feet awkwardly.

Tasha, my little sister, is here, and I say little because, like all little sisters, she will tease me about the fact Ryan and I are going to go hiking together. I don't want to talk about it with her here.

"I need to go to the bathroom," I say in the middle of the uncomfortable silence, making a beeline for the nearby Jimmy John's. I have needed to go for a while but was waiting for an opportune time like this.

Once inside, I find that the women's bathroom is occupied.

I stand and wait for a while. After deciding that the occupant is not coming out any time soon, I see if the men's room is available. It is! Oh, sweet relief!

I am about to do what needs to be done when I hear something fall into the toilet.

I go to look at what could have possibly fallen and find that it's MY KEY! What on earth???

And then, I remember.

I randomly tucked my key in the waistline of my shorts when I was sipping on my Slurpee. WHY, OH WHY didn't I stick it in the little pocket that is sewn into my running shorts? It is purposely made FOR KEYS!!

My mouth drops open in disgust as I weigh my options.

This would just HAVE to happen in the men's room, wouldn't it?

I decide the only thing to do is to reach in and pull my poor key out of its watery grave.

I scrunch up my nose and do it as quickly as possible, making sure to wash my key and my hands with soap and water. Then, and only then, can I actually have my sweet relief.

As I walk out of Jimmy John's, I wonder what I should tell my little posse. This could be quite the awkward conversation.

"So, guys, guess what I found?" I speak carefully, in a quiet voice.

"What?" They all ask as one.

"MY KEY!!!!" I hold up the newly cleaned gem.

"No way! Where was it?" Oscar inquires. "You looked everywhere, even in your socks."

"Uhhhhhh . . ." I am not sure what to say in response.

"You dropped it in the toilet, didn't you?" Ryan is eerily perceptive.

"Uhhhhhh . . . maybe."

"Ewww!" Tasha follows her proclamation of disgust with a roar of laughter.

I can't help but blush.

"And I was in the MEN'S bathroom too!"

They are all giggling now.

"Well, now that you have found your key, maybe we should let you two go for that walk." Oscar still hasn't figured out how to be subtle.

I look at Ryan out of the corner of my eye. He is looking over at me in the same manner.

"Do you want to?" he asks.

"Sure, if you still want to."

"I'm in."

"Okay. I feel bad leaving you guys though," I say, as I look over at Oscar and Tasha.

"Oh, it's NO PROBLEM," Oscar says with a wink. "I can give Tashwika a ride home. And maybe we can play some more tennis at the park."

"Sure!" Tasha says.

So, with that, I open the door to my car.

"Did you want to drive again, Ryan?"

"Oh, no." He waves his hand at me. "It is all yours."

We both take our positions, wave good-bye to our two onlookers, and head the couple miles down the road to Mavis Woods State Park.

It's the very same park I took Riley to in order to go running back in middle school. It already has its share of sweet memories, and I am hoping to make some more.

We ramble around the woods, hitting up various dirt paths and shortcuts, filling up the silence with conversation. Ryan is truly an amazing conversationalist, and I could talk with him for hours on end.

He tells me how his parents met while leading worship at a church camp.

I tell him how my parents met in math class and how my dad tried to win my mom's heart by placing a live mouse in her mailbox.

He tells me how he read his family's full set of Encyclopedia Britannica when he was younger and now has a rather extensive knowledge of the world because of it.

I tell him about how I felt neglected when I attended high school youth group back in the day.

We are in the middle of talking about Oscar's crush on Alexa, which is a whole new topic, when I suddenly run my hand along a wooden rail of a small bridge and end up with a splinter in my hand.

"Ouch," I wince, as I try to pinch it out with my barely-noticeable fingernails.

"Want me to help you, Janey?" Ryan moves in a little closer, as his green eyes sparkle a message of concern.

"Sure." I hold out my hand for him to mend it as a surge of adrenaline races through my body.

He takes my hand gently and lightly pinches my skin. He could be running my hand through with a sword and I wouldn't care.

When the little piece of wood is dislodged and I thank my knight in shining armor, we continue exploring. After about another mile, we come to a lake filled with lily pads.

"Let's have a seat." Ryan makes his way to one of the wooden benches, and I follow wholeheartedly after him.

Just before he sits down, he lies out flat on the wooden dock and reaches as far out into the water as he can. He plucks one of the bright yellow flowers that sits atop one of the lily pads and brings it back to me.

"For you," he whispers sweetly, as he takes a seat beside me.

As we look out on the glittery water, I feel as if I am in a dream.

The rest of our time at the state park is just as lovely.

I don't think I have ever enjoyed someone else's presence so much.

After our trip to Mavis Woods, we decide we are hungry and head back to the Jimmy John's with the unlucky toilet. We dine on some sandwiches and then head across the street to McDonald's for some fifty-two cent ice cream cones.

"So, I came up with a special secret handshake for us," he tells me, as we enjoy our cones.

"Yeah? I've never had a secret handshake before."

"Well, you will now. Just you wait. Put out your hand." He twitches his eyebrows mysteriously as he begins to direct me. "Up . . . down . . . pound and miss outside . . . pound and miss inside . . . STOP! . . . Outward . . . inward . . . pound with both . . . crisscross . . . punch in the head . . . HUG!"

He reaches across the table and wraps me in a warm embrace with the last directive.

"So, do you want to arm wrestle now?" He looks deeper into my eyes.

"Haha. You would KILL me. I lost in arm wrestling to one of my seventh graders two years ago."

"Well, I can play nice."

He pulls on my hand until my arm is at a ninety-degree angle.

"Ready?" He steadies his own arm. "Go!" I push on his hand as he holds it firmly in place. I know he could crush me in a matter of seconds, but he chooses not to. He just sits there, waiting, all the while staring at me with a huge grin on his face. After it seems like an eternity has passed, he lightens up on his grip and lets me push his hand to the table.

"I win!" I say lightheartedly. I could never actually win against a guy who excels at rock climbing.

Still looking into my eyes, he says, "So, I have been reading all your notes on Facebook, like the ones with the twenty-five and thirty-five random facts about yourself."

"Oh, brother." I let my head fall to the table. I wrote some pretty goofy facts on there. "You have?"

"Yep, and one of your facts was that you liked this guy for nearly half of your life."

I knew I should have deleted that post!

"Do I know him?" he asks, as he furrows his brow and waits for a response.

"Uh . . . probably not. But you don't live too far away from him."

"What's his name?"

"His name was Riley Gray."

"Did he die?"

"Noooooo." I give him a playful tap. "He just ended up being kind of a jerk to me."

"Really?"

"Yeah, like he said he was bribed to take me to homecoming and blackmailed to take me to prom . . . oh, and that I was boring."

"He said that to you?"

"Yeah."

"I can't believe ANYONE would treat you like that. You are DEFINITELY not boring, and you DEFINITELY don't deserve someone like him."

"Thanks, Ryan." It's nice to know all the guys in the world aren't going to be like Riley.

"I actually had this huge crush on Mazy Erickson for the longest time too—not for half my life but for all of freshman and sophomore year." He shares one of his secrets with me now.

"Yeah? I never knew that." I pause. "Did she like you too?"

"I don't know. I can never tell if a girl likes me."

Is he hinting at something?

"Oh."

Can he tell that I like him?

"So, Janey, do you think you ever want to get married?"

To you, I can't help but think.

"I don't know. If God wants me to, I guess I will."

"Well, you should definitely get married soon."

How am I supposed to react to that one? I just laugh somewhat awkwardly.

"Oh, hey! Let me post a new status." He pulls out his phone and opens up to Facebook. After typing a sentence or so, he holds it up for me to read.

"*Hanging with an awesome gal named Janey Lynn.*"

I smile bigger than I have all day. He thinks I am awesome. He thinks I am awesome enough to make his status just about me.

"Aww!"

"Well, we better get going!" Ryan stands up cheerfully. "You have youth group soon!"

With that, we leave McDonald's, and I drive him to his humble abode.

That night, after I get home, I send him a message thanking him for a great day. In a matter of minutes, he replies with the sweetest message of all. I read it at least a dozen times before heading to bed.

> "*To the far amazingly named Janey Lynn Eller,*
>
> *Why thank you My lady. You flatter me! The pleasure is all mine of course. Rarely does one find such an amazing lady like yourself! You are an awesome conversationalist, and I just LOVE picking your amazing brain! You're a beautiful girl and an awesome friend. I also can't wait to hangout again! (that rhymed!)*
>
> *Looking forward to next time, Ryan Lee Darling*
>
> *P.S. Don't forget that handshake! Remember, Up, Down, Pound and miss outside, Pound and miss inside, STOP! Outward, inward, pound with both, crisscross, Punch in the head, Hug! Practice at home.*"

Wow. What a message. He not only thinks I am an awesome friend, but he also thinks I am a beautiful girl. A BEAUTIFUL GIRL!! No guy has ever said that to me before. I am actually BEAUTIFUL.

My dreams can't be much better than the present reality.

The Moment of Truth

"I don't even know WHY you think Ryan likes you," Tasha huffs, as she stands up from the couch. "It's just stupid."

I am actually editing Tasha's journal entries for her when she startles me from my thoughts with a very bold and very harsh statement.

"Excuse me??? What are you even talking about?" Her words cut deep.

"I'm talking about you and Ryan . . . and how it is just stupid. He doesn't even like you."

"How do YOU know?"

"Loraine, his own sister, said he doesn't have feelings for you."

"How does she know?" I furrow my brow in annoyance.

"Well, she asked him when their family was on vacation in New Mexico. The two of them went on a hike in the mountains, and he told her he only sees you as a friend."

"Okaaaay. Well, I don't believe she was telling you the whole story. I have SEEN the way he acts around me, Tasha. I think I would know."

"Whatever. All I know is that I think it's weird you would even like him. He's like three years younger than you." She pauses. "It's just stupid."

I feel a bit sick to my stomach. Although what Tasha is saying is unnecessary and somewhat mean, could the part about Ryan be true?

Her words sit heavily in my mind all day, like a sumo wrestler squishing my brain.

I finally decide it is time to bring it up with Ryan. I NEED to know before NOT KNOWING kills me.

I mean, I am almost positive Loraine is wrong. I am nearly 100 percent certain he DOES like me. Why else would he send me a message from "The Land of Enchantment" saying he misses me and is thinking about me? Why else would he say that I was a "beautiful girl?" Why else does he flirt with me and make constant comments about marriage, relationships, and the like? Why else does he so willingly choose to spend time with me? And why does he always look into my eyes in such a loving way? To quote David Archuleta's hit single, *"I can see it in [his] eyes . . . [his] eyes don't lie."*

Finally, I decide to just bring it up over Facebook chat. That is always the place to have deep conversations. (Notice the sarcasm.)

Janey Eller: "Hey, Ryan!!! How are you doing tonight?"
Ryan Darling: "Fine and dandy, my lady!"

Who calls a friend "my lady?"

Janey Eller: "☺"
Ryan Darling: "☺ ☺"
Janey Eller: "How was New Mexico?? Did you have a bunch of fun with your family?"
Ryan Darling: "Heck yes! We climbed some amazing mountains."
Janey Eller: "Awesome!"
Ryan Darling: "Sooooooo, what is the WACKIEST thing that could happen right now???"

I just love Ryan. He can be so goofy sometimes.

Janey Eller: "Hmmmm. The cookies in my kitchen could come to life, roll on over to your house, and take you hostage."
Ryan Darling: "Nice."
Janey Eller: "☺"
Ryan Darling: "So, what have you been up to today, Janey?"
Janey Eller: "I ran, took some naps, and edited some of my sister's papers. She wasn't very nice to me though."
Ryan Darling: "I'm sorry, Janey. No one should be mean to you! What was she doing?"
Janey Eller: "Just saying stuff."
Ryan Darling: "Like what kind of stuff?"
Janey Eller: "Stuff that Loraine told her."
Ryan Darling: "What did Loraine tell her?"
Janey Eller: "Something about you . . . and me."
Ryan Darling: "Ohhhh."

This is when I decide to just say it.

Janey Eller: "Sometimes, I just wish I knew how you felt about me."

And there it is.

Ryan Darling: "I see."
Janey Eller: "Yeah."
Ryan Darling: "Well, I definitely would like to talk about this more, but I don't think we should do so on here. We should talk in person."

Yikes.

Janey Eller: "I agree."
Ryan Darling: "Are you free tomorrow night?"
Janey Eller: "Yep!"
Ryan Darling: "Okay! Well, how about I just call you around 6:00?"
Janey Eller: "Sounds good!"
Ryan Darling: "Sweet. Well, I will see you tomorrow, Janey! We can talk then! Have a good night . . . and try to get some sleep."

Sleep? Yeah, right. I haven't been able to sleep since the first night I fell for this guy.

Janey Eller: "I will! You have an amazing night yourself, Ryan! Bye!"
Ryan Darling: "Adios!"

Before closing out the chat box, I read back through the messages, seeing if there is anything that can lead me to believe he actually likes me. I can't really be sure either way. Maybe he doesn't want to talk on here because he knows it will hurt me when he tells me he DOESN'T like me. OR maybe he doesn't want to talk on here because he wants it to be special when he tells me in person that he DOES like me.
Either way, tomorrow night can't come soon enough.
There is no way I'm sleeping tonight.

*****

"I never meant to start a war. You know I never wanna hurt you. Don't even know what we're fighting for. Why does love always feel like a battlefield, a battlefield, a battlefield? Why does love always feel like a battlefield, a battlefield, a battlefield?"
I thrust my left arm out, my left leg out, my right arm out, and my right leg out. I am attempting to recreate last night's *So You Think You Can Dance* routine to Jordin Sparks' song, "Battlefield," and I'm pretty sure I'm miserably failing. Even so, I am having a blast. I am doing whatever I can to keep my mind off my impending "talk," which is going to happen in the next hour or so. I may end up wounded because of this very battlefield I am singing and dancing about, but I keep right on pounding.

"You are so weird," Tasha yawns, as she wakes up from her nap on the couch. I'm pretty sure my stomping awoke her.

I try to make my moves more technically sound for her approval, and she just rolls her eyes.

"Oh, Janey."

"*I guess you better go and get your armor, get your armor, get your armor. I guess you better go and get your armor, get your armor, get your armor.*"

I am in the middle of singing and making goofy faces at Tasha when my phone sings.

"*Doo doot do do do doo doot do do do doo doot . . .*"

I sprint to my drawstring bag and rummage through it for my phone. When I find it, I rapidly open it and head out to the front porch. I don't really like to talk to Ryan in front of Tasha, or anyone for that matter.

"Hello?"

"Heeeeeey! Janey!"

"Hey!"

"So, do you still want to hang out? I can't really go anywhere because my mom took my car, but you can come over here."

"Okay! What time should I come?"

"How about seven o'clock?"

"Works for me!"

"Okay, well, I will see you then! Bye, Janey!"

"Bye, Ryan!"

As soon as I shut my phone, I sprint into the kitchen, open the refrigerator, and take out the pan of lasagna. I haven't even had dinner yet, and I need to go to Ryan's house in five minutes! Using a metal spatula, I shovel out a lopsided piece onto a small, blue plate. After grabbing a spoon, I immediately start eating. I don't even care that it's still cold.

I eat my dinner, brush my teeth, and fix my ponytail in a total whirlwind.

Tonight is the night Ryan tells me the truth, and I don't want to wait any longer than I have to in order to hear that truth.

When I arrive at the Darling residence, Ryan answers the door and welcomes me inside.

I am super nervous, but he can't seem to tell.

"JANEY!!! Come on in!"

I head inside and follow him over to the couch.

"Here, sit down! I want to show you some of my pictures from my trip to New Mexico."

He runs through a whole series of shots, many of which are from beautiful national parks.

"Did I tell you that I almost DIED?" he says dramatically, while showing me a picture of him near a rocky, red precipice. He opens his eyes really wide in a humorous way.

"You mean when you rode your bike into a telephone pole or when your harness broke while you were rock climbing?" He has already told me about several near-death experiences he has had, so I am not sure which one he is referring to right now.

"No, this is a different one."

"Gee whiz, Ryan. You need to be careful. I don't want you to go dying on me." I nudge him with playful horror.

"Well, see this cliff right here?"

"Yeah."

"Well, the adventurous Loraine and I started to climb it. But then . . . when we were about fifty feet up . . . I slipped."

"YOU DID??!!" My eyes are bugging out of my head. I thought he was like an expert climber.

"Yeah, I started to fall backwards, surely to my death, but then Loraine grabbed my hand at the last second."

"You could have DIED!!"

"That's what I said before I told the story." He chuckles.

"I'm glad Loraine was there!"

"Me too. That sister of mine is a life saver."

All I can do is shake my head, still somewhat shocked.

He runs through some more pictures, and, then, the front door opens.

"Hey, Ryan!" It's Oscar, our tennis buddy.

"Oscar!!!" Ryan jumps up from his seat on the couch and greets him with a huge bear hug. "What is up, man? What have you been up to?"

"Well, I was just hanging with Alexa and thought I would stop by. I didn't know you had company though." He nods over at me.

I smile awkwardly back at him.

How are we going to have the chance to talk with Oscar here?

"Come look at my pictures, Oscar!"

The three of us sit on the couch together, watching a slideshow of shots and listening to more stories as mad chaos breaks out in the rest of Ryan's house.

"AHHH!! My bedroom is so scary!" Ariel, the littlest and most adorable Darling child, sprints down the wooden stairs and tries to run out the door. Her messy, strawberry-blonde pigtails swing to and fro in hypnotic fashion.

"Ariel, come back here!" Ryan's younger brother, Devin, laughs from the kitchen. He and Hayden, another brother, are busy whipping up a mixture of syrup and frosting and are leaving tracks of red, white, and brown all over the floor.

It takes everything within me not to laugh hysterically.

After observing the craziness for about a half hour, Mrs. Darling comes home and tries her best to rally the troops. Ariel is wrapped around her ankle, babbling about the monster in her closet.

"Devin, Hayden, time for bed!" She shoos the chefs from their creativity. "And you too, Ariel. You should have been in bed an hour ago." She picks up the disheveled child and looks over at us. "Ryan, can you guys go pick up Loraine from work?"

"Sure, Mama!"

I love how he calls his parents "Mama" and "Papa."

The three of us head out to his dark green Ford Taurus for a little trip to Topaz Lake.

"Janey, you can sit in the front," Oscar says with a little grin.

The ride is quite enjoyable, with lots of fun discussions, but I am kind of anxious.

When are we going to have our talk?

Once we arrive back at the Darling residence, Oscar takes off, and I am hopeful.

"Do you want to go with me to Waveland to let the dogs out, Janey? The man who owns them works weird hours, so it is kind of like my job now."

"Sure!" I answer happily.

With just the two of us together now, it will be perfect for a serious talk . . . as long as he is the one that brings it up.

We jump back into the Taurus, and he speeds over to where he cares for the dogs. (He is quite the crazy driver, but it doesn't bother me too much.)

I follow him into the cozy, blue house, and he introduces his three pups to me.

"This dog (he points to a sleepy-eyed ball of fur) is Old Faithful . . . and this dog (he points to a hyper pup with a speckled coat) is Pulse. She has a sort of heart on her forehead, see? And then, we have Bailey, the largest of the bunch."

I pet the three tail-waggers as Ryan pours food and water into six small bowls.

"Time to eat, you guys!"

The pups tear over to their food and eat with delight. Even Old Faithful seems to wake up as he munches and crunches on his meal.

Once Ryan is done giving the dogs their food and water, he leads us all outside.

As the dogs take care of business, I follow Ryan to a dilapidated, yellow shed with dusty windows. On the window closest to us, I can make out faintly written words.

"You need to add your name to the hall of fame. All of my friends who ever come with me sign it."

I lift my finger and write my name out in my best printing.

"Janey."

My name will forever be written on that window, next to *"Loraine," "Devin," "Oscar," "Will," "Jake,"* and *"Peter."*

I must be pretty special to be on his personal wall of fame, right?

Is this his prelude to telling me how he feels?

There are so many thoughts running through my head, but I feel like a dumb mute.

After taking care of the dogs, we return to Ryan's house. We head inside, but, when Ryan finds that Loraine is still awake, watching the Cubs game, we head back outside.

"Want to play some Pool?"

"Sure!"

Maybe we will talk while we play?

I follow him into a room off the garage that is decked in Cubs memorabilia. It holds a Pool table, an old piano, and a couple of couches.

I have a déjà vu moment.

Ryan and I hung out in here right before he left for New Mexico.

Maybe he just wanted to have this conversation in a meaningful spot.

We play a game of Pool, and he butters me up with each shot I take.

"That hit was CRAZY, girl!" he proclaims every so often.

I know he is merely trying to build me up because Pool is totally not my game.

He is on the verge of winning when he "accidentally" scratches by knocking in the eight ball. I say "accidentally" because this is the exact same thing he did last time we played. I think he just let me win for the second time.

"Did you do that on purpose?" I ask, scrunching up my mouth all cutesy like.

"Nooooooooo."

His face looks all suspicious as he heads over to the couch, the very same couch we sat on the last time we hung out up here.

He takes a seat and pats the cushion beside him, beckoning me over to his side.

"We can talk now," he says with a big smile.

FINALLY.

Once I sit down, Ryan looks over at me and asks, "So, Janey. What is on your mind?"

I blush and look down at my feet.

He knows what is on my mind.

"There is a lot on my mind." I squirm a little bit as I shyly look over at him. "What part do you want me to talk about?"

"I KNOW, Janey." He smirks over at me.

WHAT does he know?

"What do you want me to say?" My face is now a perpetual shade of red.

"You know what I want you to say."

"Do I?" I know what he wants me to say, but can I say it?

"Oh, you know, Janey." He nudges me playfully, pressing me for the secret information.

"You mean," I take a deep breath and continue, "that I like you?"

There, I said it.

I think I might faint.

In response, he looks into my eyes—his green, speckled eyes sparkling in their ever-mysterious way—and says the words that will stick with me all night.

"I'm totally crushing on you right now too."

My heart skips a beat, and I just sit staring back into his eyes.

I am stunned.

I am shocked.

This is not what I expected him to say.

I expected him to crush my heart, to break it into tiny pieces, just like Riley and the other Ryan had done, but he has done just the opposite.

"Tasha kept telling me that you didn't . . . because of things Loraine told her . . . but I just couldn't believe that it was true."

Studying my face, Ryan gives me a smile and pushes a strand of my hair behind my left ear.

"It is true that I told Loraine I like you just as a friend while in New Mexico, but, after saying it, I realized it just wasn't true." He keeps holding my gaze. "It was there in New Mexico that I started crushing on you pretty hard, right before I sent you that message that I missed you."

"Yeah?"

"Yeah. And now that Loraine knows about my change of heart, she has been teasing me quite a bit about you, Janey. She thinks we are pretty cute together." He gives me a quick wink as he scooches a little closer to me.

My heart starts to beat just a little faster.

"I thought it was really awesome you called me while I was on my trip, Janey."

"I hoped you didn't think it was weird."

"Aww, nah. Never. It was actually really cool." He pauses. "BUT . . . here's the thing. Even though I really like you, I don't think either of us is in a good position to date right now."

"Oh."

I don't really understand how I'm not in a good position to date. I mean, I AM twenty-four years old. But I am soaring so high from the fact this studly, amazing man of God actually likes me that I keep that fact to myself.

"Yeah, I think it is better if we just stay friends for now."

"Okay."

"Is that okay with you?"

"Yeah." I speak just a little quieter because, deep down inside, I honestly wish we could be more.

We sit in silence for a moment, gazing into each other's eyes. In the next moment, he yawns, stretches his one arm dramatically, and lets it fall softly on my shoulders. He pulls me in close to him so that we are side by side.

Didn't he just say he only wanted to be friends?

"You can rest your head on my shoulder," he whispers sweetly.

I lean my head to my left and rest it gently on his shoulder.

I can't believe I am even here in this moment.

Tasha was SO wrong!

"So, when did you first start liking me, Janey?"

"Um, kind of the first time you actually had a conversation with me."

"Are you serious?"

"Yeah. It was just so easy to talk to you."

"Aww. I kind of thought you might like me about a week after that, but I forgot about it until we started hanging out more. And then, I found out just how awesome you are. I mean, what other girl would go mountain biking with me?" I could just lose myself in his speckled eyes. "After Oscar told me you liked me, I was 95 percent sure, and, now, I'm 100 percent sure."

"Oscar told you?"

"Yeah. He also told me that I had better not lead you on, especially since you are such a nice girl." His tone becomes a little more serious. "I would never want to do that to you."

"That's good," I softly say in return.

"Didn't you say someone did that to you before?"

"Yeah. Riley Gray."

"Have there been any other guys in your life since him?"

"Only one. Ryan Graber. He was on my college cross country team, and he was awesome . . . but he ended up marrying another girl on my team." I pause for a second and bring up a silly realization I have had. "It is actually kind of funny because there was Riley, Ryan, and then you. You are Ryan Lee, so you are kind of a mixture of both of them—Ryan and Ry-Lee." I giggle to myself. "It must be a sign."

"That's kind of funny."

"Most the guys I have liked have names that start with an R. But you are the first one to REALLY like me." I am dripping with giddiness.

"Soooooo, have you really never had a boyfriend?" Ryan asks.

"Yep, never had one."

"So, I guess you have never had a guy's arm around you before then?"

"Not really, except for in pictures, like before homecoming and prom."

"So, I guess a guy has never held your hand before either?"

"No," I say shyly.

My heart is rapidly firing now.

In response to my answer, Ryan lifts my hand from my lap and interlocks our fingers.

"This is how it is done."

Woah, this is getting a little intense.

And I thought he said he just wanted to be friends?

"You can do this while watching movies or while going for walks."

I giggle somewhat stupidly because I am slightly overwhelmed.

He lightly runs circles in my hand with his fingers in a rather loving way as we continue to talk.

"So, have you ever had a girlfriend?" It is now my turn to ask.

"Well, Monica Winkle and I kind of went out back when I was sixteen, but that didn't really end up working out."

We continue talking about all sorts of things, all while he is holding my hand.

"So, Janey, remember when you said that no guy had ever called you beautiful?"

"Yeah, I remember." It was in response to his message, the one where he called me a "beautiful girl."

He lowers his voice and rubs my hand with his thumb.

"It just made me so sad, Janey, because you ARE beautiful. You really are. And I hope you know that."

I am beaming like a supernova as he says these words.

Ryan Lee Darling thinks that I, Janey Lynn Eller, am BEAUTIFUL.

For so long, I have put up with belittling comments from girls telling me that I need to change who I am to win the affections of a guy. And now, I see that all those things they told me were lies. I don't need make-up or beautiful clothes to attract a guy. All I need is to be myself. I mean, I am wearing a pair of running shorts and a faded tee-shirt right now, and he still thinks I am beautiful.

I lean a little more deeply into his shoulder and sigh. Life can't get much better than this.

I am in the middle of telling him about my struggle with food when the door to the game room swings open.

It's Loraine, Ryan's eighteen-year-old sister.

Ryan immediately drops my hand.

I can't help but blush.

Loraine grins. We can't put anything past her.

"Hey, Janey!" She looks over at me and waves. Then, she looks at her brother. "Ryan, Dad wants you in the house, NOW. It's past eleven."

Oh, crap.

I hope we aren't in trouble.

After delivering his announcement, Loraine leaves, and we both stand up, following her through the garage. I nearly trip over an old, plastic dollhouse on our way to the outside world.

"Careful, Janey!" Ryan grabs my hand before I fall all the way to the floor.

"Is your dad mad at us?" I can't help but ask when I am stable on my feet again.

"No, no. It's okay. He just doesn't like for me to hang out with girls late at night. It's kind of a rule we have."

We head to my car, and as soon as Loraine heads into the house, Ryan wraps his arm back around me. I respond by wrapping my arm around him.

"So, we probably can't hang out like this all the time. It probably wouldn't be smart," Ryan says all teacher-like when we reach my car.

"Okay."

"I mean, I know you wouldn't do anything, and I wouldn't do anything, but it is better to be safe."

"Yeah." I catch his drift.

Ryan's eyes are shining in the moonlight.

I could just melt right there on the street.

He wraps me in his biggest hug yet, pulling me slightly off the ground, and presses his lips to my bangs in a light kiss.

Holy crud.

Did he just kiss me?

Never in my wildest dreams did I ever think this night would end this way.

"Well, I better head inside," he breathes, as he lowers me to the ground. "Bye, Janey."

"Bye, Ryan."

He starts to walk away and then quickly turns back.

"Oh, Janey." He runs back over to my side, clearly having something he needs to say. "I just wanted to add that we need to also focus on staying emotionally pure and not get too emotionally attached, at least not yet." He is trying to be as serious as possible. "We still don't know if things will work out. Soooooo, when you aren't with me, try not to think about me."

Yeah, like that is possible. I have practically become an insomniac ever since Ryan entered my life.

I raise my eyebrow like he is talking a foreign language.

"Oscar didn't really understand the whole thing either when I explained it to him. But it is important to do."

I still don't really understand it, but I just hold fast to the idea that, for this moment, I am Ryan's girl.

Pulling me in for one last farewell hug, Ryan says good-bye and heads to his house.

I just stand in place for a few seconds, watching him walk away, before I step into my car and put my key in the ignition.

As I drive past, he is still waiting outside his front door, waving excitedly.

I am glad he can't see my face all too clearly because I am smiling like an idiot.

There is no way I am sleeping tonight.

And, if I do, there is NO WAY I won't be dreaming about my knight in shining armor, Ryan Lee Darling.

Just Friends? Really?

"You have really pretty eyes."

I am with Ryan once more, and we are stalled at a stoplight in his Taurus. He is taking this time to gaze into my eyes, which no one has ever called pretty before. They could be called hazel or muddy brown or maybe even yellow but not pretty.

I lock his gaze and stare back into his mysterious orbs. His look green and brown and grey and blue all at once.

Once the light turns green, he tears his eyes away and looks back to the road before us.

We sit in silence for a minute or two as we pass by the Coyote River.

It is when we are stopped at another light that he looks back over at me.

"So, are you really okay with just being friends for now?" His eyes flash with slight concern.

"Yeah." I am unsure of what else to say. I obviously want to be more than "friends," but it already seems like we are. "It seems the same as dating to me," I quietly add.

"Yeah, it does." Ryan pauses and continues hesitantly. "The only difference is that we don't have a label . . . which would only mean more pressure. There are certain implications surrounding dating, and I'm not really ready for that." He looks over at me, waiting for a reaction.

I don't have one.

What does he mean? What implications?

Does he mean MARRIAGE implications??

We sit in silence for another minute, and, as we pull into Avery Forest, he reaches over for my hand. He looks back into my eyes as he clasps it in his own.

"Your hand is cold." He grips it a little harder as if to warm it up.

"Well, you know what they say: 'cold hands, warm heart.'" My hands may not be warm but now my cheeks sure are.

He holds onto my hand for the rest of the drive. We steal small glances at each other, and, with each glance, my heart speeds up just a bit.

Do people who are "just friends" hold hands like this?

"So, have you told anyone about us?" he asks, as we enter my neighborhood.

Us.

The word makes me feel slightly giddy.

"I've told Melanie and Oscar . . . and I'm sure my family knows. I haven't told many others though."

"Yeah. I've only told my close friends and my family . . . but there are others who seem to know without me telling them." He looks over at me suspiciously. "For instance, the other day, Jared Vance gave me a hug and whispered into my ear, 'So, you and Janey?'"

"Yeah? Well, I guess I did talk to Melanie." Melanie Wales, one of my best friends in junior high and high school, married Jared Vance several years ago, so I'm sure she tells him everything I tell her.

"Elsie Olson asked me if I liked you too while we were chatting on Facebook."

"Really? Why? I never told her anything about it." I can feel the warmth returning once more to my cheeks.

"She said she saw the way we write on each other's walls and just kind of figured we had a thing. She said all of Facebook probably knows by now."

My face goes from red to crimson.

Are we that obvious?

"Oh," I mutter, as we pull into my driveway.

Our hang-out session is about to come to an end, and I feel a wave of sadness wash over me.

"Are you sure you can't come for dinner?"

"Yeah. I'm sure. I have to go to an interview soon, and I don't have a lot of time."

"Oh, okay." I am slightly deflated.

As the Taurus comes to a stop, Ryan clears his throat.

"Can I ask you something, Janey?" He looks over at me with increased attentiveness.

"Sure." What is he going to ask me? I mean, we are "just friends," right?

He clears his throat again.

"Can I give you a kiss on the cheek?"

I shudder with excitement and fear at the same time. My parents could be just behind that open window, watching us.

"Sure," I manage to say.

He reaches his arms out to wrap me in a hug and puts his head close to mine.

"You smell good," he whispers sweetly.

And then, he lightly brushes my cheek with his lips.

I feel a burst of joy spread through my veins as I sit up straight once more.

I can feel his eyes settling on me still.

"Janey, can I give you a kiss?"

It is with this question that I totally freeze. I have been waiting for such a moment for forever, and, now that it arrives, I am speechless.

He doesn't want to just kiss me on the cheek; he wants to give me a REAL kiss.

I stare back into the front window of my house to see if any of my family members are watching. I think I actually see the curtain sway just a bit.

"C . . . c . . . can we just wait until another time?" I manage to stutter.

My mom could be watching. My dad could be watching. My sisters could be watching.

Ryan responds by reaching in for another hug.

"Awwww, Janey," he breathes into my hair. "I'll call you."

I swing open the door and practically skip into my house as I wave good-bye to my Ryan, my prince.

I am a love-struck, giddy, 24-year-old mess.

The boy of my dreams asked to give me a kiss, and I turned him down.

Oh, why did I turn him down?

Best Day Ever

It is Saturday morning, one week later, and Ryan and I are finishing up a picnic lunch in the grass. The sky is blue, the air is warm, and my heart is pitter-pattering all crazy-like.

Here we are again, just Ryan and I—just the clouds, the trees, the grass, and the two of us.

If he asks me that same question today, I will NOT turn him down this time.

"Let's see whose legs are longer." Ryan grins over at me mischievously as he wipes his hands free of the orange nacho-chip crumbs.

I give him a smirk. "Okay. But mine are probably longer." Standing at five foot eight inches, Ryan isn't exactly tall for a guy.

He slides over next to me until we are side by side.

I stretch out my legs, and he does the same.

They are the exact same length.

We then compare torsos.

"My upper body is a tad bit longer," he says playfully, as he flexes his muscled arms.

"Well, my neck makes up for it," I chuckle, as I reach my head up high. I can make quite the ostrich impression. "We are practically the same person."

"Let me see your hand."

I lift my hand from my side and press it to his, making sure each finger is aligned. His pinkie is longer, but my thumb is longer.

"Yep, we are basically the same person," I say, almost inaudibly.

My heart skips a beat.

We both look out into the grassy fields, and he starts hitting his feet against mine flirtatiously. Then, he wraps his arms around me and lightly presses his lips to my glowing cheek.

I look over at him, and his face is practically radiant.

I can hear the question coming before he even asks this time.

"Can I kiss you?"

"Yeah," I whisper, not even hesitating this time.

I feel like I am at the starting line of a race, nervous as can be, as he leans in and touches his wet lips to mine.

A surge of warmth radiates from my lips to my entire being.

Ryan Lee Darling just kissed me.

When he sits back up, we just gaze into each other's eyes.

It is a magical bliss.

"Do you want to lie out in the grass and watch the clouds?" he asks, never taking his eyes off my own.

"Sure."

We both lie down in the soft grass and gaze up into the bright blue sky. Puffy white clouds roll from west to east, like a fluffy conveyor belt.

Ryan puts his left arm underneath my head like a pillow and rests his other hand lightly on my waist.

"Not many girls can say they have a six-pack."

I just laugh.

"So, Janey, on a scale of zero to ten—ten being let's get married, and zero being, I hate you, I never want to see you again—how much do you like me?" He furrows his brow, all serious-like.

"Well, DEFINITELY not a zero," I giggle. "I could NEVER hate you."

"Are you sure about that?"

"Yeah." I give him a smirk and then respond to his original question. "I'd have to say a nine . . . or even nine and a half." I want to say ten, but I don't want to freak him out.

"Yeah?"

"Yep!"

"I would say a nine too." His eyes sparkle as he leans back, resting his head on the ground.

We rest in silence for a few seconds, and then Ryan thrusts his arm upward, pointing to the sky.

"Hey, look! That cloud looks like the Batman symbol!" He is ecstatic.

"Yeah, it does." I browse the sky for a bit, looking for other pictures hidden in the cotton-ball puffs. "Hey, that cloud looks like a bunny." I point out another wisp of white that has just passed the tree line.

We both lay back, smiling at the clouds, the day, and just the fact that we are together.

"It's a good day to watch the clouds and cuddle with your girl," Ryan sighs, as he breaks the silence. He leans in to give me another kiss.

I think I must be dreaming.

Days like this do not happen to girls like me.

On cue, as if he can read my thoughts, Ryan breaks the silence once more.

"Janey, don't ever think that I'm the catch. YOU'RE the catch . . . and I'm just the lucky one."

All I can do is turn a rosy red.

Could I have found a more adorable guy?

The day continues in much of the same way. Whether we are biking or hiking or just sitting in the grass, there is endless romance. It is like I have left reality and am living in a movie.

At one point, we are crossing a stream, and he picks me up in his arms and carries me across it. He drops his gloves and sunglasses in the process, but that only makes him more adorable.

"I had been looking for an excuse to pick you up," he whispers, touching his nose to mine.

I nearly faint.

At another point, as we hike by the very same stream, he wraps me in his arms, looks into my eyes, and whispers the words I will never forget.

"I love you."

He loves me?

Ryan Lee Darling LOVES ME??

I am lost.

I am lost in a love-struck trance, and I don't ever want to awake.

Spreading the Good News

"Melly!!!"

"Hey, Janey! Come on in!"

I walk into the Vance residence and slide the glass door shut behind me.

Tasha is participating in a Bible study downstairs, but she won't be done for another thirty minutes. I figured Melanie and I could chill for the time being.

"Did you hear I went on an eighteen-mile run today with the Greenleaf Running Club?" Melanie asks, as I sit beside her on the couch. She is folding clothes.

"No, I didn't!"

"Yeah! They had water stops along the way and gave us licorice and treats too. It was really cool."

"How fast were you going?" I'm all about pace.

"I only ran like ten-minute miles, but I think I can go faster. I'm just afraid to push myself." She chuckles. "I mean, with my training regimen of one run every two weeks, I can't believe I even ran that far."

"You only run once every two weeks?" I am dumbfounded.

"Yeah . . . or maybe once a week. I'm just so busy with the kids that I don't have time." She folds a little, pink shirt, which must be Gretta's. Gretta is her adorable three-year-old daughter. She has curls just like my sister, Tasha.

"Are you doing any races before the marathon?" By marathon, I mean the Chicago Marathon. We will both be running in it in a little over a month. I will be racing it, and Melanie will be running to finish.

"I kind of want to do the Topaz Lake Half Marathon, but I'm not sure."

"I might run that too!" I exclaim excitedly.

"Yeah?? Well, even if we both run it, you will be WAYYYYY ahead of me."

I just giggle.

"So, enough about running." Melanie gives me a wink. "How are things going with Ryan?"

I blush and dive headfirst into the story of our picnic we had just yesterday.

When I finish my tale, she just sits there, stunned.

"Holy cow, Janey." She shakes her head with a smile. "You two are definitely going to get married. There's no doubt about it. Even Loraine, his own sister, is sure of it."

"You really think so?" I whisper.

"Yeah! You just had like the ultimate date with him. At this rate, he will be proposing to you tomorrow . . . or maybe even next week." Melanie nudges me, her grin growing by the second. "And, when you two do get married, I had better be a bridesmaid in that wedding."

I blush a little darker and laugh.

"Oh, you would definitely be a bridesmaid, Mel."

It feels so weird talking about the possibility of marriage, but it is exciting too.

Maybe, just maybe, Ryan is the one I have been waiting for all my life.

I Could See Myself Marrying You

"Doo doot do do do doo doot do do do doo doot . . ."

I am in the middle of taking a bite of Mom's delicious pizza as my cell phone rings. I sprint to my drawstring bag, rifle through it until I find the purple device, and see the word *"Ryan"* lighting up the screen.

I head out to the front porch and shut the door behind me.

"Hey, Ryan!"

"Hey, babe!! What are you up to?"

"Oh, just eating some pizza." A huge smile spreads across my face.

"Sounds delightful. I was maybe wondering if I could swing by to pick up my bike helmet and gloves that I left in your car."

"Sure!"

"And then you could come with me to take care of the dogs and hang out maybe too?"

"That sounds good to me!"

"Awesome. Well, I will see you in a bit."

Ryan arrives in record time, and we head off into the darkness.

"You looked really nice at church today," he says, as he jimmies open the door of the house in which the dogs make their residence.

"Aww, thanks."

"It made me nervous to talk to you."

I blush.

"I've worn that dress since the fifth grade." And it's true. My sisters have told me a dozen times to stop wearing it because they say it makes me look like a little kid. But, if Ryan likes it, they must be wrong.

He pours a cup of dry dog food into each bowl as the pups wag their tails. Once they have devoured what is set before them, Ryan opens the back door to let them run around and take care of business. As we follow the dogs outside, he fixes his gaze on me. Gently taking me by the hand, he twirls me in a circle.

I feel like a princess, even in this grassy lawn.

"I can't believe the most beautiful girl in the world would like me," he sighs, as he kisses me tenderly on the cheek.

My grin is so huge that I feel like my face is about to burst . . . if my heart doesn't burst with love and adoration first.

I kiss him on the cheek in return, relishing every moment of our time together.

After we are done taking care of the dogs, we meander over to a little park in the neighborhood next to mine.

"Let's go for a walk, Janey."

We both hop out of the car and head around the short half-mile loop circulating the baseball fields.

As we walk, we shove each other playfully, trying to knock the other one off the path.

"You are just too strong," Ryan laughs.

Yeah right. He could fling me into the grass at a moment's notice. I'm a weakling compared to him.

I shiver as we head farther down the path. I should have brought my long-sleeve shirt.

Ryan must sense I am chilly because he wraps his arms around me as we walk.

I am instantly warmed.

After we circle the fields, Ryan leads me by the hand to the playground. After swinging around on the monkey bars like a couple of kids, we climb the steps to the very top of the structure.

Wrapping me in a huge embrace, he leans his forehead against mine and just breathes.

He looks like an adorable Cyclops from this view.

"I never would have thought a half an hour ago that I would be standing at the top of a playground holding you."

His breath is warm on my face.

All I can do is smile. This kid is such a romantic.

We dance in the moonlight, under the twinkle of the stars. He lightly gives me a peck on the cheek every so often, and I think I am in heaven.

"So, Janey. I was thinking about a message you sent to me the other day, a message where you said you hoped this would all work out." He pauses and appears to be contemplating what he is about to say next. "Honestly, before this week, I had never thought about this going all the way to marriage, but I am starting to see it as a possibility now. I COULD see myself marrying you."

Did he just say the word "MARRIAGE??"

Breathe, Janey, breathe. He only declared he was crushing on you less than a month ago.

"I do think it is a good thing to keep this a friend's thing for now so that we can get to know each other better." He pauses and thinks some more.

And there he goes with the "friends" line again.

How is dating going to be different than all that is going on right now?

"And then, if we do get married, we can save up money from your job and my job and do missions for a while, maybe two years or so. Then, we could settle down and have kids."

Kids? WOAH. This boy is sounding serious.

"I wouldn't want to have ten kids or anything crazy like that," he chuckles, "but maybe four. Four would be ideal. The oldest should be a boy though and the second a girl, just like in my family. Then her brother could look out for her."

I remain fairly silent, marinating in all that he is saying.

After he finishes his monologue, we stare longingly into each other's eyes and sway in the moonlight.

I wish we could stay this way forever.

When it is time to go, he leads me by the hand, down from our mountaintop view.

As we descend, I smack my leg on one of the plastic columns.

I yelp.

"Are you okay, Janey?" He pulls me closer to his side, with a look of pretend terror in his eyes.

I laugh at myself and reply, "Yeah. I'm always running into stuff."

And just when I think he can't be any more romantic, he is.

"Well, I'm glad you ran into me." And, with that, he lifts me into his arms and carries me down the rest of the steps, across the woodchips, and to his car.

I rest my head on his chest and smile.

"I'm sorry if I'm too heavy."

"You are a twig," he quietly replies.

When we reach the car, he sets me down on my feet, opens the passenger door, and guides me to my seat.

"Your chariot, madam."

"Why thank you, my good sir." I am giddy.

When we are both seated in the confines of his car, he studies my face for a few moments, as he starts the engine.

"I definitely don't deserve you, Janey . . . I deserve death."

"Don't be so hard on yourself," I whisper.

This kid could feed lines to the movie stars.

I am floating on a cloud as we drive back to my house.

This must be what a magic carpet ride feels like.

I don't want this night to end.

When we pull into my driveway, he wraps me in one last hug, gives me one last peck on the cheek, and says goodbye.

"Later, babe."

"Bye, Ryan."

As I lightly frolic to my front door, I look over my shoulder one last time.

Ryan, the boy who thinks I am "the most beautiful girl in the world," waves at me happily.

I hope with all my might that I marry this boy. There is no one sweeter than him.

Sub-Three Isn't What It's Cracked up to Be

"Go, Janey!"

"Good job, Janey!"

How do these people know me? I wonder, as I run through the streets of Chicago. It is the day of the Chicago Marathon, the day that I hope to break three hours, and, as of right now, I am not sure that is going to happen.

At just about the eight-mile mark, my hip flexors started to tighten, and they are now throbbing.

I punch my upper thighs, hoping to loosen them up a little.

It doesn't seem to help.

It only makes me look like a goofy monkey.

"Go, Janey!"

I twist my head to the right, seeing if I recognize the person calling out my name.

I don't.

"Nice job, Janey!"

That voice almost sounded like Ryan's.

I twist my head to the left, hoping to see that familiar, beloved face.

Instead, there is no one I recognize.

Ryan.

He said he would LOVE to come watch me run my big race last month when I asked, but, this week, he made up tons of excuses as to why he couldn't come. *"It's too early." "I have to let the dogs out." "I didn't know it was on a Sunday."* Excuse after excuse after excuse. What happened to my knight in shining armor that declared I was "the most beautiful girl in the world?"

My heart sinks.

But I must be strong.

"Way to go, Janey!"

Seriously, HOW do these people know me?

And then, I remember.

My first name is written on the race bib on the front of my tank top. HELLO!!

I inwardly laugh at my stupidity.

This sudden realization boosts my spirits for just a moment as I head towards the half-marathon mark.

"1:27:21."

So far, so good.

Still at about 6:40 pace, I know I am doing just fine.

If only these aching, tight-as-a-rubber-band, hip flexors aren't the death of me!

I partake in the monkey dance, where I beat on my quads like I am pounding on a bongo drum, at least once every 200 meters. But it is of no use.

Maybe my legs are so tight because I waited around in shorts in this thirty-nine-degree weather for at least twenty minutes before the gun sounded at the start of the race. Or maybe my legs are just tight because I can't help but pound my feet when I run.

At the eighteen-mile mark, my legs are already wobbling like they do at the end of an 800-meter dash.

Good grief.

How will I ever make it 8.2 more miles?

I must be running over eight-minute pace by now.

But, I'm not. According to my most recent split, I'm still running faster than seven-minute pace. I have no clue how, but I am.

Help me, Jesus.

The miles drag on and on and on. But, somehow, through the throbbing and the wobbling, I continue to put one foot in front of the other.

"Go, Janey!"

This time, when I look, I recognize the face. It is Marla Keyes, a girl who used to run for Bayer High School.

This puts enough pep in my step to keep me from mentally or physically unraveling.

With three miles to go, I pass Emily Moffle, another familiar face. She was also a runner for Bayer High School and a stud runner at that.

She looks exhausted.

If I just passed her, I must still be running well.

With two miles to go, I am passed by Jamie Aubertson, a girl I trained with several times before this race. She seems upbeat, energetic, and not one bit tired. And she has never run a marathon before, has she? Shouldn't I still be ahead of her? Maybe I'm actually not running well anymore.

"Good job, Janey!" she says cheerily.

I wish I had that much energy.

The pain in my legs is excruciating, but when I pass the *"one mile to go"* marker, I know I will meet my goal.

All I have to run is a nine-minute mile.

My heart starts to soar as I know the end is in sight. I dig deep and push just a little harder, past the pain and past the worries that I am not going to make it.

That is when I feel my shoe filling with a wet sort of goop.

I look down at my right foot and see that the entire toe box is red.

A blood blister must have popped.

Oh well.

I fix my eyes back up on the horizon and start to pass several runners.

I am going to make it.

As I climb the last small hill, I hear my family cheering my name.

I push even harder.

"Go, Janey, go!!"

"You can do it, Janey!"

"You are AWESOME, Janey!!"

As I charge down that last 200-meter stretch, I am overcome with joy.

I pass one last group of runners as I cross the finish line.

"2:58:11."

I made it.

All I want to do is lie down right there, but I don't. I continue like the walking wounded to the medical tent. I need someone to bandage up my bloody foot.

I collapse into a chair and shiver as my wound is cleansed and covered with a Band-Aid. Thirty-nine degrees is perfect for running a marathon but not for just sitting still.

Once I am finished, I lift myself up and begin to hobble away. I am physically trashed but find strength in the fact my family is waiting for me somewhere in the enormous crowd of spectators.

I wrap my arms around myself to try and stay warm. This tank top and shorts get-up is no longer conducive to the weather.

"Young lady, are you okay?" I am nearly free when a woman in the medical tent calls out to me with worry.

"Yeah, I think so. I'm just cold . . . and tired."

Cold is an understatement.

And tired . . . well, that is a GIGANTIC understatement.

"You don't look so good. I think you need to come back here with me."

"Why?" I whisper.

I just want to find my family! I want them to know I broke three hours.

"I want to make sure you are okay."

I turn around and hobble back into the white shelter.

"Have a seat here on the cot. I will bring you some hot broth to drink."

Hot broth? Gag me.

After a few seconds, the woman returns with a cup of bright yellow liquid.

Can't I just have some water?

"Here you go."

I woefully accept the drink offering and take a sip.

Ugh. I do not think this will help my nausea, not at all

"I want you to drink ALL of it. And when you are done, I will give you another."

Disgusting.

"I think I will take your temperature," the lady adds.

"But I'm not sick," I mutter.

"It is a precautionary measure."

"Oh, okay."

She sticks the thermometer in my mouth and cringes.

"Ninety-one degrees."

"What?"

My mind isn't functioning all too well, but I'm pretty sure that is REALLY low.

"I think you are a little hypothermic."

Am I like dying?

"Here, lie down."

I fall back onto the cot as she places an electric blanket over me.

"I'm going to get you an IV."

WHAT?? An IV?? As in a NEEDLE??? Noooooooo!!!! I cannot STAND needles!!!!!

Breaking three hours is supposed to be a happy time.

I close my eyes and wait . . . and wait.

Let's just get this over with already!

"Hold out your arm."

I lift my limb, eyes still closed.

When I feel the bite of the needle, I squirm.

When I feel that same bite in a different location, I squirm again.

"You are so dehydrated that I can't even find a vein!"

I squint and detect that the nurse is shaking her head with frustration.

She continues to poke me and prod me as I start to whimper.

When she finally has found a location she is happy with, I am able to relax just a tad.

I will not be able to fully relax until this needle is removed.

Even though the warm blanket is now covering my body, I am still shivering. I am shivering so much that I am practically shaking.

"I will bring you another blanket," the nurse says, "and another cup of soup too."

Blah.

After seven cups of glowing broth and sixty minutes of IV torture, the nurse finally allows me to leave.

"Put these on before you go." She hands me an extra-large red hoodie and an extra-extra-large pair of grey sweatpants.

They are enormous, but they look warm.

I put them on and shuffle out into the daylight.

FREEDOM!!

I am walking for no more than thirty seconds when I hear my name called in jubilation.

"JANEY!!!!!" Tasha jogs over to me.

"Oh, Janey," Mom whimpers, as she and Dad follow close behind.

I try to smile, but all I can manage is a haggard half-grin.

"Why were you in the medical tent for so long?"

"My temperature was really low, and I was really dehydrated, so they put a stinking IV in my arm FOR AN HOUR."

"That doesn't sound fun," Tasha responds.

"No, not at all. I HATE needles."

"You broke three hours though!!" Tasha adds, cheerfully.

"Yeah. 2:58:11."

"We are so proud of you, Janey." Mom wraps me in an enormous hug.

"You looked like you even had a kick," Dad says with a smile, also giving me a hug.

"Yeah. For some reason, even when I'm about to die in a marathon, I always get this burst of energy when I'm close to the finish."

"So, what is up with your outfit?" Tasha scans me up and down, trying not to laugh.

"They gave it to me in the medical tent to keep warm."

Tasha chuckles.

"You look HUGE."

"Thanks." I pause. "I'm still freezing though."

"Here, take my windbreaker." Dad whips off his extra-large jacket, and soon I look like I am seriously obese. But I could care less. I did what I came to do, and now all I want to do is pass out in my bed . . . and maybe grab a bite to eat. I am famished.

Tasha chuckles again.

"So, are you ready to head to the train station?" Mom asks.

"I guess . . . although I'm not sure how I am going to walk all the way there."

"Dad should carry you," Tasha suggests.

"No, Janey should walk some more to loosen up her legs."

WHY?? I already ran at least twenty-seven miles when adding in the warm up. I just want to sleep.

I give him a pained look, and we start our journey to the train. One of my arms is wrapped around Tasha's shoulder and the other around Mom's.

At each light, we barely beat the countdown clock. Tasha and Mom are practically dragging me because my legs are no longer functioning.

"Seriously, Dad. Why don't you just carry her?" Tasha asks with exasperation.

Yeah, why Dad? Why don't you just carry me? Lying down in the medical tent for so long did a number on my legs . . . oh yeah, and so did that marathon. You know the one where I ran 26.2 MILES??!!

"No, she's doing fine."

And thus we continue or lethargically slow journey. I swear we are plodding along slower than one mile per hour. But it is all I can manage.

Once we reach the station, Dad buys us some milkshakes. I am starving, but this is all my queasy stomach can handle at the moment.

Soon, we are on the train, heading back home.

"Are you going to call Ryan and tell him how you did?" Mom asks, as the world rolls by in a blur.

"Probably." I look away. I wish he could have just been here with me today.

When we arrive home, I hobble into my bedroom with my cell phone. Falling onto my bed, I dial his number and wait . . . and wait.

He doesn't pick up.

I guess I will try back later.

To pass the time, I call various other people that would love to know how I ran, such as Coach McDevitt, Beth, Kerin, and my training buddy for the marathon, Carly Settler.

After all these conversations, I call Ryan again.

He still doesn't answer.

When I punch in his number a third time, he finally answers.

"Janey!"

He sounds excited that I called.

So far, so good.

"Hey, Ryan!"

"Hey! What's up?"

"I just wanted to tell you how I did in the Chicago Marathon! I broke three hours!"

"Yeah?!"

"Yeah! I averaged 6:48 pace and took fifty-fifth out of all the girls! It was so awesome . . . except for the part where I had to get an IV in my arm for over an hour."

"That is awesome, except for the IV part."

"I know! Ugh. I hate needles!" I pause. "I wish you could have been there."

"That would have been cool. Originally, when you told me about it, I thought it was on a Saturday, not a Sunday. And I had no idea I would have to wake up at 4:00 am. That is WAY too early to wake up."

"Oh, it's okay," I say, even though I am inwardly thinking that he could have manned up just this once.

"Janey, I got your card in the mail the other day."

"You mean your birthday card?"

"Yeah."

There is silence for a few seconds.

Did he not like it or something? I spent at least two hours making it.

"Janey . . . I think you might be a little too emotionally attached to me."

"Oh," I whisper.

That's my reward for trying to be thoughtful.

"I mean, we aren't even dating."

"Oh," I whisper once again.

What does that mean? I know he has SAID we are only friends before, but his actions have NEVER backed up that notion. I mean, if the amount of kisses he has given me equals the amount of love in his heart for me, he has to totally be head over heels for me. He even SAID that he loved me on two different occasions.

"I just want to make sure that you are giving your heart and emotions only to God, Janey. One day, we might get married, BUT, for now, you need to make sure to not get emotionally attached to me . . . just in case things don't work out."

"Oh." I feel like a broken record.

A tear rolls down my warm cheek as we sit in silence. Neither of us knows what to say.

"Are you okay, Janey?"

By the time he asks this question, I am crying steadily.

"I don't think so," I mumble through the water works, as my lips quiver.

"Aww, Janey. I wish you could be here with me so I could give you a really big hug."

He is breathing deeply, feeling my hurt right along with me.

I gulp and try to calm my aching heart.

"Can I pray for you right now, Janey?"

"Sure."

I close my eyes and listen as he offers up a heartfelt cry to the Creator of the universe. Even when he is making me cry, Ryan truly is the sweetest guy I have ever met. He always knows exactly what to pray.

When he finishes, Ryan sighs.

"Janey, I better let the dogs out now."

"Okay."

"I hope you have a good night."

"You too."

"Love ya, Janey."

"Love ya too, Ryan."

And with that, the conversation ends.

I lay my phone beside me on the bed and let the tears continue to fall. I don't know what to think.

He didn't say he doesn't like me anymore. I mean, he even used the words "love ya." Not only that, but he said, "One day, we might get married." He still cares. He just doesn't want me to be "too emotionally attached."

Then, if he still likes me and still cares, why am I so brokenhearted?

Today was supposed to be a joyful day. Breaking three hours was supposed to be the pinnacle of my running career thus far.

But now . . . I can see the truth.

Running sub-three isn't what it's cracked up to be.

"Hey, Miss Eller!"

"Hi, Miss Eller!!"

"Miss Eller!!! What's up?"

Alison Fru, Elsa Maki, and Monique Tipper bounce into my room, babbling on and on as they make their way to my desk.

I had them all in my class as seventh graders last year, but, even as eighth graders, they stop by my room each and every day.

"Hey, guys! How are you all doing today?"

"Awesome!" Monique's face is radiant. "I shimmied in band."

Oh brother.

"Yeah?"

"Yeah. I'm like a pro at it now. I did it while we were shopping in the store the other day too, but my dad yelled at me." She giggles as she practices her shimmying once more. Monique is bubbly, outgoing, and far from shy.

Alison laughs as she shakes her head.

Oh dear.

"So, Miss Eller, how are your classes going this year?" Elsa inquires, as she takes a seat next to my desk.

"Pretty good! I don't have any kids as crazy as Harrison or Parker this year."

We both laugh, remembering just how wild those two could be.

"That's good."

"Remember when they wouldn't believe me that a rhombus with two VERY obtuse and two VERY acute angles WASN'T a square?"

"Yeahhhhhhh. That was interesting."

"I mean, even Mrs. Trumello's son, who is FIVE, knows what a square is. He even knows what a cylinder is." I look over at the lovely lady that shares my classroom with me. She nods her head in agreement as she picks up a stack of papers to go make copies.

"Didn't they like go to the vice-principal to tell him you didn't know what you were talking about?"

"Yeah. It was RIDICULOUS."

"Soooooooooo, Miss Eller, I have heard through the grapevine that there is a special guy in your life now?"

I jerk my head over to Alison and try to keep a straight face.

"Huh?"

"The Shirtless Wonder," she replies. "Remember him? Strawberry-blonde hair . . . green eyes . . . very muscular?"

Oh no.

"Yeah, Serena Hamm told me you had a picture on your camera of you and this really cute guy in swim trunks."

I lower my head and try not to make eye contact as I blush.

"Well, is he your boyfriend?" Monique jumps in, very excited to know.

"I . . . I don't know." My heart aches to even think of Ryan. I haven't heard from him in two weeks.

"You don't know?"

"Well, it's confusing."

"How?"

"Well, he doesn't really talk to me anymore. He used to, but now he doesn't."

I can see even Monique's exuberance diminish at this statement.

"Boys are dumb," Alison states, folding her arms across her chest, and then she brightens for a moment, "except for Edward Cullen, of course."

Monique sighs.

I just roll my eyes.

I think Elsa is following suit.

Some things never change, such as Monique and Alison's obsession with the *Twilight* series.

We all sit in silence for a few moments.

That's when a mob of energetic eighth-grade boys enters my room.

"Hey, Miss Eller!! Can we have some candy?"

"Sure! Just take one though." I smile their way as they rifle through my container of treats.

Once they have found what they are looking for, they thank me for my generosity and leave as quickly as they appeared.

Alison huffs as soon as they are gone. "You shouldn't let them take candy from you anymore, Miss Eller."

"Why not?" I wonder.

"Because . . . they aren't as nice as you think."

"What do you mean?"

"Well . . . um . . . I don't think you really want to know."

Okay, now I REALLY want to know what the heck she is talking about.

"Tell me, Alison."

"Noooo . . . I don't think I should."

"Why not?"

"Because they are saying mean things about you."

"Like WHAT?" I am desperate to know.

"Some of them are spreading a rumor that you are a lesbian."

Come again?

"WHAT??" I am dumbfounded, in shock really. "Why on earth would they say that??"

"They think that because you live at home, share a track phone with your parents, and have never had a boyfriend that you must be a lesbian."

"Oh my word! That is horrible. And it is SO not true."

Seriously, I have liked boys since I was in first grade.

"We know it isn't true, Miss Eller," Monique reassures me. "I mean, we KNOW about 'The Shirtless Wonder.'"

I just shake my head.

"And I let them have candy nearly every day." I am processing out loud.

"They are just jerks, Miss Eller. We know the truth." Alison tries to comfort me.

If they weren't in the room right now, I would definitely be crying.

"What does sharing a track phone even have to do with being a lesbian? Or living at home? I like being with my family." I am hurt and outraged but need to contain myself.

"I don't know." Elsa frowns.

"I shouldn't have told you." Alison lowers her head.

"No. I'm glad you told me. I'd rather know what people are saying about me."

The trio stays in my room for a bit longer, talking to me and doodling on my whiteboard. It helps to take my mind off the bit of news I just received, but it still lingers in my thoughts.

When they leave, I just sit staring for a few minutes.

I already have been feeling super stressed over the Ryan situation, and THIS has only increased my stress level.

The kids I used to teach think I'm a lesbian.

What is with this world?

Raging Sea

"Don't know where to begin. It's like my world's caving in. And I try but I can't control my fear. Where do I go from here? Sometimes it's so hard to pray, when You feel so far away. But I am willing to go where You want me to. God, I trust You. There's a raging sea, right in front of me, wants to pull me in, bring me to my knees. So let the waters rise, if You want them to. I will follow You. I will follow You. I will follow You."

I am beyond nervous as I drive the five miles to Ryan's house. Today is the day he will tell me how he feels about me for the second time. Today is the day of reckoning. I have been chasing him around for nearly a month, telling him that we NEED to talk, and, after a month of waiting, it is going to happen.

All I can do is sing along with the radio to keep from puking.

One of my favorite songs, "Let the Waters Rise," by MIKESCHAIR, is playing, and it seems to be almost prophetic for what I am sure is bound to happen. I am nearly positive he is about to break up with me, if that is what you can even call the end of a relationship that was never an official relationship.

"I will swim in the deep, 'cause You'll be next to me. You're in the eye of the storm and the calm of the sea. You're never out of reach. God, You know where I've been. You were there with me then. You were faithful before. You'll be faithful again. I'm holding Your hand. There's a raging sea, right in front of me, wants to pull me in, bring me to my knees. So let the waters rise, if You want them to. I will follow You. I will follow You. I will follow You."

There IS a raging sea in front of me, but I need to step into it if I want to know the truth.

God, please help me with what is coming.

"God, Your love is enough. You will pull me through. I'm holding onto You. God, Your love is enough. I will follow You. I will follow You."

But what if RYAN doesn't love me? What will I do then?

As I pull into Ryan's street, I listen to the chorus play once more.

God, give me strength.

"There's a raging sea, right in front of me, wants to pull me in, bring me to my knees. So let the waters rise, if You want them to. I will follow You. I will follow You. I will follow You."

"So, Janey, how have you been?"

He doesn't know? He doesn't know after ALL the messages I've sent to him???

"Um, well, not very good."

Where do I even start?

Seated next to Ryan in his Ford Taurus, I am suddenly unsure of how to start this conversation. I thought he would be the one to just man up and say what he's actually feeling, but I guess it's up to me.

I decide to start with something totally unrelated to our relationship.

"Well, for starters, on Friday, I found out that a bunch of eighth graders are spreading a rumor that I'm a lesbian."

"Wow. That's not very nice."

"Yeah, I know. And these are kids that I thought LIKED me. It is just dumb."

And you are the boy I thought LOVED me. Maybe that was just dumb too.

"Hmmm. So, why else have you not been doing all that well?"

"Basically, this whole month has been stressful."

"And why is that?"

Oh, you know why.

"Well, Ryan . . . I guess what made me most sad and stressed out is the fact that . . . is the fact that I didn't know what had become of us." We make brief eye contact. "It was just like everything completely changed one day. You know?"

"Yeah . . ."

"So, what happened?"

"Well, Janey, it had just been a long time since we hung out." He pauses. "And during that time, I got to thinking and praying and realized I shouldn't even like a girl right now."

"And why is that?" I ask in a near whisper.

"I guess I just don't really have time to put in the effort."

"Oh."

"Does that make sense?"

Um, no, that doesn't make any sense. How busy can you be? Busier than a teacher like me who makes PLENTY of time for you?

"Uh, maybe."

I sit pondering his reasoning as he pulls through the Burger King drive-thru.

"Do you want anything, Janey?"

"No, that's okay."

I just want to know the TRUTH.

Once he is equipped with two double cheeseburgers and a Cherry Pepsi, we are on our way.

"Can you unwrap one of the cheeseburgers for me?" he asks kindly, as he starts to drive.

"Sure."

I open one and hand it to him as he makes a right-hand turn.

Where are we going now?

"You can have a sip of my Cherry Pepsi if you want, Janey."

"Okay."

I NEVER drink pop, but if it is a chance to feel just a little closer to Ryan before the bomb is dropped, I will take it.

I breathe in the bubbly, sweet liquid and hope I can handle whatever he is about to tell me.

Well, he doesn't really tell me anything for quite some time.

Instead, he drives me around his old neighborhood, pointing out favorite parks, ponds where he would catch fish, and the house where the scariest dog lived.

"This is the first time I've been over here in a long time . . . like since we moved ten years ago."

He drives slowly, quietly reminiscing on the past.

When we finally exit the neighborhood, Ryan looks back over at me.

"So, Janey, I honestly thought you'd have more questions than that."

"Questions?"

"Yeah, that is why we are driving around."

Okay, so I guess it's my duty to uncover the truth.

If only my nerves would allow me to articulate what I am feeling.

"So, um, do you think there is any hope for the future . . . for us?"

There, I've said it.

Ryan studies my face for a second and then looks back to the road.

"I would have to say yes . . ."

YES?? He said YES??

". . . because I don't know what God has in store. God could say, in the future, 'Hey Ryan, you and Janey, make it work.' And I would have to listen. But that doesn't mean anything will happen."

But it COULD happen.

There IS hope.

"Any other questions?"

"Um, yeah . . ."

Courage, Janey, courage.

"So, do you not like me at all then?"

I hope he just heard what I asked because I'm practically whispering again.

"I wouldn't say that. I just think I may have led you to believe there was more there than there ever was."

"Oh."

"I liked you at like a five on a scale of zero to ten—ten being let's get married."

Zero being, I hate you, I never want to see you again.

"That isn't what you said the day we had the picnic," I mutter.

"I know." He looks like he might start crying. "I wasn't trying to lead you on . . . but I think I did."

You THINK??

"I also think I may have said things and done things that made you give me more of your heart than you should have . . . and, for that, I'm to blame."

He is still looking at the road but is almost cowering.

"Do you think you don't like me the way you used to because this isn't the time for you to like somebody?"

"That is probably part of it." He appears to be searching for words to say. "I guess I just see you more as a sister now than as a wife."

A wife? He saw me as a WIFE??

This kid.

"I mean, I just don't see you in a romantic way anymore. I still care though. I still like you . . . just in a different way than before."

But WHY?? WHY do you see me in a different way??

"Can we at least still be friends?" I squeak, scared of the answer.

"I would prefer that."

"And can I still send you messages?"

"I would prefer that too."

"And can we still get to know each other?"

The questions are coming out rapid-fire now.

"Yes, Janey. I WANT for you to get to know me better."

I smile and relax a little more in my seat.

But then, I decide to ask the other questions I have been waiting over a month to ask.

"So, Ryan, did I do something wrong to make you change your mind about me?"

A look of sorrow crosses his face once more.

"If anyone made mistakes, Janey, it was me. You have EVERY right to be angry with me. And you SHOULD be angry."

I'm more sad and heartbroken than mad.

"It's okay, Ryan," I quietly say.

"No." He shakes his head. "No, it's not. I did not treat you how you deserve to be treated."

We sit in silence for nearly a minute, but, then, I decide it is time for one last question.

"Ryan?"

"Yeah, Janey?"

"Why did you say I was the most beautiful girl in the world if you didn't mean it?"

I want to ask why he said he loved me if he didn't mean it or why he said he could see himself marrying me if he didn't mean it, but I settle with this question instead. It will be the last one I ask, for now at least.

"Because you ARE a very beautiful girl, Janey. I MEANT that."

Just kill me now.

He cups my head in his hands and gazes with concern into my eyes.

I gulp down the tears that are about to escape. I have to be strong.

"I never meant to hurt you, Janey . . . but I did."

For a few minutes, Ryan just breathes in and out, so slowly that it seems like time is about to stop. He is definitely trying to hold back tears of his own.

"I'm just a little boy trying to play the part of a grown-up," he quietly adds, when we are less than a mile from his house.

Once we arrive back where we started, Ryan leans over and gives me a warm embrace.

"Can I pray for you, Janey?"

"Sure."

As he prays, a few tears drip down my cheeks.

When he is finished, he takes my hand and looks it over.

"You need to stop picking at your nails, Janey," he says quietly.

He gently kisses my hand . . . and then my cheek.

We gaze into each other's eyes, just like we used to, and I can see the empathy pouring from those green orbs.

"I feel like this all happened for nothing," I say, after a while.

"Don't think that, Janey. EVERYTHING happens for a reason. This could either be the foundation if something does happen in the future or help us in a relationship with someone else."

Some foundation.

I feel like this foundation is cracked in at least a dozen places.

"This was the most exciting summer of my life, Ryan."

"I'm happy I could make it such."

Ryan smiles and tenderly kisses my cheek once more.

And then, he heads down our memory lane.

"There was hiking," he smiles.

"And biking," I join in.

"And reading the Bible," he continues.

"And playing tennis," I add.

"And dancing on the jungle gym," he nudges me.

"And tubing at the lake," I breathe.

"And watching the clouds," he sighs.

"Don't forget shoveling dirt," I giggle.

At least I no longer feel like bawling.

"See, we had a lot of good memories, you and me."

Yes, we did.

"I just hope what I did won't keep you from trusting others in the future. I would never want that."

"Ryan." Okay, so I want to ask one more question. "What should I do since I still like you? It's not like I can just stop."

"Time is the only cure for that," he responds.

Time.

Like a WHOLE lot of time.

I have never been one to move past anyone quickly.

"Janey, you are an amazing girl. ANY guy who ends up marrying you is lucky. Trust me on that."

But I don't want just ANY guy. I want YOU.

"I love how you always have hope, like when everyone told you I didn't like you. You stuck to what you knew was true, and you were right."

Well, I'm not right any more.

"And Janey, I solemnly promise, hand over my heart," he places his hand over his heart, "to NEVER ignore you again. And here, just to show you that I still want to be friends, would you be up to seeing a movie, *The Blindside*, with me and my friends in two weeks, like on a Friday or Saturday?"

"Sure! But not on Saturday. I have a wedding that day."

"Your own?"

"Haha. NO."

"Okay, then I will NOT pick Saturday, just so you can come. I still want to be your friend, Janey, okay?"

"Good," I weakly smile.

After talking a little more in the car, we head into his house and watch some baseball (the Cubs, NOT the Sox).

We say nothing.

We just sit in silence.

It is all so awkward, but I don't want to leave. Once I leave, it is over... unless, of course, God tells him something different. So, I choose to stay.

"Well, I had better go let the dogs out," he says, after about a half hour.

"Yeah, and I had better go to my leaders' meeting," I respond reluctantly.

"I will walk you out to your car then, just in case a hobo jumps out at you." He nudges me playfully.

I can't help but chuckle.

As we walk, I relish in each moment I still have him by my side.

I am going to miss him so much.

"You doing okay, Janey?" he asks, worried about me.

"Yeah, I think so."

I am sure that will all change when I drive away.

When we reach my car, he gives me one last hug. Putting his forehead to mine, he leans back and lifts me so my feet are no longer touching the ground.

"I forgive you," I whisper, while in his embrace. I want him to know that. I don't WANT to be mad at him.

When he lowers me back down, he asks a question I never thought he would ask again.

"Can we kiss?"

I know I should probably say "no," but I can't bring myself to say it.

"Yeah."

I mean, didn't he just say he sees me as a sister?

He puts his lips to mine, and at least ten seconds pass before he pulls away.

What a way to go.

"Bye, Ryan," I whisper, as I open my car door.

"Bye, Janey."

And, it is then, as soon as I start to drive away, that the water works begin.

I am NOT okay.

As I drive through the shower of tears, "More Beautiful You" starts to play.

Now, I am sobbing.

This is the song Ryan sang as he drove my car that one day.

I sit there, wishing that any other song than THIS would be playing, but I am unable to change the station.

It is like I WANT to feel the pain.

It is like I WANT to remember how I am like the girl in the song.

"So turn around, you're not too far
To back away, be who you are
To change your path, go another way
It's not too late, you can be saved
If you feel depressed with past regrets
The shameful nights hope to forget
Can disappear, they can all be washed away
By the one who's strong, can right your wrongs
Can rid your fears, dry all your tears
And change the way you look at this big world
He will take your dark, distorted view
And with His light, He will show you truth
And again you'll see through the eyes of a little girl."

Oh, to see through the eyes of a little girl again, to see through the eyes of someone who has not yet discovered how difficult life can be.

Writing Away the Sorrows

I go to sleep, you're in my thoughts
I dream, you are there too
When I awake, it's you I find
You're always somewhere in my mind
I can't escape, it's like a trap
A trap of sadness holds me back
Why can't it just be you and I?
I'm sure to always wonder why
My prince, you left me like a frog
Will a kiss change you back?
Don't lie to me, my heart is weak
Be honest when to me you speak
My heart's a treasure, tear it not
You consistently tie it in a knot
I love you
You liked me
Are you sure it wasn't more?
Are you sure there isn't more?
Do you think this is the end?
I just want you as a friend
At least
If that is all you can give
Acquaintances we cannot be
Can you not see you're hurting me?

Still Writing

Refreshing kisses, warm embraces
You gaze at me, and my heart races
Face to face and cheek to cheek
You're eyes, they sparkle when you speak
You hold me, and my whole world shines
We sway, forgetting about time
We laugh, we grin, make goofy smiles
You say, "I love you, stay a while"
But then the summer fades to fall
Your love, it dies, we've lost it all.

You're Beautiful, Baby!

The air is crisp, yet warm, as I pull into Cherry Lake Forest Preserve. It is a beautiful December day for a run.

After changing from my school clothes into my running clothes, I take off down the hill that will lead me between the two lakes.

This is where I once destroyed the field of runners at the cross country conference meet in seventh grade.

This is also where you and Ryan spent several summer days, hiking and biking and being in love.

I try to brush the thought from my mind, but it is there—front and center.

I will never be able to run in my favorite place again without thinking of him.

As I head around the lake to my left, I can feel the ache in my heart returning. It is like the muscle has been replaced with a gaping hole. This awful pain has been here for the past two months, and I don't know if it will ever leave.

As I head around the lake to my right, I see the place where Ryan and I read Bibles together. I want to just stop and reminisce, but I can't. I have to move on.

But you don't want to move on, Janey.

But I have to.

But do I?

He said there was a chance you would get back together someday.

BUT he also promised, crossed his heart, to never ignore me, and he already has.

AND he said he was going to round up a group of people to watch *The Blindside*, but THAT never happened.

I guess I am the one that was blindsided.

I wish someone could just make an intervention.

If only someone could make him SEE that we belong together.

I bet Melanie could do it. She thinks he is secretly still madly in love with me.

"Why can't you see? You belong with me. You belong with me."

The Taylor Swift lyrics flit through my head as I continue my jaunt.

His mom said he could never stop smiling when he was hanging out with me. That has to account for something, doesn't it?

As I cross the road and race down the gravel path that heads towards the town of Waveland, I feel some sort of hope returning.

He DID kiss me that last time we said good-bye.

He wouldn't do that unless he felt something, right?

But he also wouldn't have ignored me for over a month if he still cared, would he?

He PROMISED he wouldn't do that . . . but he did.

As I continue to run, I feel my hope return, then vanish, return, and then vanish.

I am descending into madness!

I circle Wave Lake and am heading back to where my car is parked when I hear someone hollering at me.

"I LOVE YOU!!!"

What on earth?

Some random young man, who I have never seen before or since, is shouting at me from his sparkly red convertible.

"I SERIOUSLY REALLY LOVE YOU!!!"

I can't help but smile at the ridiculousness of it.

"YOU'RE BEAUTIFUL, BABY!!!!"

The random stranger gives me one last look and drives away.

Remember when Ryan used to call you "babe?"

I brush away the thought and choose to continue smiling instead.

I am still beautiful to someone.

"1."

I see the bright red number flash onto the screen under *"messages."*

Ooh, someone has sent me a message!

I click onto the link at the top of my Facebook page to see who has sent me this delightful note.

When I see the name of the sender, I freeze.

"Ryan Darling."

Holy moly.

Maybe he's apologizing for forgetting about the whole movie idea?

Maybe he's written to say he wants to work on being friends?

All I know is that after a month-long drought of communication, he has written me.

And, for that, I can be excited!

When I open up the message, however, I stop dead.

"Please Janey, for real now. I kinda hoped you would pick out all the hints I desperately tried to drop you, but it looks like you weren't paying attention."

This is NOT what I was expecting.

"Your eyes were probably blinded by 'love,' a.k.a. human, desperation-based emotion. I KNOW, beyond a shadow of a doubt, that it is partially my fault. I kissed you, hugged you, told you that you were pretty. All dumb things to do in the presence of ANY girl, much less a 24-year-old who has never been in any relationship before."

Who do you think you are?

You are talking to me like I'm a child.

I was NOT "blinded" by a "desperation-based emotion."

I DID love you, for crying out loud!

And I STILL love you. I'm not sure why, but I do.

And wow, thanks for making me feel like I'm too ancient to even be pursued by a guy.

"But it is NOT, repeat NOT, all my fault. It is completely 100% ridiculous to expect us to just be BFF's after you went out and spilled your guts in front of EVERY SINGLE PERSON that MIGHT talk to me soon."

Okay . . . so maybe I shouldn't have told so many people, but YOU wouldn't talk to me. YOU ignored me for so long, and when you DID break up with me, if that is what you can even call it, you left me with a kiss. What does THAT mean? And then, after you PROMISED you would never ignore me, you kept right on doing it.

I continue reading, even though all I want to do is crush the computer.

"*I kinda liked you, we hung out a few times, had fun! But your lack of talking, coupled with your basic worship of me, just scared me.*"

You KINDA liked me??

We hung out a FEW times??

Um, NO. We hung out like twice a week for a majority of the summer.

And I was WORSHIPPING you???

YOU were the one gushing romantic one-liners that would make ANY girl melt!!

And YOU were the one literally sweeping me off my feet.

"*There was maybe hope for the future. Now there will never be.*"

It is this line that brings a hot fire to my face.

It is ALL over.

There is no longer ANY hope.

Summer has faded into an ETERNAL fall.

"*I'm sorry to come down on you like this, but I can't think of anything else. I don't hate you, but you are going to have to earn my friendship. FYI, we never really were that great of friends. You do not know me very well, and I do not know you.*"

The fire in my face converts into hot tears brimming from my eyes.

I have to earn HIS friendship??

We were NEVER friends???

I don't KNOW him????

I could list six pages front and back of all that I know and love about him.

But I am not about to do that right now.

RIGHT NOW, I just want to scream and send him the nastiest message ever in return.

I would never do that though.

Instead, I reach for my phone and immediately dial Melanie's number.

When she answers, I shakily tell her about the message and read it to her line by line.

I am not even sure how I am able to speak through the tears, but I manage.

By the end, she is fuming on the other end.

"Janey, that seriously makes me SO MAD!!! I just want to go over there and slit his tires."

"No, don't do that," I mutter, choking out a garbled sort of laugh.

"Seriously, you DO NOT deserve that. UGH!!! That makes me SO MAD!!!!"

Oh, Melanie. She can make me smile even when it is the last thing I would ever want to do.

"I cannot BELIEVE him. And here I thought he was still madly in love with you."

"I wish," I murmur.

"No, don't wish that. He doesn't deserve someone as sweet as you."

"He can be sweet too," I mutter.

"No, Janey, NO. He is NOT sweet and NOT someone that deserves you, not at all. AHHH!! This makes me so angry!"

Maybe I shouldn't have told Melanie. She sounds even more outraged than I am.

"Did you reply to the message yet?"

"No, not yet. I'm not sure what to say."

"Well, you better say EXACTLY what you feel."

"I will," I almost whisper.

What am I going to even say in return? I mean, I still love the kid . . . even after this. I will ALWAYS love him.

"Well, I better go, Melanie."

"Okay. Bye, Janey. And you stand up for yourself!"

"Okay. I will. Bye, Mel."

Silence.

I look down at the keyboard and lift my fingers to reply.

I write the first thing that comes to mind.

"Oh my gosh, no joke, this is seriously without a freaking doubt the meanest, cruelest email I think I have ever received . . ."

I do what Melanie has told me to do.

I tell that boy EXACTLY what I feel.

In the end, I've nearly written a book, but it has helped.

There is nothing on my mind I've left unsaid.

Fresh Start

> *"One pair of feet belongs to a businessman from America. The other pair belongs to a young Thai girl who just sold him her body for the night. Would you like to help us change her life? Bangkok, Thailand has thousands of bars, with thousands of women who believe that selling themselves is their only option. Some have been forced into this life; some have been trafficked and work because of fear. Our goal is to prevent this. Here's your chance to be a part of her redemption story. What happens in Thailand is only the beginning. The World Race: September 2010."*

I sit staring at the computer, mesmerized by the email on the screen.

It has only been one day since I was glued to the screen because of ANOTHER message, but this is for a different reason.

The World Race.

It has always been a crazy idea in the back of my mind, but would I ever be daring enough to try it? Would I ever be courageous enough to just leave the country for eleven whole months?

I click on the link that says *"September 2010 Race Route"* and become even more mesmerized.

"India, Nepal, Central Asia, Thailand, Cambodia, Kenya, Uganda, Central Africa, Romania, Ukraine, Eastern Europe."

I have always wanted to go to Kenya! That is where the fast runners are. And Uganda! That is where the child soldiers have suffered. And I've always wanted to go to these specific Asian countries where trafficking is at its worst, especially Thailand. Ooh, and then there's Nepal. Maybe I could see Mt. Everest!!

Suddenly, I feel this joyous anticipation well up within me.

Maybe, just maybe, this is why God didn't allow things with Ryan to work out. I mean, would I have ever been willing to do something like this if we WERE dating?

"This is so interesting," I quietly say to myself.

"What's interesting?" Mrs. Trumello peers over her computer at me. It is our free period, and we are both enjoying the down time.

"I just received an email about The World Race, and it is something I've always been interested in."

"What is it? Do you run around the world?"

"No . . . although that would be AWESOME. It is this eleven-month mission trip to eleven countries, and, on it, you have the chance to fight injustice, share the gospel, and serve people living in poverty."

"Wow! That sounds exciting!"

"Yeah, it does."

"And right up your alley."

"Yeah, I know."

"You should totally do it!"

"But . . . I couldn't just quit teaching, could I?"

"Why not? What do you have to lose? I wanted to do something like that when I was your age, but I was in a relationship. You're not. You are FREE."

She's right. I am NOT in a relationship. I AM free.

"Janey, you should definitely think about it. Pray about it. Maybe even give the organization a call."

"Okay, I think I will!"

I feel all jittery inside as I think about the possibility of what could be a reality.

I can't even remember the last time I was excited about anything.

On one hand, if I left, I would miss Tasha's senior year, leave my cross country kids behind, probably say goodbye to my hopes of ever qualifying for the Olympic Trials Marathon, and potentially never have the chance to teach at Frost Junior High again. BUT, on the other hand, if I left, I would have the chance to go ALL over the world, come to see people through the eyes of Jesus, provide justice for the weak and poor, have the chance to scout out possible places to serve long-term, leave all this frivolous materialism, find healing from my relationship with Ryan, and grow as a leader, Christian, and individual. And, what's more, I have no more college loans to pay back and have nothing, other than this job, tying me down.

Maybe, just maybe, God sent me this email today to show me life DOES go on. There can be healing. There can be freedom from heartache.

And suddenly, as I dwell in this happy moment, I know that I want Ryan to feel free as well.

I can forgive him, and I can move on.

"*Let the waters rise, if You want them to. I will follow You. I will follow You.*"

"Hi, there!"

"Hey!"

I am sitting on the dock, feet drawing circles in the hot Georgian water (seriously, this place is scorching hot), when an angelic girl with bright blue eyes and golden-brown waves of hair sits beside me.

"My name is Corey. What's yours?" She reaches out to shake my hand.

"Janey."

"So, are you one of the World Racers?"

"Yep! I'm here for training camp. Are you?"

"No, I'm here for music camp."

"Cool. I didn't know they had that."

"Yep. It's with Joseph Daniel Helms, the man that leads worship for you guys at camp." She pulls her sandals off and, like me, dips her feet in the water. "So, Janey, why did you decide to go on the World Race?"

I look over Corey, the girl I just met, and start in on my story.

She listens intently, especially when I talk about what happened between me and Ryan.

"It was just really hard. I LOVED him, you know? And I thought he loved me. Never before in my life had a guy told me I was beautiful or that he loved me. Guys just don't ordinarily like me like that. They usually see me as someone to compete with or tease. I mean, I am someone that has been made fun of my WHOLE life. Everyone has always thought I was weird or that I needed to change to become something I'm not. For the first time, with Ryan, I thought someone truly loved me for who I was. But it was all a lie."

I look down into the water and swirl my feet a little faster.

"I'm sorry, Janey." When I look up, I can see that Corey's eyes are filled with hurt. "But you know what? You ARE loved! You are loved by an amazing, incredible, AWESOME God that will NEVER leave you nor forsake you. With Him, there is ALWAYS hope for the future. He will never change His mind, ignore you, or reject you. He LOVES you." The hurt in her face turns to joy.

And as she speaks, my hurt begins to turn to joy.

But something is still holding me back.

"I know that is true. And I know all I need is Him, but I still don't feel free. I thought I was free way back when I decided to go on the World Race, but I really wasn't. I still couldn't let go of the memories. I still couldn't stop myself from trying to win him back. And I still can't."

"Janey, it is because you are a loyal person. You CARE about him. But, at the same time, God WANTS you to be free. He wants you to LET GO, and let

Him take control."

What she says brings me back to when I struggled with the eating disorder. Back then, it was all about giving up control too. It was all about letting go of what I thought was best and giving it up to Him.

"Janey, can I pray for you?"

"Sure."

I would never say "no" to prayer.

Putting her hand on my shoulder, Corey, this random, radiant angel, begins to pray as boldly as I have ever seen. And, as she prays, the heavens open, and rain begins to fall.

I feel like slowly, but surely, God is washing away the hurt and the pain.

Slowly, but surely, the chains are being broken.

They aren't completely gone, but there aren't as many as there used to be.

When she finishes, she looks me in the eye and stands me to my feet.

It is still pouring, but neither of us minds.

This is a healing rain, the kind that refreshes and mends the soul.

"Janey, God is calling you on this trip to fully romance you." Corey is grinning from ear to ear as the rain runs down her face. "It is just going to be you and Him."

Listening to her, I know it is true.

"He wants to take you to places you have never been and make you stand in awe of His beauty." She throws her hands up into the air and twirls. "He wants to show you incredible sunsets and amazing mountains. He wants to woo you, like only the one true Lover can do."

I continue to listen, and the encouragement keeps right on coming.

"Janey, you are a beautiful, amazing girl. You have a BIG heart. You are loyal and courageous and ready to follow Jesus wherever He goes, even if it is to a third-world country. I so wish I was in your position."

"You should go on the World Race!" I cheerfully respond.

I would LOVE to have this inspirational girl along for the trip. We could be the best of friends.

"I'm not old enough," she pronounces. "I'm only twenty."

"You should definitely go when you are twenty-one then!"

"I would love that. But, for now, it is your turn, Janey. It is your turn to go on a honeymoon with the King of Kings and Lord of Lords. He wants you to fall COMPLETELY in love with Him."

I have nothing to say in response. All that she is saying is too wonderful to need one.

"Well, Janey, I think I had better go. The music camp has a meeting in five minutes!"

She gives me a huge hug.

"Thank you so much, Corey. Talking to you meant so much to me."

"Same here. You have a beautiful story, Janey, and it deserves to be told."

Slipping her feet back into her sandals, Corey adds, "Now, remember, this trip is about you and Jesus."

"I will."

"Bye, Janey."

"Bye, Corey."

And, with that, the angel with the piercing blue eyes walks up the hill and through the trees.

In less than ten seconds, she is gone.

I will never see her again, but I will never forget the wise words she has spoken.

Postlude

A 25-year-old girl dances with a group of Indian children in the moon-filled, Malaysian night air. You can tell she is a bit wary of making a complete fool of herself, but she is loosening up as the minutes pass. Her wavy, brown ponytail slightly bobs as her sandals shuffle across the cement floor.

She has had a rough couple of months, from coming down with Dengue Fever within the first week of the trip to not really fitting in with her teammates, and she is not sure she really even belongs.

But when it is time for her and her World Race teammates to leave, the oldest boy in the most-welcoming Indian family shakes her hand. With a big smile on his face, he blushes and says, "You are very beautiful."

He doesn't say it to anyone else, only to this 25-year-old girl, who we recognize as Janey.

She can't help but smile just a little brighter.

It is like God himself has spoken to her.

She follows the group to the van and finds a seat next to the window. Staring out into the darkness, she notices that the blushing boy is running down the road. She strains to see where he is headed, but he is gone.

As the van starts to move, the girl notices that no one has chosen to sit beside her. Her heart sinks just a bit, but she focuses her eyes back on the road. She wants to know where the boy has gone.

When they reach the end of the particular dirt road they are traveling down, she sees that the blushing boy is waiting there, waiting for them to pass. Looking directly at her, the boy shyly reaches his hand to his lips and blows her a farewell kiss.

She cannot contain the joy that spreads across her face.

It is like God is blowing a kiss to her from Heaven.

As the screen fades to black, we hear a faint whisper—a whisper from the one true Lover.

"You are very beautiful, my daughter."

"Make me broken
So I can be healed
'Cause I'm so calloused
And now I can't feel
I want to run to You
With heart wide open
Make me broken

Make me empty
So I can be filled
'Cause I'm still holding
Onto my will
And I'm completed
When you are with me
Make me empty

Make me lonely
So I can be Yours
'Til I want no one
More than You, Lord
'Cause in the darkness
I know You will hold me
Make me lonely

'Til You are my one desire
'Til You are my one true love
'Til You are my breath, my everything
Lord, please keep making me."

"Keep Making Me," Sidewalk Prophets

Made in the USA
Lexington, KY
12 April 2017